Bismillah
May Allah
health

Love
Naheed & Farhan
May 2013

The Guiding Light

A blessed collection of verses and Sūrahs recited by Ḥaḍrat Khalīfatul Masīḥ V[aba] during various daily prayers, along with their commentary

Compiled by Professor Amtul Razzaq Carmichael

2012

Islam International Publication Ltd.

The Guiding Light

A blessed collection of verses and Sūrahs recited by Ḥaḍrat Khalīfatul Masīḥ V[aba] during various daily prayers, along with their commentary

Compiled by Professor Amtul Razzaq Carmichael

First Published in the UK: 2012

Published by:
Islam International Publication Ltd.
"Islamabad"
Sheephatch Lane
Tilford, Surrey GU10 2AQ
United Kingdom

Printed and bound by CPI Group (UK) Ltd, Croydon, CR0 4YY

For further information you may visit
www.alislam.org

ISBN 978-1-84880-080-9

Contents

Sunday

Monday

Thursday

Friday and Eid Prayer

Introduction

[1]It was reported in Al-Fazl International weekly that Ḥaḍrat Khalīfatul Masīḥ V (May Allāh strengthen him with His Mighty Hand) generally recites a certain set of verses and chapters of the Holy Qur'ān while leading the congregational Ṣalāt. It should also be mentioned that Ḥaḍrat Khalīfatul Masīḥ III and IV (May Allāh have mercy on them) had a set routine to recite certain verses of the Holy Qur'ān during the Ṣalāt. The Khulafā' of the Promised Messiah[as] chose these verses during their blessed period, in accordance with the wishes of our God and to address the needs and demands of the time. Therefore, people should recite these verses in their Ṣalāt as many times as possible. May Allāh enable us all to do so, Āmīn.

The subject matter covered in the verses and chapters that are recited by Ḥaḍrat Khalīfatul Masīḥ V (May Allāh strengthen him with His Mighty Hand) are diverse and thought-provoking. While reflecting on these, it appears that raising the standard of worship in order to achieve one's true spiritual potential is a strong theme of these

---

[1] Adapted from Al-Fazl International Weekly, London 16th to 22nd of July 2010

blessed words. To believe and to perform good deeds is not without challenges; persecution by non-believers is one of the difficulties faced by believers. The people of the Cave suffered atrocious persecution for their belief in the Unity of God and during their long period of suffering resorted to sincere prayers to beseech for Allāh's help.

An account of the people of elephants is given to remind believers that Allāh the Exalted helps those who work to safeguard His religion. Allāh the Exalted helped the custodians of the Ka'bah and protected the Holy Ka'bah from the attack of a powerful, well equipped army by employing small insignificant birds who eventually led to the complete destruction of the aggressors. For the believers there is reassurance that their fear will be allayed and security will be granted to them. A promise of ultimate success of the believers is associated with strong Divine commandments to safeguard the welfare of the weaker segments of society such as orphans and deprived. Believers are enjoined to relay the bounties of their God to others.

The attention of believers is drawn to the great migrations of the past Prophets as a result of bitter persecution that ultimately led to the success of the Divine missions. It is emphasised that humans are Allāh's best creations and they

have been given a choice to act in a way so that they can either progress to spiritual heights or can end up as the worst of the worst. Allāh the Exalted is best of all Judges and believers are enjoined to do good deeds. A detailed description of good deeds is given and the concept of believers, non-believers and hypocrites are introduced. Allāh the Exalted has promised a fitting punishment for the Hypocrites. Believers are taught prayers to seek protection against discord, jealousy and evil speculations whilst drawing their attention to God's attributes which are magnificent, manifold and all-encompassing.

It is explained that the rejection of Divine Prophets is a heinous act and will be punished severely. While those who will accept the message of the prophets, believe in God and do good deeds will be duly rewarded. They will be granted vital blessings of composure, tranquillity and peace of mind. Believers are enjoined to follow the commandment of "we hear and we obey" and are taught prayers to seek Allāh's forgiveness for their shortcomings. The believer is encouraged to seek "the good end" of being with the righteous in the next world. It is explained that each soul will have to be accounted for their deeds and the Holy Qur'ān is the ultimate Guide book for the believers. It is explained that the Holy Qur'ān is the word of God Who has all the best attributes and beautiful names and subject

of intercession is explained. Only God knows the state of the heart of a person and hence has the authority to grant right to intercession, respect and acceptance to man.

A code of conduct of prayers and seeking forgiveness is given to the believers when the final triumph arrives. A picture of life in the latter days is given when the treasures of earth will be discovered and extensively utilised. The concept of accountability for one's actions is re-emphasised. Believers are also warned not to fall in the trap of materialism in the days of affluence and remain focussed in their belief.

It was prophesised that the sun and the moon will bear witness to the truthfulness of the Divine reformer of the latter days and a bad ending of those is reminded who attempted to hinder the mission of the Prophet(s) of God. It is indicated that hardship faced by the Reformer of the latter days and his followers will turn into triumph and it is commanded that believers turn to Allāh the Exalted with keenness.

May Allāh the Exalted help us to understand these blessed words and act upon them to gain the ultimate goal of our lives of achieving *Taqwā* or righteousness. Āmīn.

I should most humbly acknowledge the hard work, dedication and commitment of the following Jamā'at members in preparation of this book.

Typing (Urdu and Arabic) was helped by Miss Mufazah Arooj, Dr Mashood Mansoor, Mrs Alia Arif, Mr Mohammad Arif Nasir, Dr Amtul Salam Sami and Miss Zartasht Sami Carmichael. The task of proof reading was helped by Mrs Shahida Syed, Mr Mansoor Syed, Dr P Ali Carmichael and Miss Natasha Sami Carmichael. For research and references invaluable advice was given by Maulana Ataul Mujeeb Rashed Sahib, Imam Fazl Mosque London, Mrs Qanita Shahida Rashed, Dr Amtul Shafee Sami and Dr Amtul Musawwar Sami. The task of formatting and typesetting was diligently carried out by Maulana Muhammad Tahir Nadeem Sahib. The title page was designed by Zartasht and Natasha Sami Carmichael under the able guidance of Mr Tanveer Khokhar. May Allāh the Exalted reward them all for this hard work, Āmīn.

I am most grateful to Allāh the Exalted for granting me (late) parents, Dr Abdus Sami Sahib and Mrs Amatul Rahman Sahiba who most kindly infused the love of Ahmadiyyat in our hearts and with the grace of God gave

us teaching and training to enable us to humbly serve Ahmadiyya Muslim Jamā'at.

It is only fair that kind and unrelenting support and guidance of the Additional Wakīlut-Taṣnīf, Munir-ud-Din Shams Ṣāḥib is gratefully acknowledged. He kindly and painstakingly edited the manuscript and invested time and energy to teach the skills of transliteration to a complete novice with extreme patience. I am greatly in debt to his helpfulness. I learnt a great deal from his thoroughness and his ability to pay great attention to detail. May Allāh the Exalted reward him abundantly for his help. Āmīn.

May Allāh the Exalted accept this humble effort, Āmīn.

With request for Prayers

A humble servant of Islam Ahmadiyyat

Professor AR Carmichael

About the book

- This book is compiled under the supervision of Additional Wakīlut-Taṣnīf, Munir-ud-Din Shams Ṣāḥib, according to the guidance given by Ḥaḍrat Khalīfatul Masīḥ V[aba].
- The list of Tilāwat schedule is taken from a report published in Al-Fazl and inserted as a table of Tilāwat Schedule.
- All verses and Sūrahs are presented in the chronological order of recitation during the week.
- The translation is taken form the English Translation by Maulawī Sher Ali[ra], revised edition; 2004.
- The references of the Holy Qur'ān are given as Chapter number: verse number.
- The commentary of the Holy Qur'ān is taken from the Five Volume Commentary. The Holy Qur'ān with English Translation and Commentary. 3rd ed. Islam International Publications Limited; 2002.

- Some technical discussion about the detailed meanings of Arabic words have been referenced and not added in this booklet.
- Transliteration of Arabic words is added.
- A section about the importance of the Sūrahs has been added based on *Tafsīr-ul-Qur'ān* by the Promised Messiah, Ḥaḍrat Mirzā Ghulām Aḥmad[as] of Qadian, *Ḥaqā'iqul-Furqān* by Ḥakīm Maulānā Nūr-ud-Dīn,[ra] Ḥaḍrat Khalīfatul Masīḥ I and *Tafsīr-e-Kabīr* by Ḥaḍrat Mirzā Bashīr-ud-Dīn Maḥmūd Aḥmad[ra], Khalīfatul Masīḥ II.
- A self-reflection exercise is added at the end of every section.

Amatullah Khurshid Memorial Fund

With great humility, I express my deepest gratitude to Allāh the Exalted who has enabled us to prepare this book as part of Amatullah Kurshid Memorial Fund. This fund was set up by the revered and great scholar of the Ahmadiyya Community Maulānā Abul 'Aṭā Jālundhrī in memory of his pious and dedicated eldest daughter Amatullah.

Mrs Amatullah Khurshid was a highly learned scholar. She completed a 4-year course in Theology or religious education. She graduated (Maulawī Fāḍil) from the University of Punjab. She served Lajnah in many capacities since 1945. She had the honour to serve as the Secretary Iṣlāḥo-Irshād for Lajnah Imā'illah Qadian.

Mrs Amatullah Khurshid was appointed in 1947 as the first woman editor of *Miṣbāḥ* (meaning a lamp or source of light) the first ever magazine dedicated for the education of Ahmadi women. She had the privilege to serve as the Editor of *Miṣbāḥ* for 15 years, right up to the time of her death. She had no children and regarded *Miṣbāḥ* as her

child. She passed away in 1960 and was buried in the *Bahishtī Maqbarah* in Rabwah, Pakistan.

My mother Mrs Amatul Rahman Sami Sahiba had a special bond with her elder sister Mrs Amatullah Khurshid and lovingly called her *Āppā Achchī* (good big sister).

A book that enhances the Qur'ānic knowledge of Lajnah is a fitting tribute to a woman who spent all her life striving to improve Lajnah's knowledge. The fact remains that it is only the real fortunate ones amongst us, who get the privilege to serve their faith with as much dedication and commitment as Mrs Amtullah Khurshid did. May Allah enable us all to follow her shining example. Āmīn.

Humble servant of Islam Ahmadiyyat
Professor Amtul Razzaq Carmichael

Foreword

The Holy Qur'ān is the word of God and guidance for all the humanity for all the time. All blessings are associated with reading, understanding and following the teachings of the Holy Qur'ān[1]. In a Ḥadīth it is stated that the best among you is the one who learns the Holy Qur'ān and teaches it to others[2].

The Promised Messiah[as] came to this world to revive the practice of Islam as mentioned in the Holy Qur'ān. He says, "You have an obligation not to cast aside the Holy Qur'ān like a thing forsaken; it is the source of your life. Those who honour it will be honoured in heaven. Those who give precedence its teachings over all other traditions and sayings will be given preference in heaven[3]". He also said, "Strive hard so that not even a single iota of the Holy Qur'ān may testify against you and cause you to be punished".

---

[1]. This is a perfect Book; there is no doubt in it; it is a guidance for the righteous. (The Holy Qur'ān 2: 3)

[2] Bukhārī, Kitābo Faḍā'ilil-Qur'ān Bāb, *Khairokum man ta'allamal- Qur'āna wa 'allamahu*

[3] *Kashti-e-Nūḥ*, Ḥaḍrat Mirzā Ghulām Aḥmad[as] of Qadian' *Ruḥānī Khazā'in*, Vol 19, p 13, published by Islām International Publication Limited, 2009

After the Promised Messiah (on whom be peace) passed away, his Khulafā' carried on with the mission of enhancing and promoting the reading, understanding and following the education of the Holy Qur'ān. Ḥaḍrat Khalīfatul Masīḥ I[ra] said, "Abiding by the teachings of the Holy Qur'ān saves us from the humiliation of depending on and begging from other human beings[4]". Ḥaḍrat Khalīfatul Masīḥ II[ra] expounded, "If you read this with care and attention, you can find an answer to anything from this book[5]". Ḥaḍrat Khalīfatul Masīḥ III[rt] further explained that the real purpose for the revelation of the Holy Qur'ān is to let these guiding rules influence every sphere of your life by making a true bond with the teachings given in the holy book[6]. Ḥaḍrat Khalīfatul Masīḥ IV[rt] has strongly emphasised the importance of understanding the Holy Qur'ān, "The Holy Qur'ān is a living book, it is important to make a bond of commitment to this Holy Scripture, so that the true meanings and the real concepts given in the Holy Qur'ān will find the way to your heart.[7]"

---

[4] *Ḥaqā'iqul-Furqān*. Ḥaḍrat Ḥakīm Maulānā Nūr-ud-Dīn[ra], Khalīfatul Masīḥ I, Print well Focal Point Amritsar 2005,Vol 2, Page 57

[5] *Anwārul-'Ulūm*. Ḥaḍrat Khalīfatul Masīḥ II, Mirzā Bashīr-ud-Dīn Maḥmūd Aḥmad[ra] Faḍl-e-'Umar Foundation, Islam International Publications Limited, Vol 10, Page 92

[6] *Khuṭabāt-e-Nāṣir*, Nazarat Nashro Ishaat, December 2005, Vol 4, Page 254

[7] *Mash'al-e- Rāh,* Khuddamul-Ahmadiyyah Pakistan, June 2004, Vol. 3, Page 111

Ḥaḍrat Khalīfatul Masīḥ V[aba] admonished that we must be mindful that we do not end up like people who have turned their backs to the Holy Qur'ān. Ḥaḍrat Khalīfatul Masīḥ V[aba] stressed that we can truly respect every word of the Holy Qur'ān only by following its commandments. In addition, Allāh will resolve all our problems through the Holy Qur'ān[8].

Ḥaḍrat Khalīfatul Masīḥ V[aba] generally recites a certain set of verses and chapters of the Holy Qur'ān while leading the congregational Ṣalāt[9]. It should also be mentioned that Ḥaḍrat Khalīfatul Masīḥ III[rt] and IV[rt] also had a set routine to recite certain verses of the Holy Qur'ān during the Ṣalāt. The Khulafā' of the Promised Messiah[as] chose these verses during their blessed period, in accordance with the wishes of our God and to address the needs and demands of the time. Therefore, as much as possible, people should recite these verses in their Ṣalāt. The subject matter covered in the verses and chapters recited by Ḥaḍrat Khalīfatul Masīḥ V[aba] is diverse and thought-provoking

Professor Amtul Razzaq Carmichael wished to collect and present the details of the recitation of various verses and

---

[8] *Mash'al-e- Rāh*, Khuddamul-Ahmadiyyah Pakistan, June 2006, Vol. 5, part 3, Pages 132-133

[9] Adapted from Al-Fazl International Weekly, London 16th to 22nd of July 2010

Sūrahs that Ḥaḍrat Khalīfatul Masīḥ V[aba] recites in various daily prayers. On my suggestion, she and her team have collected the commentary and the importance of all the verses recited by Ḥaḍrat Khalīfatul Masīḥ V[aba] in one place for the benefit of all Ahmadis. May Allah grant them the best reward for this noble service, Āmīn.

This is a useful book to understand the meanings of these revered words, self-reflect and enhance one's spiritual capacity. It is important that this book is read and understood and the beneficence of the Holy Qur'ān is appreciated as applicable to today's world. May Allāh the Exalted help us all to benefit from these holy words as said by the Promised Messiah[as], "So read the Qur'ān with due diligence and love it more than anything else. God has revealed to me, That is, "all good is contained in the Holy Qur'ān[10]." Āmīn.

Munīr-ud-Dīn Shams
Additional Wakīl-ut-Taṣnīf
August 2012

---

[10] *Kashti-e-Nūḥ*, Ḥaḍrat Mirzā Ghulām Aḥmad[as] of Qadian, *Ruḥānī Khazā'in*, Vol 19, p 26-27, Islām International Publication Limited, 2009

Publishers' Note

Please note that, in the translation that follows, all references, unless otherwise specified, are from the English translation of the Holy Quran by Ḥaḍrat Maulawī Sher Ali[ra]
The following abbreviations have been used. Readers are urged to recite the full salutations when reading the book:

sa *ṣallallāhu 'alaihi wa sallam*, meaning 'may peace and blessings of Allah be upon him,' is written after the name of the Holy Prophet Muhammad[sa]

as *'alaihis-salām*, meaning 'may peace be on him,' is written after the name of Prophets other than the Holy Prophet Muhammad[sa]

ra *raḍiyallāhu 'anhu/'anhā/'anhum*, meaning 'may Allah be pleased with him/her/them,' is written after the names of the Companions of the Holy Prophet Muhammad[sa] or of the Promised Messiah[as].

rt *raḥmatullāhi 'alaihi*, meaning 'may Allah shower His mercy upon him,' is written after the names of deceased pious Muslims who are not Companions of the Holy Prophet Muhammad[sa] or of the Promised Messiah[as].

aba *ayyadahullāhu Ta'ālā binaṣrihil-'Azīz*, meaning 'may Allah the Almighty help him with his powerful support,' is written after the name of the present Head of the Aḥmadiyya Muslim Jamā'at, Ḥaḍrat

Mirza Masroor Ahmad, Khalīfatul-Masīḥ V[aba].

In transliterating Arabic words we have adopted the following system established by the Royal Asiatic Society.

ا	at the beginning of a word, pronounced as *a*, *i*, *u* preceded by a very slight aspiration, like *h* in the English word *honour*.
ث	*th*, pronounced like *th* in the English word *thing*.
ح	*ḥ*, a guttural aspirate, stronger than *h*.
خ	*kh*, pronounced like the Scotch *ch* in *loch*.
ذ	*dh*, pronounced like the English *th* in *that*.
ص	*ṣ*, strongly articulated *s*.
ض	*ḍ*, similar to the English *th* in *this*.
ط	*ṭ*, strongly articulated palatal *t*.
ظ	*ẓ*, strongly articulated *z*.
ع	‘, a strong guttural, the pronunciation of which must be learnt by the ear
غ	*gh*, a sound approached very nearly in the *r* *grasseye* in French, and in the German *r*. It requires the muscles of the throat to be in the ‘gargling’ position whilst pronouncing it.
ق	*q*, a deep guttural *k* sound.
ء	’, a sort of catch in the voice.

Short vowels are represented by:

a	for (like *u* in *bud*)
i	for (like *i* in *bid*)
u	for (like *oo* in *wood*)

Long vowels by:

ā for or آ (like *a* in *father*);
ī for ی or (like *ee* in *deep*);
ū for و (like *oo* in *root*);

Other:

ai for ی (like *i* in *site*);
au for و (resembling *ou* in *sound*)

The consonants not included in the above list have the same phonetic value as in the principal languages of Europe. While the Arabic ن is represented by *n*, we have indicated the Urdu ں as *ń*. Curved commas are used in the system of transliteration, ‘ for ع, ’ for ء.

Normally we have not transliterated Arabic words which have become part of English language, e.g. Islam, Quran, Hadith, Mahdi, jihad, Ramadan and Ummah. The Royal Asiatic Society rules of transliteration for names of persons, places and other terms, could not be followed throughout the book as many of the names contain non-Arabic characters and carry a local transliteration and pronunciation style which in itself is also not consistent either.

The Publishers

Ṣalāt Tilāwat Schedule of Ḥaḍrat Khalīfatul Masīḥ V[ABA]

DAY	SALAT	FIRST RAK'AH	2ND RAK'AH
FRIDAY	Fajr	Sūrah Banī Isrā'īl 17:79-85	Sūrah al-Kahf 18:1-11
	Maghrib	Sūrah al-Fīl Ch:105	Sūrah Quraish Ch:106
	'Ishā'	Sūrah aḍ-Ḍuḥā Ch:93	Sūrah at-Tīn Ch:95
SATURDAY	Fajr	Sūrah al-Baqarah 2:1-8	Sūrah al-Baqarah 2:9-17
	Maghrib	Sūrah al-Falaq Ch:113	Sūrah an-Nās Ch:114
	'Ishā'	Sūrah al-Baqarah 2:256 (Āyatul-Kursī)	Sūrah al -Baqarah 2:287
SUNDAY	Fajr	Sūrah al-Kahf 18:103-107	Sūrah al-Kahf 18:108-111
	Maghrib	Sūrah al-Falaq Ch:113	Sūrah an-Nās Ch:114
	'Ishā'	Sūrah Ḥā Mīm as-Sajdah 41:31-33	Sūrah Ḥā Mīm as-Sajdah 41:34-37
MONDAY	Fajr	Sūrah al-Baqarah 2:285-287	Sūrah Āl-e-'Imrān 3:191-195
	Maghrib	Sūrah al-Falaq Ch:113	Sūrah an-Nās Ch:114
	'Ishā'	Sūrah al-Ḥashr 59:19-22	Sūrah al-Ḥashr 59:23-25
TUESDAY	Fajr	Sūrah al-Baqarah 2:255-258	Sūrah Āl-e-'Imrān 3:26-31
	Maghrib	Sūrah al-Kāfirūn Ch:109	Sūrah an-Naṣr Ch:110
	'Ishā'	Sūrah az-Zilzāl Ch:99	Sūrah at-Takāthur Ch:102
WEDNESDAY	Fajr	Sūrah al-Kahf 18:103-107	Sūrah al-Kahf 18:108-111
	Maghrib	Sūrah al-Falaq Ch:113	Sūrah an-Nās Ch:114
	'Ishā'	Sūrah ash-Shams Ch:91	Sūrah aḍ-Ḍuḥā Ch:93
THURSDAY	Fajr	Sūrah al-Baqarah 2:285-287	Sūrah Āl-e-'Imrān 3:191-195
	Maghrib	Sūrah al-Falaq Ch:113	Sūrah an-Nās Ch:114
	'Ishā'	Sūrah aḍ-Ḍuḥā Ch:93	Sūrah al-Inshirāḥ Ch:94
JUMU'AH AND EID PRAYERS		Sūrah al-A'lā Ch:87	al-Ghāshiyah Ch:88

FRIDAY

DAY	SALAT	FIRST RAK'AH	2ND RAK'AH
FRIDAY	Fajr	Sūrah Banī Isrā'īl 79-85	Sūrah al-Kahf 2-11
	Maghrib	Sūrah al-Fīl	Sūrah Quraish
	'Ishā'	Sūrah aḍ-Ḍuḥā	Sūrah at-Tīn

First Rak'ah of the Friday Fajr Prayer

First Rak'ah of the Friday Fajr Prayer

Importance of Sūrah Banī Isrā'īl

- Sūrah Banī Isrā'īl is also known as Sūrah al-'Isrā', as it gives details of this highly spiritual event in the life of the Holy Prophet[sa].

- This Sūrah is called Banī Isrā'īl because it explains the history of Israelites and details accounts of their life.

- The Holy Prophet[sa] was called akin to the Prophet Moses[as] and hence Muslims are likened to Israelites in a metaphorical sense.

- [1]Because of this similarity, this Sūrah prophesises the trials and tribulations that Muslims will have to face.

---

[1] *Tafsīr-e-Kabīr*. Ḥaḍrat Mirzā Bashīr-ud-Dīn Maḥmūd Aḥmad[ra], Printwell Amritsar 2004. Volume 4 pages 277

- [2]Also mentioned in this Sūrah is the national destruction that followed Jews after they categorically defied two Prophets of God, namely Dāwūd[as] and 'Īsā[as], reminding Muslims that a similar fate would befall them if they were to become disobedient and transgressors. This is followed by the glad-tiding of the ultimate triumph of Islam.

- [3]This Sūrah explains the blessings that can be achieved by a righteous person and gives details of the punishment for disbelievers, mischievous and those who renegade on their promises. This Sūrah serves as a warning for the Jews residing in Medīnah.

---

[2] The Holy Qur'ān with English Translation and Commentary. 3rd ed. Islam International Publications Limited; 2002. Volume 3, Page 1402

[3] *Ḥaqā'iuql Furqān*. Ḥaḍrat Ḥakīm Maulānā Nūr-ud-Dīn[ra], Khalīfatul Masīḥ I, Printwell Focal Point Amritsar 2005. Volume 2, Page 521

أَقِمِ ٱلصَّلَوٰةَ لِدُلُوكِ ٱلشَّمْسِ إِلَىٰ غَسَقِ ٱلَّيْلِ وَقُرْءَانَ ٱلْفَجْرِ ۖ إِنَّ
قُرْءَانَ ٱلْفَجْرِ كَانَ مَشْهُودًا ۝ وَمِنَ ٱلَّيْلِ فَتَهَجَّدْ بِهِۦ
نَافِلَةً لَّكَ عَسَىٰٓ أَن يَبْعَثَكَ رَبُّكَ مَقَامًا مَّحْمُودًا ۝ وَقُل رَّبِّ
أَدْخِلْنِى مُدْخَلَ صِدْقٍ وَأَخْرِجْنِى مُخْرَجَ صِدْقٍ وَٱجْعَل لِّى مِن
لَّدُنكَ سُلْطَٰنًا نَّصِيرًا ۝ وَقُلْ جَآءَ ٱلْحَقُّ وَزَهَقَ ٱلْبَٰطِلُ ۚ إِنَّ
ٱلْبَٰطِلَ كَانَ زَهُوقًا ۝ وَنُنَزِّلُ مِنَ ٱلْقُرْءَانِ مَا هُوَ شِفَآءٌ
وَرَحْمَةٌ لِّلْمُؤْمِنِينَ ۙ وَلَا يَزِيدُ ٱلظَّٰلِمِينَ إِلَّا خَسَارًا ۝ وَإِذَآ
أَنْعَمْنَا عَلَى ٱلْإِنسَٰنِ أَعْرَضَ وَنَـَٔا بِجَانِبِهِۦ ۖ وَإِذَا مَسَّهُ ٱلشَّرُّ كَانَ
يَـُٔوسًا ۝ قُلْ كُلٌّ يَعْمَلُ عَلَىٰ شَاكِلَتِهِۦ فَرَبُّكُمْ أَعْلَمُ بِمَنْ
هُوَ أَهْدَىٰ سَبِيلًا ۝

Translation

Observe Prayer at the declining and paling of the sun on to the darkness of the night, and the recitation *of the Qur'ān in Prayer* at dawn. Verily, the recitation *of the Qur'ān* at dawn is *specially* acceptable *to God.* And wake up for it (the Qur'ān) in *the latter part of* the night as a supererogatory service for thee. It may be that thy Lord will raise thee to an exalted station. And say, 'O my Lord, make my entry a good entry and *then* make me come forth with a good forthcoming. And grant me from Thyself a helping power.' And say, 'Truth has come and falsehood has vanished away. Falsehood does indeed vanish away *fast*.' And We are *gradually* revealing of the Qur'ān that which is a healing and a mercy to the believers; but it only adds to the loss of the wrongdoers. And when We bestow favour on man, he turns away and goes aside; and when evil touches him, he gives *himself* up to despair. Say, 'Everyone acts according to his own way, and your Lord knows full well who is best guided.'

أَقِمِ ٱلصَّلَوٰةَ لِدُلُوكِ ٱلشَّمۡسِ إِلَىٰ غَسَقِ ٱلَّيۡلِ وَقُرۡءَانَ ٱلۡفَجۡرِۖ إِنَّ

قُرۡءَانَ ٱلۡفَجۡرِ كَانَ مَشۡهُودٗا ﴿٧٩﴾

[17:79] Observe Prayer at the declining and paling of the sun on to the darkness of the night, and the recitation *of the Qur'ān in Prayer* at dawn. Verily, the recitation *of the Qur'ān* at dawn is *specially* acceptable *to God.*

[4]Commentary

The words of this verse denote the hours of the five daily Prayers of Islam.

The three meanings of the word دلوک (*dulūk*) i.e.

1. The sun declined from the meridian,
2. Or it became yellow
3. Or it set

[4] The Holy Qur'ān with English Translation and Commentary. 3rd ed. Islam International Publications Limited; 2002. Volume 3, Page 1455-1460

indicate the time of ظهر (*Ẓuhr*) afternoon Prayer and عصر ('*Aṣr*) late afternoon Prayer and مغرب (*Maghrib*) sunset Prayer.

The words غسق اليل (*ghasaqal-lail*) include the times of مغرب (Maghrib) sunset Prayer, but particularly refers to عشا ('Ishā') night Prayer. The words the recitation of Qur'ān at dawn قرآن الفجر (*Qur'ānal-Fajr*) indicates the hour of فجر (*Fajr*) morning Prayer.

In this and the following verses Muslims are warned to be prepared to meet great hardships and privations at the hands of the Jews of Medīnah. These people were very punctilious about outward acts of worship. The slightest slackness in Prayers on the part of Muslims would make them criticise Islam and the Holy Prophet[sa]. Moreover, Islam was destined to make great headway in Medīnah in the near future and as success and prosperity generally make men prone to a life of ease and they become indifferent towards Prayers, so Muslims are particularly warned to be on their guard against any slackness in Prayers.

وَمِنَ ٱلَّيْلِ فَتَهَجَّدْ بِهِۦ نَافِلَةً لَّكَ عَسَىٰٓ أَن يَبْعَثَكَ رَبُّكَ مَقَامًا

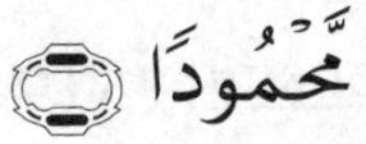

[17:80] And wake up for it (the Qur'ān) in *the latter part of* the night as a supererogatory service for thee. It may be that thy Lord will raise thee to an exalted station.

Commentary

The word نافلتہ لک (*nāfilatan-laka*) (the supererogatory service of thee) refers to the Tahajjud Prayer offered in the latter part of the night.

- The word نافلتہ لک (*nāfilatan-laka*) as its meanings (a supererogatory service) show, implies that the Tahajjud Prayer is not obligatory for Muslims.
- The verse may also be taken to indicate that this Prayer was obligatory only for the Holy Prophet[sa], and not for any other Prophet.
- The word نافلت (*nāfilat*) further means a special favour and signifies that Prayers are not a burden to weary the flesh, but a privilege and a favour from God.

The expression, *it may be that thy Lord will raise thee to an exalted station*, embodies a great prophecy.

- The implied prophecy; Perhaps no other person has been so much maligned and abused as the Holy Prophet[sa] of Islam and certainly no other person has been the recipient of so much Divine praise and the object of invocation of so many Divine blessings and favours upon him as he. The implied prophecy was that whereas the sons of darkness would abuse and condemn the Prophet[sa], the good, the noble and the righteous would invoke God's blessings upon him and God Himself would proclaim his praises from His Exalted Throne. Thus the Prophet's praise by God and His Elect would far outweigh the undeserved abuse heaped upon him by the sons of darkness.

- The expression مقام محمود (*maqām-e-maḥmūd*) exalted station may also be understood to imply the special prerogative of شفاعت (*shafā'at*) intercession which God bestowed upon the Holy Prophet[sa]. There is a well-known ḥadīth that the followers of all other Prophets, having despaired of the intercession of

their own Prophets on the Day of Judgement, will seek the Holy Prophet's intercession and he will intercede for them, and thus they will acknowledge his greatness.

- The advent of the Promised Messiah and Mahdi[as] is another manifestation of this مقام محمود (*maqām-e-maḥmūd*)) exalted station of the Holy Prophet[sa]. When denunciation of him reached its climax, and he was also deserted by his own so-called followers and friends, God raised the Promised Messiah[as] and Mahdi from among his followers and through him vindicated his honour. The Promised Messiah[as] refuted and rebutted the charges of his enemies, and by imparting to his followers true knowledge of the manifold excellences and beauties of his teaching and character inspired them with the new love and veneration for him.

- The mention of the grant of مقام محمود (*maqām-e-maḥmūd*)) the exalted station after the command for obligatory and supererogatory Prayers implies the hint that the real remedy for him who receives mockery and abuse from the people of the world is

not to retaliate with mockery and abuse but to turn to God and seek His help. This is sure to turn enemies into friends, as happened in the Prophet's case. His bitterest enemies became his most devoted followers. Of the many exalted stations the Holy Prophet[sa] was destined to obtain the first was his possession of Medīnah from where spread his praise and holiness to the ends of the earth. This is why the next verse refers to his emigration to Medīnah.

وَقُل رَّبِّ أَدۡخِلۡنِی مُدۡخَلَ صِدۡقٍ وَأَخۡرِجۡنِی مُخۡرَجَ صِدۡقٍ

وَٱجۡعَل لِّی مِن لَّدُنكَ سُلۡطَـٰنًا نَّصِیرًا ۝

[17:81] And say, 'O my Lord, make my entry a good entry and *then* make me come forth with a good forthcoming. And grant me from Thyself a helping power.'

Commentary

In acceptance of his prayers and supplications, the Prophet[sa] in this verse has been vouchsafed the glad tidings

that in fulfilment of the prophecy made in the words, '*Glory be to Him, Who carried His servant by night from the Sacred Mosque to the Distant Mosque*,' he would be taken to Medīnah, which would constitute the first of the various 'exalted positions' مقام محمود (*maqām-e-maḥmūd*) which are to be bestowed upon him.

In anticipation of the fulfilment of this prophecy the Prophet[sa] is commanded to pray that his entry in Medīnah may be doubly blessed and so may be his departure from the town in which he is now living (Makkah). This prayer of the Prophet[sa] was amply fulfilled. His enemies desired to expel him from Makkah in ignominy and disgrace but he was foretold by God of their evil designs and in accordance with divine plan he left Makkah of his own accord and arrived in perfect safety in Medīnah, where he succeeded in gathering round him a band of most faithful and devoted followers.

The question may be asked why the entry of the Prophet[sa] in to Medīnah has been mentioned before his 'coming forth' from Makkah, which is contrary to events as they took place. The answer to this seeming historical anomaly is that the order in the statement of events as they took place has been reversed in order to console the Holy

Prophet[sa]. The news of his departure from Makkah would naturally have caused him great pain. In order to relieve him of this mental anguish God preceded the news of his departure from Makkah by the news of his entry into Medīnah, where power and honour awaited him.

The word مدخل (*mudkhala*) entry might also be taken to refer to the Holy Prophet's subsequent victorious entry into Makkah. Read in this sense, the said 'entry' may be understood to constitute another stage in the Holy Prophet's march to his promised مقام محمود (*maqām-e-maḥmūd*) exalted station because with his triumphant re-entry into Makkah ended all opposition to Islam and the Prophet's erstwhile opponents became his devoted followers.

The prayer contained in the words, *And grant me from Thyself a helping power*, was necessary because power is a great corrupter of men. The Prophet[sa] is taught to pray that instead of corrupting him the acquisition of power may prove a source of real help to him.

The prayer contained in this verse supports the interpretation of اسراء (*Isrā'*) the Vision about the Prophet's

Night Journey mentioned in verse 2, namely that the flight of the Holy Prophet[sa] from Makkah to Medīnah was sure to take place.

وَقُلْ جَآءَ ٱلْحَقُّ وَزَهَقَ ٱلْبَـٰطِلُ ۚ إِنَّ ٱلْبَـٰطِلَ كَانَ زَهُوقًا ۝

[17:82] And say, 'Truth has come and falsehood has vanished away. Falsehood does indeed vanish away *fast*.'

Commentary

This verse implies a beautiful hint that with the entry of the Holy Prophet[sa] into Medīnah his power would continue to grow and that of his enemy decline till it would be finally broken. So it came to pass when by the conquest of Makkah idolatry disappeared from Arabia for ever.

The word زهق (*zahaq*) which has been translated as 'has vanished away' actually conveys, the sense of gradual weakening and ultimate disappearance. It is among the marvels of Qur'ānic diction that to convey a certain sense it selects that particular word which points to a long sequence of events. In this particular instance the sense of the

vanishing of falsehood might as well have been expressed by the word هلك *(halaka)* perished or بطل (*baṭala*) became useless, vain or ineffective) but neither of these words would have conveyed the sense of gradual weakening and ultimate disappearance which is expressed by the word زهق (*zahaq*). This word, in fact, implies a prophecy of the gradual weakening and an ultimate disappearance of idolatry from Makkah, which was literally fulfilled as foretold.

It is another marvel of the style of the Qurān that, without being poetry, its verses possess that poetic rhythm and cadence, without which it is not possible to give full expression to feelings of extreme delight. The verse under comment furnishes one such example.

After the conquest of Makkah when the Holy Prophet[sa] was busy clearing the Ka'bah of the idols which had desecrated it, he repeated as he struck each of the idols the following verse of the Qur'ān; i.e. **And say, Truth has come and falsehood has vanished away. Falsehood does indeed vanish away fast**. One can imagine the deep emotion the Prophet's Companions must have felt when they watched him strike down the idols one after the other and repeat this

Qur'ānic verse in a measured tone. It is only natural that they spontaneously joined him in reciting this verse on that august occasion.

وَنُنَزِّلُ مِنَ ٱلْقُرْءَانِ مَا هُوَ شِفَآءٌ وَرَحْمَةٌ لِّلْمُؤْمِنِينَ ۙ وَلَا يَزِيدُ ٱلظَّٰلِمِينَ إِلَّا خَسَارًا ﴿٨٣﴾

[17:83] And We are *gradually* revealing of the Qur'ān that which is a healing and a mercy to the believers; but it only adds to the loss of the wrongdoers.

Commentary

The verse purports to say that as to a jaundiced eye all objects appear yellow, similarly to a mind which is swayed by jealousy and prejudice, even most pure and noble teachings appear impure and ignoble. Such was the case with disbelievers in regard to the teachings of the Qur'ān.

The word 'Qur'ān' in this verse may also be taken to refer the portions of the Qur'ān already revealed, the portion containing prophecies about the prosperity and success of the Faithful and the ruin and destruction of disbelievers.

The verse means to say that the time has come for the fulfilment of those prophecies and that the flight of the Prophet from Makkah would usher in an era of triumph for Islam and would bring discomfiture and humiliation to disbelievers.

وَإِذَآ أَنْعَمْنَا عَلَى ٱلْإِنسَـٰنِ أَعْرَضَ وَنَـَٔا بِجَانِبِهِۦ ۖ وَإِذَا مَسَّهُ ٱلشَّرُّ كَانَ يَـُٔوسًا ۝

[17:84] And when We bestow favour on man, he turns away and goes aside; and when evil touches him, he gives *himself* up to despair.

Commentary

The verse means to say that Muslims were subjected to tortures and suffered all sorts of hardships for thirteen long years, but they bore them with fortitude and patience. The case of disbelievers, however, is different. When their turn came to be visited with divine punishment they would give way to despair, because they had no faith in God.

قُلْ كُلٌّ يَعْمَلُ عَلَىٰ شَاكِلَتِهِۦ فَرَبُّكُمْ أَعْلَمُ بِمَنْ هُوَ أَهْدَىٰ

[17:85] Say, 'Everyone acts according to his own way, and your Lord knows full well who is best guided.'

Commentary

Everyman acts according to his own motives, way of thinking, aims and purposes. The aim and object of disbelievers is to attain worldly gains. Therefore when they suffer a worldly loss they give themselves up to despair. But a believer's whole aim in life is to win God's pleasure, so the loss of worldly wealth leaves him unperturbed. He faces all trials and hardships with a brave heart.

The verse means to say that God treats men, according to their motives and intentions. He takes into consideration not only the actions of man but also his intentions and motives. As all the efforts of disbelievers are for this world, they do not deserve to be the recipient of God's help and favour. This and the preceding verse apply as much to the Jews as to the idolaters of Makkah.

What is the key message of this portion of the Holy Qur'ān?

How does this message apply to your personal life?

Second Rak'ah of the Friday Fajr Prayer

Importance of Sūrah al-Kahf

- [1], [2]It is mentioned in Ḥadīth that whoever would learn the first and the last ten verses of Sūrah al-Kahf would be protected from the evil influence of Dajjāl or antichrist (Musnad).
-
    - [3], [4]According to the Arabic lexicon, Dajjāl signifies a group of people who present themselves as trustworthy and pious, but are neither trustworthy nor pious. Rather, everything they say is full of dishonesty and deceit. This characteristic is to be found in the class of Christians known as the clergy. Another group is that of the philosophers and

---

[1] The Holy Qur'ān with English Translation and Commentary. 3rd ed. Islam International Publications Limited; 2002. Volume 3, Page 1478

[2] *Tafsīr-e-Kabīr*. Ḥaḍrat Mirzā Bashīr-ud-Dīn Maḥmūd Aḥmad[ra], Printwell Amritsar 2004. Volume 4, Pages 403-404

[3] The *Essence of Islām*. The Promised Messiah[as], Ḥaḍrat Mirzā Ghulām Aḥmad of Qadian: First edition. Islam International Publications Limited; 2005. Volume III, Pages 279-287

[4] *Kitabul-Bariyyah, Ruḥānī Khazā'in*, vol. 13, Pages. 243-244.

thinkers who are busy trying to assume control of machines, industries and the Divine scheme of things. They are the Dajjāl because they deceive God's creatures by their actions and tall claims as if they are partners in God's dominion. The clergy are arrogating to themselves the status of Prophethood because they ignore the true heavenly Gospel and spread a perverted and corrupted version as the supposed translation of the Gospel. For detailed discussion about the concept of Dajjāl, please see Essence of Islam, Volume 3)

- It is stated in the Ḥadīth when Sūrah al-Kahf was revealed, 70,000 angels descended to protect it (Manthūr Vol 4, Page 210). This is a metaphorical expression that means that in order to fulfil the Divine prophecy of the final triumph of Islam given in this Sūrah, Allāh the Exalted, in accordance with His Divine law, will appoint thousands of angels to help bring about this success.
    - This chapter gives the information about the challenges of Gog and Magog; huge powers of Christian nations and their attempts to

misrepresent and distort the Islamic teachings. Despite the might of Gog and Magog, weak Muslims will be helped by Allāh the Exalted to bring true the prophecy of triumph of Islam, Allāh Almighty will assign angels to help them

- ([5,6]*Yājūj* [Gog] and *Mājūj* [Magog] are two peoples who have been mentioned in earlier scriptures. The reason why they are so called is that they make extensive use of *Ajīj* [fire], and would reign supreme on earth and dominate every height. At the same time, a great change will be ordained from heaven and will usher in days of peace and amity.
- [7]I have also proved that it is essential for the Promised Messiah to appear at the time of Gog and Magog. Since *Ajīj*, from which the

[5] The *Essence of Islām*. The Promised Messiah[as], Ḥaḍrat Mirzā Ghulām Aḥmad of Qadian: First edition. Islam International Publications Limited; 2005. Volume III, pages 305

[6] *Lecture Siālkot, Rūḥānī Khazā'in*, vol. 20, Page. 211

[7] *Ayyāmuṣ-Ṣulḥ, Rūḥānī Khazā'in*, vol. 14, Page. 424-425

words Gog and Magog are derived, means 'fire', God Almighty has disclosed to me that Gog and Magog are a people who are greater experts in the use of fire than any other people. Their very names indicate that their ships, trains and machines will be run by fire. They will fight their battles with fire. They will excel all other people in harnessing fire to their service. This is why they will be called Gog and Magog. These are the people of the West, as they are unique in their expertise in the use of fire. In Jewish scriptures too it was the people of Europe who were described as Gog and Magog. Even the name of Moscow, which is the ancient capital of Russia, is mentioned. Thus it was preordained that the Promised Messiah would appear in the time of Gog and Magog. [8]For detailed discussion about the concept of Gog and Magog, please see Essence of Islam, Volume 3).

---

[8] The *Essence of Islām*. The Promised Messiah[as], Ḥaḍrat Mirzā Ghulām Aḥmad of Qadian: First edition. Islam International Publications Limited; 2005. Volume III, Pages 305-310

Sūrah al-Kahf, Chapter 18, Verses 1-11

بِسۡمِ ٱللَّهِ ٱلرَّحۡمَٰنِ ٱلرَّحِيمِ ۝

ٱلۡحَمۡدُ لِلَّهِ ٱلَّذِيٓ أَنزَلَ عَلَىٰ عَبۡدِهِ ٱلۡكِتَٰبَ وَلَمۡ يَجۡعَل لَّهُۥ عِوَجَاۜ ۝
قَيِّمٗا لِّيُنذِرَ بَأۡسٗا شَدِيدٗا مِّن لَّدُنۡهُ وَيُبَشِّرَ ٱلۡمُؤۡمِنِينَ ٱلَّذِينَ
يَعۡمَلُونَ ٱلصَّٰلِحَٰتِ أَنَّ لَهُمۡ أَجۡرًا حَسَنٗا ۝ مَّٰكِثِينَ فِيهِ
أَبَدٗا ۝ وَيُنذِرَ ٱلَّذِينَ قَالُواْ ٱتَّخَذَ ٱللَّهُ وَلَدٗا ۝ مَّا لَهُم بِهِۦ مِنۡ
عِلۡمٖ وَلَا لِأٓبَآئِهِمۡۚ كَبُرَتۡ كَلِمَةٗ تَخۡرُجُ مِنۡ أَفۡوَٰهِهِمۡۚ إِن
يَقُولُونَ إِلَّا كَذِبٗا ۝ فَلَعَلَّكَ بَٰخِعٞ نَّفۡسَكَ عَلَىٰٓ ءَاثَٰرِهِمۡ إِن
لَّمۡ يُؤۡمِنُواْ بِهَٰذَا ٱلۡحَدِيثِ أَسَفًا ۝ إِنَّا جَعَلۡنَا مَا عَلَى ٱلۡأَرۡضِ
زِينَةٗ لَّهَا لِنَبۡلُوَهُمۡ أَيُّهُمۡ أَحۡسَنُ عَمَلٗا ۝ وَإِنَّا لَجَٰعِلُونَ مَا عَلَيۡهَا
صَعِيدٗا جُرُزًا ۝ أَمۡ حَسِبۡتَ أَنَّ أَصۡحَٰبَ ٱلۡكَهۡفِ وَٱلرَّقِيمِ كَانُواْ
مِنۡ ءَايَٰتِنَا عَجَبًا ۝ إِذۡ أَوَى ٱلۡفِتۡيَةُ إِلَى ٱلۡكَهۡفِ فَقَالُواْ رَبَّنَآ ءَاتِنَا
مِن لَّدُنكَ رَحۡمَةٗ وَهَيِّئۡ لَنَا مِنۡ أَمۡرِنَا رَشَدٗا ۝

Translation

In the name of Allah, the Gracious, the Merciful. All praise belongs to Allah Who has sent down the Book to His servant and has not put therein any crookedness. *He has made it* a guardian, that it may give warning of a grievous chastisement from Him, and that it may give the believers who do good deeds the glad tidings that they shall have a good reward, Wherein they shall abide for ever. And that it may warn those who say, 'Allah has taken unto Himself a son.' No knowledge have they thereof, nor *had* their fathers. Grievous is the word that comes from their mouths. They speak naught but a lie. So haply thou wilt grieve thyself to death for sorrow after them if they believe not in this discourse. Verily, We have made all that is on the earth as an ornament for it, that We may try them as to which of them is best in conduct. And We shall make all that is thereon a barren soil. Dost thou think that the People of the Cave and the Inscription were a wonder among Our Signs? When the young men betook themselves for refuge to the Cave and said, 'Our Lord, bestow on us mercy from Thyself, and provide for us right guidance in our affair.

بِسۡمِ ٱللَّهِ ٱلرَّحۡمَـٰنِ ٱلرَّحِيمِ ۝

In the name of Allah, the Gracious, the Merciful.

[9]Commentary

(i) The verse بسم الله الرحمن الرحيم (*Bismillāhir-Raḥmānir-Raḥīm*) is the first verse of every chapter of the Qur'ān, except the Chapter *Barā'at* which, however, is not an independent chapter but a continuation of the chapter al-Anfāl. There is a saying reported by Ibn-e-'Abbas to the effect that whenever any new chapter was revealed, *Bismillāh* was the first verse to be revealed, and without *Bismillāh* the Holy Prophet[sa] did not know that a new chapter had begun (Sunan Abū Dāwūd).

This Ḥadīth goes to prove that

(1) The verse *Bismillāh* is part of the Qur'ān and not something supernumerary and

(2) The chapter *Barā'at* (*at-Taubah*) is not an independent Sūrah (chapter).

[9] The Holy Qur'ān with English Translation and Commentary. 3rd ed. Islam International Publications Limited; 2002. Volume 1, Pages 6-8

It also refutes the belief expressed by some that *Bismillāh* is a part only of *Al-Fātiḥah* and not of all the Qur'ānic chapters. Such views are further refuted by the Ḥadīth in which the Holy Prophet[sa] is reported to have said definitely that the verse *Bismillāh* is a part of all the Qur'ānic chapters (Ṣaḥīḥ Bukhāri & Sunan Dār Quṭnī).

(ii) The Holy Prophet[sa] attached very great importance to the verse *Bismillāh*. He is reported to have said that any important work which is done without reciting *Bismillāh* is apt to prove devoid of God's blessings. So it is a general practice among Muslims to commence every work with a recital of this prayer.

(iii) The place of this verse in the beginning of every chapter has the following significance:

1. The Qur'ān is a treasure of Divine knowledge to which access cannot be had without the special favour of God. In 56:80 God says regarding the Qur'ān, *None shall touch it except those who are purified*, meaning that except the favoured ones who have been purified by the hand of God, none shall grasp the deeper meaning of the Qur'ān. Thus *Bismillāh* has been placed at

the beginning of each chapter to remind the reader that in order to have access to, and benefit by, the treasures of Divine knowledge contained in the Qur'ān, he should not only approach it with pure motives but also constantly invoke the help of God and try to lead a righteous life.

ٱلْحَمْدُ لِلَّهِ ٱلَّذِىٓ أَنزَلَ عَلَىٰ عَبْدِهِ ٱلْكِتَٰبَ وَلَمْ يَجْعَل لَّهُۥ عِوَجَا ۜ ۝

[18:2] All praise belongs to Allah Who has sent down the Book to His servant and has not put therein any crookedness

قَيِّمًا لِّيُنذِرَ بَأْسًا شَدِيدًا مِّن لَّدُنْهُ وَيُبَشِّرَ ٱلْمُؤْمِنِينَ ٱلَّذِينَ

يَعْمَلُونَ ٱلصَّٰلِحَٰتِ أَنَّ لَهُمْ أَجْرًا حَسَنًا ۝

[18:3] *He has made it* a guardian, that it may give warning of a grievous chastisement from Him, and that it may give the believers who do good deeds the glad tidings that they shall have a good reward,

[10]Commentary

The Qur'ān has been called قيم (*qayyim*) guardian in this verse.

According to the different meanings of the Arabic word قيم (*qayyim*); the Qur'ān performs a double function. It is a guardian of the previous Scriptures inasmuch as it corrects and removes the errors that have found their way into them.

It is also a guardian for future generations of men because it takes upon itself their spiritual up-bringing and guides them to the paths which lead to the realisation of the sublime object of their life.

The believers have been promised اجراحسنا (*ajran Ḥasanan*) good reward in this verse. The significance of 'good reward' being implicit in the word اجر (Ajr) reward which in many places in the Qur'ān has been promised to believers, the addition of the qualifying word حسنا (*ḥasanan*) good points to the fact that the reward of the believers would be productive of particularly good results. It would not spoil them, but would make them deserving of

[10] The Holy Qur'ān with English Translation and Commentary. 3rd ed. Islam International Publications Limited; 2002. Volume 3, Page 1481-1490

still greater reward as they would turn God's favours to good account.

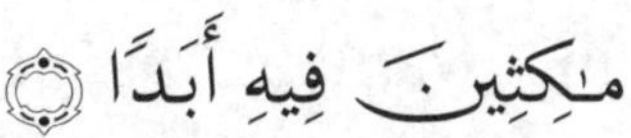

[18:4] Wherein they shall abide for ever

<u>Commentary</u>

If the verse be taken as referring to the reward of believers in Paradise, it would mean that that reward will last for ever and will know no end or diminution. But if it refers to the good reward of this world, then the verse would mean that believers would get a good reward so long as they do good deeds. The continuity of their good reward would depend upon the continuity of their good and righteous deeds.

وَيُنذِرَ ٱلَّذِينَ قَالُواْ ٱتَّخَذَ ٱللَّهُ وَلَدٗا

[18:5] **And that it may warn those who say, 'Allah has taken unto Himself a son.'**

Commentary

It is worthy of special note that the Qur'ān is first spoken of as 'giving warning', next as 'giving glad tidings' (v 3) and then again as 'giving warning' as in the present verse. Disbelievers have been warned twice and in between these two warnings the believers have been given glad tidings. This seems rather queer and the words appear to have been used haphazard. But it is not so.

They serve a very useful purpose.

The two 'warnings' and the one 'glad tidings' point to three important periods of the history of Islam. The first 'warning' mentioned in v. 3 pertains to the disbelievers of Makkah and all those people in the time of the Holy Prophet[sa], who had rejected his Message and were punished for their rejection and opposition. The 'glad tidings' spoken of in the same verse applies to Muslims who after their enemies had been destroyed enjoyed divine favours for a very long time and this fulfilled the divine promise embodied in the words, "Wherein they shall abide for ever".

For long centuries Muslims ruled over a large part of the globe and enjoyed great power and prestige. The 'second

warning' embodied in the present verse refers to Christian nations of the "latter days" and implies a prophecy that after Muslims had enjoyed power and dominion for a long time, their glory would depart and Christian nations would again come into their own and spread over the entire world and would prove as a bar sinister to the expansion of Islam.

These present-day Christian nations of the West have been warned of a severe punishment that is in store for them in the words, ***that it may warn those who say, Allāh has taken unto himself a son***.

Thus this giving of warnings twice and interspersing these two warnings with glad tidings for Muslims implied three great prophecies *viz*.,

a. The discomfiture and destruction of the Holy Prophet's opponents in his own time
b. The phenomenal rise of Muslims to power and glory and, after the departure of Muslim glory,
c. The punishment that is in store for the nations who say that ***Allāh has taken unto Himself a son***. The signs of this divine punishment are already becoming too manifest to be overlooked.

مَّا لَهُم بِهِۦ مِنۡ عِلۡمٍ وَلَا لِأَبَآئِهِمۡۚ كَبُرَتۡ كَلِمَةً تَخۡرُجُ مِنۡ أَفۡوَٰهِهِمۡۚ إِن يَقُولُونَ إِلَّا كَذِبًا ۝

[18:6] No knowledge have they thereof, nor *had* their fathers. Grievous is the word that comes from their mouths. They speak naught but a lie.

Commentary

The expression كبرت كلمة (*kaborat kalimatan)* grievous is the word is really كبرت هى كلمة (*kaborat hiya kalimatan*) which means that the saying of this word is very grievous, or that it is very grievous even to open the lips with this word and it is against reason and common sense to utter it.

The verse constitutes a severe indictment of the doctrine that Jesus[as] is the son of God. This doctrine is not only blasphemous but also revolting to human intellect. It is an insult to human understanding to say that a weak and helpless man who could not save himself from being hung on the Cross was God or the son of God. Misguided and erring leaders of the Christian church fabricated a most heinous and blasphemous doctrine without even a

modicum of sense or reason to support it. They were fully aware of the fact that the disciples of Jesus[as] and early Christians were strict monotheists and yet they departed from their pristine Faith. The later Christians, however, had with them the excellent Islamic teaching about the Unity of God, but they did not benefit by it, nor by the monotheistic beliefs of their own forebears. Without rhyme or reason they ascribed Godhead to a weak human being.

The words, *they speak naught but a lie*, signify that Jesus[as] never taught such a foolish doctrine but later Christians themselves invented it and they are to blame for it. In fact, even the canonical Gospels lend no support to this blasphemous doctrine. No doubt the Bible has used the epithet "son of God" about Jesus[as] but so has it also done about several other persons. For instance in Exod. 4:22 we have, "Thus saith the Lord, Israel is my son, even my first born." See also Gen. 6:2, John 10:35, etc.

فَلَعَلَّكَ بَـٰخِعٌ نَّفْسَكَ عَلَىٰٓ ءَاثَـٰرِهِمْ إِن لَّمْ يُؤْمِنُوا۟ بِهَـٰذَا ٱلْحَدِيثِ أَسَفًا ۝

[18:7] So haply thou wilt grieve thyself to death for sorrow after them if they believe not in this discourse.

Commentary

It is clear from the context that the people spoken of in these verses are the Western Christian nations. God had blessed them with material comforts and wealth and had bestowed upon them power, prestige and dominion. But they fell into the grievous error of taking a frail human being as the son of God. The Holy Prophet's solicitude and concern for the spiritual well-being of these people and his deep grief over their opposition to truth had almost killed him. But such is human ingratitude that from the very people for whom he felt and grieved so much he received nothing but abuse, invective and ridicule. Never, indeed, were selfless love and kindness so ill requited!

The words, *if they believe not in this discourse*, allude to the reason of the Prophet's grief. They mean to say that the Qur'ān contains the solution of all those difficult problems that Christian nations had to face in this life, yet these people who have made so much progress in material sciences are so backward in the spiritual science that they are inviting death and destruction by refusing to accept true guidance.

إِنَّا جَعَلْنَا مَا عَلَى ٱلْأَرْضِ زِينَةً لَّهَا لِنَبْلُوَهُمْ أَيُّهُمْ أَحْسَنُ عَمَلًا ۝

[18:8] Verily, We have made all that is on the earth as an ornament for it, that We may try them as to which of them is best in conduct

Commentary

The words, *We have made all that is on the earth as an ornament for it*, point to the great moral lesson that nothing in this world has been created in vain. Of all the innumerable things that God has created there is not one which has not its particular use or is devoid of all good. All of them add to the beauty of human life. Muslims were expected always to keep in view the great truth underlined in these simple words and to devote their time and energy to delving into the great secrets of nature and to exploring the unlimited properties of its elements. But they ignored this supreme lesson while the Christian peoples of the West remembered it well with the result that they became the most advanced and powerful nations in the world.

It is to be regretted, however, that while Western nations greatly benefited by the lesson taught in the words, *We have made all that is on the earth as an ornament for it*,

they neglected the one embodied in the words, *that We may try them as to which of them is best in conduct*. No doubt they sought after knowledge and made great advances in science. But the object of the advance and expansion of knowledge is that man's conduct may become pure and human life more peaceful. But these nations, instead of employing their knowledge and resources to the service of man, have ended by making human life miserable and unliveable. They have failed to set an example of good conduct and have put their scientific researches to evil use and have thereby laid the foundations of injustice, tyranny and corruption in the world. It is probably to this fact that the present verse refers.

[18:9] And We shall make all that is thereon a barren soil

Commentary

The verse means to say that all the things of this world are transitory. Their acquirement is not the end and object of human life. On the contrary, they have been created to serve higher and sublimer purposes- to be used for the

service of humanity. But Christian nations of the West, after having acquired wealth, power and dominion and after having made great discoveries and inventions, have not turned their scientific achievements to the service of mankind, but instead have employed them generally to add to human misery. As these scientific discoveries and inventions have not fulfilled the purpose of making human life more peaceful and beautiful, all the works of these peoples would be brought to naught and entirely obliterated. The expression, *And We shall make all that is thereon a barren soil*, does not mean that the whole world will be destroyed. It only refers to the destruction of the works of Christian nations to whom these verses particularly apply.

- Since a similar expression صعیدازلقا (*ṣa'īdan zalaqan*) barren ground used in verse 41 of this Sūrah in connection with the parable of "two gardens" clearly applies to the works of Western nations, as shown by the context, the expression صعیداجرزا (*ṣa'īdan jorozan*) barren soil must also be taken as applying to them. The words صعیداجرزا (*ṣa'īdan jorozan*) mean, a land without herbage or a land of which the

herbage has been cut or eaten. Now, ‘herbage’ in Qur’ānic terminology stands for the works of men, and according to this sense of the word, the words would mean that all the progress that the Western nations were to make and all their handiworks, their lofty and stately buildings, the beautiful scenery of their land and all their pomp, glory and grandeur would be destroyed. This means that a terrible visitation is in store for them.

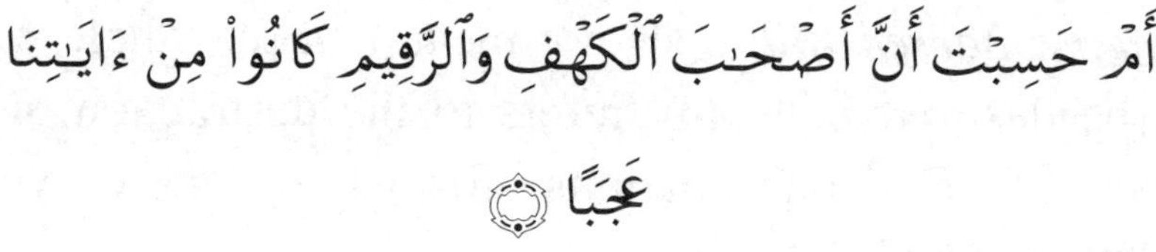

[18:10] Dost thou think that the People of the Cave and the Inscription were a wonder among Our Signs?

<u>Commentary</u>

The verse declares the Dwellers of the Cave to be no novel or out of the ordinary thing but as only one of the so many Signs of God. There was nothing about them which might be considered a departure from the ordinarily laws of nature. It is, however, very regrettable that while according to this verse the Dwellers of the Cave were no object of

wonder but were only a sign of God, many Commentators of the Qur'ān have woven fantastic legends around them.

Who were these Dwellers of the Cave, where did they live and what were the conditions and circumstances under which they had to live, are some of the questions that have agitated the minds of Commentators for hundreds of years. A good clue to the solution of these baffling questions is to be found in some of the stories related by Muslim historians, Ibn Ishaq being most prominent among them.

[11]A detailed account of these can be seen elsewhere. Based on these accounts following facts unmistakeably emerge.

1. That early Christians were believers in the Unity of God and that they suffered great persecution for their beliefs.

2. That some of these Christians fearing persecution and death took refuge in a cave in the time of a king, variously known as Dacyuse, Dacyanuse or, in Latin, Decius.

---

[11] The Holy Qur'ān with English Translation and Commentary. 3rd ed. Islam International Publications Limited; 2002. Volume 3, Page 1486-1488

3. That the persecutors of these Christians were idol-worshippers who sought to compel them to worship their own idols and offer sacrifices to them.
4. That these young men came out of the cave in the time of a King named Nandusis or, as Gibbon says, Theodosius

From the inscriptions on the tomb-stones in the catacombs it appears that the early Christians were strict monotheists. There is not a single word on the inscriptions which indicated that they believed in Jesus as 'God or the son of God'. He has been represented only as a shepherd or a Prophet of God, which he really was. Nor has Mary, his mother, been mentioned as anything more than a pious woman. The story of the tribe of the Prophet Jonah and that of Noah's flood find repeated and prominent mention in the inscriptions and engravings. This clearly shows that early Christians regarded the Old Testament with greater respect then do present-day Christians. It also appears that Christians who took refuge in the catacombs kept dogs at their entrance which would announce the approach of strangers by their barking.

To be brief, the account of the dwellers of the cave constitutes a representation of the history of early Christians and shows how they conducted a vigorous campaign against idolatry and polytheistic beliefs and suffered untold persecutions for their belief in the Unity of God and how their successors ended by disowning almost all the fundamental doctrines of their Faith. The position of "the cave", however, is of secondary importance; though from the facts narrated above its description as given in verse 18 applies more fully and in greater detail and exactness to the catacombs at Rome then to any other place.

Similarly, very strange and widely divergent accounts of الرقيم *(ar-Raqīm)* the Inscription have been given by the Commentators. According to some it was a tablet of lead or copper or a slab of stone on which the names of the Dwellers of the Cave, their ancestry, etc., were inscribed. Some say it was the name of the town or village from which they came or the name of the mountain or valley in which that "cave" was situated, yet according to others it was the name of their dog or the coin which they used. Leaving aside the mental wanderings of Commentators, these two words – "cave" and "inscription"- represent the

two most prominent aspects of the Christian Faith, viz., that it began as a religion of renunciation and withdrawal from the world and ended by becoming a religion of entire engrossment in worldly affairs, a religion of business and trade in a world of writings and inscriptions.

إِذْ أَوَى ٱلْفِتْيَةُ إِلَى ٱلْكَهْفِ فَقَالُوا۟ رَبَّنَآ ءَاتِنَا مِن لَّدُنكَ رَحْمَةً
وَهَيِّئْ لَنَا مِنْ أَمْرِنَا رَشَدًا ۝

[18:11] When the young men betook themselves for refuge to the Cave and said, 'Our Lord, bestow on us mercy from Thyself, and provide for us right guidance in our affair.

Commentary

The verse means to say that the Dwellers of the Cave prayed to God for His Mercy and deliverance from the difficult situation in which they found themselves.

What is the key message of this portion of the Holy Qur'ān?

How does this message apply to your personal life?

First Rak'ah of the Friday Maghrib Prayer

First Rak'ah of the Friday Maghrib Prayer

Importance of Sūrah al-Fīl[1]

- This chapter gives an account of the historical incidence which took place in Arabia, when a powerful and strong army of trained soldiers equipped with arms and powerful elephants, attempted to attack the House of God, and was defeated by actions of small birds.
- The Holy Prophet[sa] is given reassurance in this chapter that God, who can destroy powerful armies by agency of mere birds, has got the power to make the Holy Prophet[sa] successful against powerful enemies
- This chapter contains a promise that the protection of Allāh the Exalted will last till the day of judgement.
- These days Islam is under attack by powerful enemies who are attacking the fundamental basis of this religion. Allāh the Exalted has promised that strong enemies will be defeated by small and apparently insignificant righteous people.

---

[1] *Tafsīrul-Qur'ān* by The Promised Messiah, Ḥaḍrat Mirzā Ghulām Aḥmad[as] of Qadiān, Pages 487-489 available on www.alislam.org

بِسۡمِ ٱللَّهِ ٱلرَّحۡمَـٰنِ ٱلرَّحِيمِ ۝

أَلَمۡ تَرَ كَيۡفَ فَعَلَ رَبُّكَ بِأَصۡحَـٰبِ ٱلۡفِيلِ ۝ أَلَمۡ يَجۡعَلۡ كَيۡدَهُمۡ

فِي تَضۡلِيلٍ ۝ وَأَرۡسَلَ عَلَيۡهِمۡ طَيۡرًا أَبَابِيلَ ۝ تَرۡمِيهِم بِحِجَارَةٍ

مِّن سِجِّيلٍ ۝ فَجَعَلَهُمۡ كَعَصۡفٍ مَّأۡكُولِۭ ۝

<u>**Translation**</u>

In the name of Allah, the Gracious, the Merciful. Hast thou not seen how thy Lord dealt with the People of the Elephant? Did He not cause their plan to miscarry? And He sent against them swarms of birds, *Which ate their carrion*, striking them against stones of clay. And *thus* made them like broken straw, eaten up.

بِسۡمِ ٱللَّهِ ٱلرَّحۡمَـٰنِ ٱلرَّحِيمِ ۝

[105:1] **In the name of Allah, the Gracious, the Merciful.**

أَلَمۡ تَرَ كَيۡفَ فَعَلَ رَبُّكَ بِأَصۡحَـٰبِ ٱلۡفِيلِ ۝

[105:2] **Hast thou not seen how thy Lord dealt with the People of the Elephant?**

Commentary[2]

This verse refers to Abrahah, who marched on Makkah with a large army in 570 A.D., the year of the Holy Prophet's birth, in order to destroy the Ka'bah. The Holy Prophet's birth taking place in the year of Abrahah's attack on the Ka'bah and the utter destruction of his army implied a Divine hint that because the great Prophet for whose sake the Ka'bah had been built and who was to preach the last Heavenly Message from there was about to be born, it militated against God's eternal plan that it should suffer

[2] The Holy Qur'ān with English Translation and Commentary. 3rd ed. Islām International Publications Limited; 2002. Volume 5, Pages 2886-2889

destruction at the hands of an arch-infidel. Abrahah had a number of elephants with him. They were destroyed by a plague or epidemic, of the nature of small-pox, and their rotting bodies were eaten up by swarms of birds.

Detailed account of the incident

Dhu Niwas, the Jewish Himyar ruler of Yemen had put to death in cold blood 20,000 Christians. The Kaiser of Rome has ordered the Negus, the King of Abyssinia, which then formed part of the Roman Empire, to avenge this cruel act of Dhu Niwas. The Negus sent Abrahah to Yemen. He defeated the Himyar ruler and Yemen became part of the Abyssinian dominion and Abrahah was appointed its viceroy. In order to curry favour with the Negus and to break the unity of the Arabs or, as tradition goes, to stem the apprehended tide of Arab nationalism under a great Prophet whose appearance was eagerly awaited and was expected to take place very soon, and in order also to divert the attention of the Arabs from the Ka'bah, and to preach and disseminate Christianity in Arabia, Abrahah built a church at Sana, the capital of Yemen.

When, however, he failed to cajole or intimidate the Arabs into accepting the church at Sana in place of the Ka'bah as their central place of worship he was stung with rage, and being intoxicated with his great military power he marched on Makkah with an army of 20,000 strong in order to raze the Ka'bah to the ground.

Arriving at a place, a few miles from Makkah, he sent for the leaders of the Quraish in order to negotiate with them about the fate of the Ka'bah. The Quraish deputation, led by the venerable 'Abdul-Muṭṭalib', grandfather of the Holy Prophet[sa], met Abrahah who treated 'Abdul-Muṭṭalib' with great honour. But to Abrahah's great surprise, 'Abdul-Muṭṭalib', instead of beseeching that the Ka'bah be spared, only requested that his two hundred camels which Abrahah's men had seized be restored. 'Abdul-Muṭṭalib' on being told by Abrahah that he had not expected such a paltry request from him, poured out the anguish of his heart and expressed his firm faith in the invulnerability of the Ka'bah in the words إني أنا رب الإبل وإن للبيت ربًّا يمنعه i. e. "I am the master of the camels and the Ka'bah has a master who will protect it" (Al-Kāmil vol 1).

The negotiations, however, broke down and finding that they were too weak to offer effective resistance to Abrahah,

'Abdul-Muṭṭalib'advised his compatriots to repair to the surrounding hills. Before leaving the city, 'Abdul Muṭṭalib', holding the skirts of the Ka'bah, prayed in the following words full of extreme pathos:

لا هم إن المرء يمنع رحله فامنع حلالك

لا يغلبن صليبهم ومحالهم غدوا محالك

i.e., just as a man protects his house and property from plunder, so do thou O Lord, defend Thine own House and suffer not the Cross to triumph over the Ka'bah ("Tārikh Al-Kāmil", by Ibn-e- Athīr.Vol; 1. P 156 & Muir).

Abrahah's army had hardly moved when the Divine scourge overtook them. "A pestilential distemper," says Muir, "had shown itself in the camp of Abrahah. It broke out with deadly pustules and blains and was probably an aggravated form of smallpox. In confusion and dismay the army commenced retreat. Abandoned by their guides, they perished among the valleys and a flood swept multitudes into the sea. Scarcely any recovered who had once been smitten by it and Abrahah himself, a mass of malignant and putrid sores, died miserably on his return to Sana." It is to this incident particularly that the Sūrah refers.

The fact that the disease which destroyed Abrahah's army was smallpox in a virulently epidemic form is supported by the great historian Ibn-e-Isḥāq. He quotes 'Ā'ishah[ra] as saying that she saw two blind beggars in Makkah and on enquiring who they were, she was told that they were the drivers of Abrahah's elephants (Durr-e-Manthūr).

The expression كيف فعل (*kaifa fa'ala*) refers more to the dreadfulness of the scourge which destroyed Abrahah's army than to the manner of their destruction.

أَلَمْ يَجْعَلْ كَيْدَهُمْ فِي تَضْلِيلٍ ۝

[105:3] Did He not cause their plan to miscarry?

Commentary

How Abrahah was foiled in his design is writ large on the pages of history.

وَأَرْسَلَ عَلَيْهِمْ طَيْرًا أَبَابِيلَ ۝

[105:4] And He sent against them swarms of birds,

تَرۡمِيهِم بِحِجَارَةٖ مِّن سِجِّيلٖ ۝

[105:5] ***Which ate their carrion*, striking them against stones of clay**.

Commentary

Swarms of birds feasted themselves upon dead bodies of the invaders, striking the severed pieces against stones, as birds generally do when eating the small and severed pieces of the dead body of an animal.

فَجَعَلَهُمۡ كَعَصۡفٖ مَّأۡكُولِۭ ۝

[105:6] **And *thus* made them like broken straw, eaten up**.

What is the key message of this portion of the Holy Qur'ān?

How does this message apply to your personal life?

Second Rak'ah of Friday Maghrib Prayer

Second Rak'ah of the Friday Maghrib Prayer

Importance of Sūrah Quraish

- [1]An Arab while looking at the bewildering loneliness of Qadian commented to the Promised Messiah[as] that it was only in his honour that so many people visited such a remote place, otherwise who would want to bother to come to such a bleak and arid place? At which the Promised Messiah[as] smiled and said, "The example of this place is like Makkah, where people had to bring in provisions for routine use from distant places. The same is hinted about this place as mentioned in Sūrah Quraish".

- [2]In continuation with Sūrah al-Fīl, which explained the bad endings of those who have animosity against the Holy Ka'bah, Sūrah Quraish promises the reward for people who hold the Holy Ka'bah as a place of reverence.

---

[1] *Tafsīrul-Qur'ān* by The Promised Messiah[as], Ḥaḍrat Mirzā Ghulām Aḥmad of Qadiān, Page 490 available on www.alislam.org

[2] *Tafsīr-e-Kabīr*. Ḥaḍrat Mirzā Bashīr-ud-Dīn Maḥmūd Aḥmad[ra], Printwell Amritsar 2004. Volume, 10, Pages 79-80

- [3]Allāh the Exalted has stated the level of sacrifice of the Quraish as the gold standard for generations of Muslims to follow. Muslims are enjoined to emulate this degree of commitment to Islām.

- In accordance with the prayer of the Prophet Ibrāhīm[as], followers of Islām are promised peace and provisions.

[3] *Tafsīr-e-Kabīr*. Ḥaḍrat Mirzā Bashīr-ud-Dīn Maḥmūd Aḥmad[ra], Printwell Amritsar 2004. Volume 10, Page 121

بِسۡمِ ٱللَّهِ ٱلرَّحۡمَـٰنِ ٱلرَّحِيمِ

لِإِيلَـٰفِ قُرَيۡشٍ ۝ إِۦلَـٰفِهِمۡ رِحۡلَةَ ٱلشِّتَآءِ وَٱلصَّيۡفِ ۝

فَلۡيَعۡبُدُواْ رَبَّ هَـٰذَا ٱلۡبَيۡتِ ۝ ٱلَّذِىٓ أَطۡعَمَهُم مِّن جُوعٍ

وَءَامَنَهُم مِّنۡ خَوۡفٍۭ ۝

Translation

In the name of Allah, the Gracious, the Merciful. To bind the Quraish together and to promote their alliance We have devised trade journeys of the winter and summer. Hence they should worship the Lord of this House, Who has fed them against hunger, and has given them security against fear.

بِسۡمِ ٱللَّهِ ٱلرَّحۡمَٰنِ ٱلرَّحِيمِ ۝

[106:1] In the name of Allah, the Gracious, the Merciful.

لِإِيلَٰفِ قُرَيۡشٍ ۝

[106:2] To bind the Quraish together

إِۦلَٰفِهِمۡ رِحۡلَةَ ٱلشِّتَآءِ وَٱلصَّيۡفِ ۝

[106:3] and to promote their alliance *We have devised trade* journeys of the winter and summer -

Commentary[4]

As ل (*lām*) is a particle and in Arabic a new sentence never begins with a particle, a sentence or clause or expression therefore must be taken as understood before the words لِإِيلَٰفِ قُرَيۡشٍ (*Li Īlāf-e-Quraishin*) as before

[4] The Holy Qur'ān with English Translation and Commentary. 3rd ed. Islām International Publications Limited; 2002. Volume 5, Pages 2891-2892

بِسۡمِ اللّٰہِ الرَّحۡمٰنِ الرَّحِیۡمِ the word أقرء (*aqrā'o*) "I read" or أشرع (*ashra'o*) "I begin" is taken to be understood. In the present case the understood expression, according to some Commentators, is اعجب يا محمد (*a'jabo yā Muḥammad*) and the verse is supposed to read something like this:

اعجب يا محمد لنعم الله على قريش فى ايلافهم رحلة الشتاء والصيف

i.e., do thou wonder O Muhammad at God's great favour upon the Quraish that He has created in their hearts love for journeying in winter and summer. The Divine favour consisted in the fact that by taking trade caravans in winter to Yemen and in summer to Syria and Palestine, the Quraish brought necessities of life to Makkah. By this trading activity, they developed a certain prestige and also became acquainted with the prophecies about the appearance of a great Prophet in Arabia by coming into contact with Jews of Yemen and Christians of Syria who knew those prophecies.

It was indeed a great Divine favour that God created in the hearts of the Quraish a liking, for making journeys to Yemen and Syria. They were so rooted in the soil and had such great attachment for the Ka'bah that they would rather

starve than leave it, even temporarily. It was by the exhortation of Hāshim, the Holy Prophet's great grandfather, that they took to this calling. Thus it constituted a great Divine favour upon the Quraish that by their journeys to these places they, besides other advantages of these journeys, were being prepared to accept the coming Prophet when he appeared.

Apart from the expression اعجب يا محمد لنعم الله على قريش taken as understood, there is another explanation of the verses which fits in, perhaps more appropriately, with the context. This is as follows: "Thy Lord destroyed the Owner of the Elephant to attach the hearts of the Quraish to their journeying freely in winter and summer, which constituted a great Divine favour upon them."

This because if Abrahah had not been destroyed it would have been impossible for the Quraish to make journeys to Yemen. The destruction of Abrahah thus besides opening the way for trade-journeys to Yemen, made the Ka'bah all the more sacred in the eyes of the Arabs for whom it was already a place of pilgrimage. This in its turn gave added impetus to the trade of the Quraish.

فَلۡيَعۡبُدُواْ رَبَّ هَـٰذَا ٱلۡبَيۡتِ ۝

[106:4] Hence they should worship the Lord of this House

ٱلَّذِىٓ أَطۡعَمَهُم مِّن جُوعٍ وَءَامَنَهُم مِّنۡ خَوۡفٍۭ ۝

[106:5] Who has fed them against hunger, and has given them security against fear.

Commentary

It was indeed a great Divine favour that as servants of the Ka'bah the Quraish were granted perfect security from fear, while all around them raged fear and insecurity. Besides, they were provided round the year, with every kind of fruit and food. All this was not due to mere chance. It was in pursuance of a Divine Plan and in fulfilment of a prophecy made by the Patriarch Abraham 2500 years before (14: 36, 38 & 2: 127,130).

The verse drives home to the disbelieving Quraish their guilt of ingratitude by telling them that they had taken to the worship of gods made of wood and stone.

What is the key message of this portion of the Holy Qur'ān?

How does this message apply to your personal life?

First Rak'ah of Friday, Second Rak'ah of Wednesday and First Rak'ah of Thursday 'Ishā' Prayer

Importance of Sūrah Aḍ-Ḍuḥā

- [1]This chapter explains that as it is a natural phenomenon for day and night to alternate, similarly to have breaks between periods of Divine revelations (akin to spiritual day) with a duration of no Divine revelation (akin to night) is the normal course of action. This natural variation motivates the Prophets for more impassioned prayers
- [2]Ḥaḍrat Muṣleḥ-e-Mau'ūd[ra] elucidated that these periods of breaks in the Divine revelations have a purpose; they prepare and train the recipient of the Divine message for the next set of revelations and commandments.
- [3]In his Eid sermon on 27th December 2000, Ḥaḍrat Khalīfatul Masīḥ IV, Ḥaḍrat Mirzā Ṭāhir Aḥmad[ra] gave a discourse of verse 7-12 of Surāh Aḍ-Ḍuḥā

---

[1] *Tafsīrul-Qur'ān* by The Promised Messiah[as], Ḥaḍrat Mirzā Ghulām Aḥmad of Qadiān, Pages 404-405 available on www.alislam.org

[2] *Tafsīr-e-Kabīr*. Ḥaḍrat Mirzā Bashīr-ud-Dīn Maḥmūd Aḥmad[ra], Printwell Amritsar 2004. Volume 9,Page 70

[3] *Khuṭabāt-e.Īdain*, Ḥaḍrat Khalīfatul Masīḥ IV[rt], Khuṭbah Īdul Fitr. Ṭahir Foundation. December 27th 2000, Pages 341-345 available on www.alislam.org

- Ḥaḍrat Khalīfatul Masīḥ IV[ra] explained that Allāh the Exalted likes to see that His blessings have made an impact on his servant, thus that it is matter of virtue to make the most of blessings endowed by Allah the Exalted.
- One way to value the blessings given to one is to deliberate about less fortunate people and not to envy the person who has been granted more blessings. Not everybody is equally blessed, if one always looks at people more fortunate than oneself, it is possible that one may become jealous. However, if one gets to give some thought to those less prosperous than one, then one is inspired to be grateful for the blessings.
- Another way to value one's blessings is to serve others.
- It is mandatory to show gratitude for one's blessings, this enhances one in the love of Allah and motivates one to be obedient.

بِسۡمِ ٱللَّهِ ٱلرَّحۡمَـٰنِ ٱلرَّحِيمِ ۝

وَٱلضُّحَىٰ ۝ وَٱلَّيۡلِ إِذَا سَجَىٰ ۝ مَا وَدَّعَكَ رَبُّكَ وَمَا قَلَىٰ ۝

وَلَلۡأَخِرَةُ خَيۡرٌ لَّكَ مِنَ ٱلۡأُولَىٰ ۝ وَلَسَوۡفَ يُعۡطِيكَ رَبُّكَ

فَتَرۡضَىٰٓ ۝ أَلَمۡ يَجِدۡكَ يَتِيمًا فَـَٔاوَىٰ ۝ وَوَجَدَكَ ضَآلًّا

فَهَدَىٰ ۝ وَوَجَدَكَ عَآئِلًا فَأَغۡنَىٰ ۝ فَأَمَّا ٱلۡيَتِيمَ فَلَا تَقۡهَرۡ ۝

وَأَمَّا ٱلسَّآئِلَ فَلَا تَنۡهَرۡ ۝ وَأَمَّا بِنِعۡمَةِ رَبِّكَ فَحَدِّثۡ ۝

Translation

In the name of Allah, the Gracious, the Merciful. By the growing brightness of the forenoon, And *by* the night when it becomes still, Thy Lord has not forsaken thee, nor is He displeased *with thee*. Surely *every hour* that follows is better for thee than *the one* that precedes. And thy Lord will soon give thee and thou wilt be well pleased. Did He not find thee an orphan and give *thee* shelter? And He found thee wandering in search *for Him* and guided thee *unto Himself*. And He found thee in want and enriched *thee*. So the orphan, oppress not, And as for the begger, childe not, And as for the bounty of your Lord, do relate it to others.

بِسۡمِ ٱللَّهِ ٱلرَّحۡمَٰنِ ٱلرَّحِيمِ ۝

[93:1] In the name of Allah, the Gracious, the Merciful.

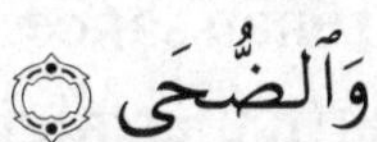

[93:2] By the growing brightness of the Forenoon,

[4]<u>**Commentary**</u>

"The brightness of the Forenoon" signifies the rise and progress of Islam. The verse therefore purports to say that the phenomenal rise of Islam will establish the truth of the Holy Prophet[sa] الضحى (aḍ-Ḍuḥā) may also refer to the particular forenoon, when the Holy Prophet[sa] entered Makkah at the head of an army of 10,000 holy warriors and the Ka'bah was cleared of idols.

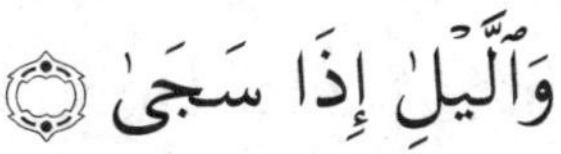

[93:3] And *by* the night when its darkness spreads out,

---

[4] The Holy Qur'ān with English Translation and Commentary. 3rd ed. Islām International Publications Limited; 2002. Volume 5, Pages 2840-2843

Commentary

The verse signifies that the prolonged period of the decline of Islam will also bear witness to the truth of the Holy Prophet[sa] in that according to his prophecies the decline will be followed by its renaissance. "The Night" may also have reference to that particular night when after the fall of darkness the Holy Prophet[sa] went out of his house and took refuge in Cave Thaur along with Abū Bakr[ra]. In fact the night when the Holy Prophet[sa] left Makkah and the day Makkah fell, give in a nutshell the various ups and downs of the Holy Prophet's whole career.

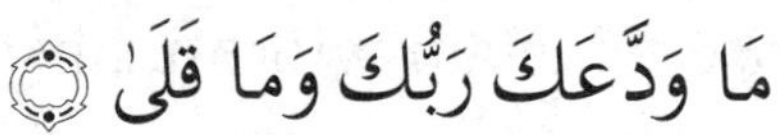

[93:4] Thy Lord has not forsaken thee, nor is He displeased *with thee*.

Commentary

Every day and night of the Holy Prophet[sa]: his great successes and temporary setbacks; his joys and tribulations; his devotions at night and activities in the day, all bear out that God was with him.

وَلَلْآخِرَةُ خَيْرٌ لَّكَ مِنَ ٱلْأُولَىٰ ۞

[93:5] Surely *every hour* that follows is better for thee than *the one* that precedes.

Commentary

The verse means that every succeeding moment of the Holy Prophet's life is better than the preceding. To mention a few landmarks in his career, one may observe that he left Makkah with a single Companion, a price having been put on his head. He entered the same town after a brief period of eight years at the head of 10,000 devoted followers.

At Badr there were only 313 Muslims with him and at Uhud more than double that number, and in the Battle of the Ditch the number grew to several thousand, till at the Last pilgrimage more than 100,000 believers marched under his banner. The successes of the Holy Prophet[sa] continued after his death. Islam went from strength to strength till it spread, within a few decades, over a large part of the then known world. The reference in the verse may also be to the latter days when the renaissance of Islam was to take place. The verse may also mean that Divine Reformers will continue to appear among Muslims

during periods of decline to impart to the Faith a new life and a new vigour.

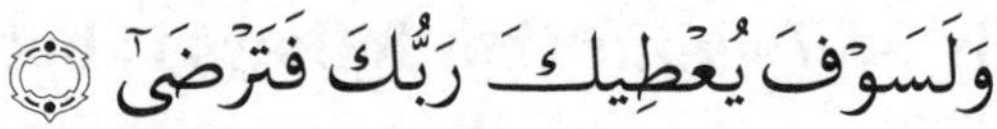

[93:6] And thy Lord will soon give thee and thou wilt be well pleased.

Commentary

The Sūrah being one of the earliest revelations received at a time when those who had responded to the Call of the Holy Prophet[sa] could be counted on one's fingers, the verse under comment contains a message of hope and good cheer wherein the Prophet[sa] is told that the time is fast approaching when his cause will triumph and he will be blessed with Divine favours-- in this life and the Hereafter-- to his heart's content.

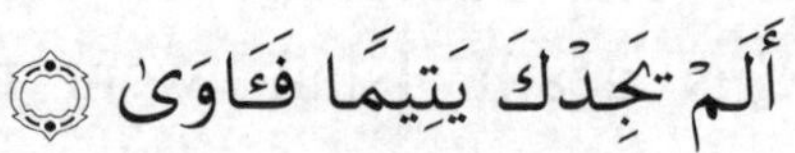

[93:7] Did He not find thee an orphan and give *thee* shelter?

Commentary

The Holy Prophet[sa] was an orphan in fact, as well as figuratively. His orphanhood was of the extreme kind. His father died before he was born, leaving no property. His mother died when he was hardly six years old and his grandfather 'Abdul-Muṭṭalib' who took charge of him after his mother's death, died two years later, leaving him under the care of his uncle, a man of scanty means. Thus the Prophet[sa] was deprived of parental care and love in his early childhood. Yet he received love and affection from his juniors and seniors, his Companions and compatriots in a large measure such that no woman-born had ever received the like of it before or after him or is likely to receive in future.

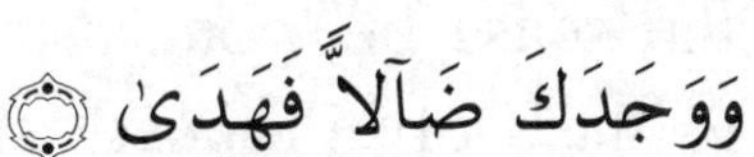

[93:8] And He found thee wandering in search *of Him* and guided thee *unto Himself*.

Commentary

In view of different meanings of the word ضل (*ḍalla*), the verse may be interpreted thus

1. The Holy Prophet[sa] wandered in search of the ways and means to attain to God, and God revealed to him the law which guided him to the desired goal.
2. He was perplexed and did not know how to find the path that led to the attainment of his quest and God guided him to it (42:53)
3. He was entirely lost in the love of God and did not know how to find Him but God led him to Himself (12:9)
4. He was hidden from the eyes of the world. God discovered him and chose him for the task of leading people to him. Thus the word ضال (*ḍāll*) has not been used in disapprobation but in praise of the Holy Prophet[sa].

The word in the sense of 'gone astray' does not and cannot apply to the Holy Prophet[sa] since according to another Qur'ānic verse (53:3) he was immune to error or going astray. Moreover, the six concluding verses of the Sūrah reveal a certain sequence—verse 7,8 & 9 standing in close relationship to 10,11&12 respectively; the ضال (*ḍāll*) of verse 8 being substituted by سائل (*sā'il*) of verse 11, explains the significance of the former word which is, 'one who sought God's help to be guided to

Him'. The verse may also be interpreted as: And He found thee lost in thy love for thy people, and provided thee with guidance for them.

وَوَجَدَكَ عَآئِلًا فَأَغْنَىٰ ۝

[93:9] And He found thee in want and enriched *thee*.

__Commentary__

The Holy Prophet[sa] started life as a poor orphan but ended by being the undisputed master of the whole of Arabia.

فَأَمَّا ٱلْيَتِيمَ فَلَا تَقْهَرْ ۝

[93:10] So the orphan, oppress not,

وَأَمَّا ٱلسَّآئِلَ فَلَا تَنْهَرْ ۝

[93:11] And as for the begger, chide him not,

وَأَمَّا بِنِعْمَةِ رَبِّكَ فَحَدِّثْ ۝

[93:12] And as for the bounty of your Lord do relate it to others.

Commentary

Verses 7,8 and 9 speak of God's favours on the Holy Prophet[sa] and in verses 10, 11 and 12, the Prophet[sa] is enjoined to show his gratitude for Divine favours by doing similar favours to his fellow beings. The commandment applies equally to his followers.

What is the key message of this portion of the Holy Qur'ān?

How does this message apply to your personal life?

Second Rak'ah of Friday 'Ishā' Prayer

Second Rak'ah of Friday 'Ishā' Prayer, Sūrah at-Tīn

Importance of Sūrah at-Tīn

- [1]It is incumbent upon man to have a true and strong bond with God and aspire to emulate the attributes of God, which will make man the best of Allah's creation; otherwise one runs the risk of becoming lowest of the lowest of creatures of God. Even a sheep can be useful to others. If one chooses not to work for the benefits of others, one is worse than a sheep.

- [2]This chapter points to the four historical emigrations that took place. Prophets Adam[as], Noah[as] and Moses[as] all of them were ultimately triumphant after having suffered the hardships of having to leave their

---

[1] *Tafsīrul-Qur'ān* by the Promised Messiah[as], Pages 414-416 available on www.alislam.org

[2] *Tafsīr-e-Kabīr*. Ḥaḍrat Mirzā Bashīr-ud-Dīn Maḥmūd Aḥmad[ra], Printwell Amritsar 2004. Volume 9, Pages 151-153

homelands. A similar destiny is prophesised for the Holy Prophet[sa] in this chapter of the Holy Qur'an.

- This chapter concludes to say that with the advent of the Holy Prophet[sa] the Divine Law became complete and perfect in all its manifold aspects, and man attained his complete intellectual, social, moral and spiritual development; therefore following the teachings of Islam will make a person the best of the best and not following the teachings of Islam will make him the worst of the worst of Allah's creations.

بِسۡمِ ٱللَّهِ ٱلرَّحۡمَٰنِ ٱلرَّحِيمِ ۝

وَٱلتِّينِ وَٱلزَّيۡتُونِ ۝ وَطُورِ سِينِينَ ۝ وَهَٰذَا ٱلۡبَلَدِ ٱلۡأَمِينِ
۝ لَقَدۡ خَلَقۡنَا ٱلۡإِنسَٰنَ فِيٓ أَحۡسَنِ تَقۡوِيمٖ ۝ ثُمَّ رَدَدۡنَٰهُ أَسۡفَلَ
سَٰفِلِينَ ۝ إِلَّا ٱلَّذِينَ ءَامَنُواْ وَعَمِلُواْ ٱلصَّٰلِحَٰتِ فَلَهُمۡ أَجۡرٌ غَيۡرُ
مَمۡنُونٖ ۝ فَمَا يُكَذِّبُكَ بَعۡدُ بِٱلدِّينِ ۝ أَلَيۡسَ ٱللَّهُ بِأَحۡكَمِ
ٱلۡحَٰكِمِينَ ۝

<u>Translation</u>

In the name of Allah, the Gracious, the Merciful. By the Fig and the Olive, And *by* Mount Sinai, And *by* this town, the abode of peace. Surely, We have created man in the best of creative plans. Then We reverted him to the state of the lowest of the low, Except those who

believe and do good works; so for them is an unending reward. Then what is there to give the lie to thee after *this* with regard to the Judgment? Is not Allah the Best of judges?

بِسۡمِ ٱللَّهِ ٱلرَّحۡمَـٰنِ ٱلرَّحِيمِ ۝

[95:1] In the name of Allah, the Gracious, the Merciful.

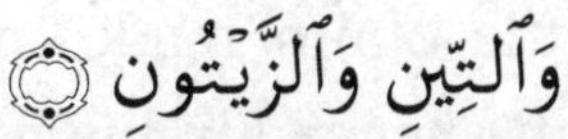

[95:2] By the Fig and the Olive,

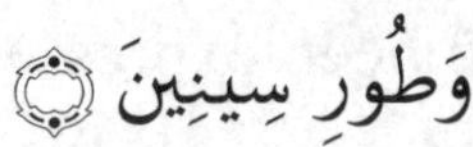

[95:3] And *by* Mount Sinai,

[3]**Commentary**

The word سينين (Sīnīn) being in the plural shows that there are several mountains of this name in that region. On one of these God manifested Himself to Moses.

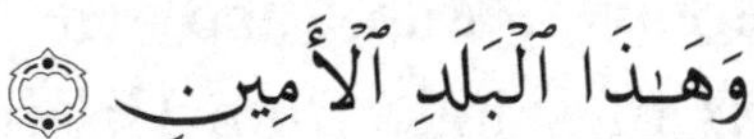

[95:4] And *by* this Town, the abode of peace.

---

[3] The Holy Qur'ān with English Translation and Commentary. 3rd ed. Islām International Publications Limited; 2002. Volume 5, Pages 2848-2851

Commentary

The Fig, the Olive, Mount Sinai and "this City of Security" have been invoked as witnesses to support and substantiate the claim made in the Sūrah that the Holy Prophet[sa] will succeed in his mission.

Various views have been expressed as to what is meant by these things and how do they support the above-mentioned claim? Here are some of these views:

1. "The Fig" and "the Olive" are symbolic of Jesus[as], "Mount Sinai" of Moses[as]; and "this City of Security" of the Holy Prophet[sa]. These three verses together point to the well-known Biblical reference, *viz.*, "The Lord came from Sinai, and rose up from Seir with them; and He shined forth from Mount Paran, and He came with ten thousands of saints: from His right hand went a fiery law for them." (Deut 33:2).

2. "The Fig" is symbolic of the Mosaic Dispensation and "the Olive" of the Islamic Dispensation. In the Bible good people and the bad among the

Israelites have been likened to two baskets of good and bad figs (Jer. Chap. 24: 1-5); and in the Qur'ān Islamic Teaching has been likened to "the oil of a blessed Olive tree which is neither of the East nor of the West" (24:36). This simile has been further expressed in more concrete form by the words "Mount Sinai" and "this City of Security". The simile is very apt, since "the Fig" and "the Olive" are both used as medicines and as articles of food, with this difference that the former tastes sweet but rots very soon, while the latter is used as fruit, it's oil is in general use and when mixed with condiments it preserves and protects pickled article from rotting and decaying.

3. According to some Commentators "The Fig" stands for Buddhism, the, "the Olive" for Christianity, "Mount Sinai" for Judaism and "this City of Security" for the Holy Prophet[sa] of Islam.

4. But perhaps the best explanation of the symbolism used in these verses is the one according to which the four words represent four periods in the history of human evolution, "The Fig" representing the era of Adam[as], "the Olive'

that of Noah[as]", "Mount Sinai"' that of Moses[as] and "this City of Security" the Islamic epoch.

This explanation finds ample support from the Bible and the Qur'ān. When Adam[as] and Eve ate the forbidden fruit and found themselves naked, they sewed fig leaves together, and made themselves aprons (Gen. 3:7). About Noah[as] we read: "And the dove came into him in the evening; and lo! In her mouth was an olive leaf plucked off; so Noah[as] knew that the waters were abated from off the earth" (Gen 8:11). And it is an accepted fact that Moses[as] received the Divine Law on Mount Sinai and that Makkah, the birthplace of Islam was, from time immemorial, regarded as, and proved to be, the "City of Security".

These four periods represent the four cycles through which man had to pass to reach the stage of complete development. In the cycle of Adam[as] the foundations of human civilisation were laid. Noah[as] was the founder of the Sharī'at. In the cycle of Moses[as] the details of the Sharī'at were revealed, while with the advent of the Holy Prophet[sa] the Divine Law became complete and perfect in all its manifold aspects, and man attained his complete intellectual, social, moral and spiritual development.

The verse signifies that the circumstances of the Holy Prophet[sa] resemble those of Adam[as], Noah[as], and Moses[as]. Like them he will suffer hardships in the beginning and like them will succeed in the end.

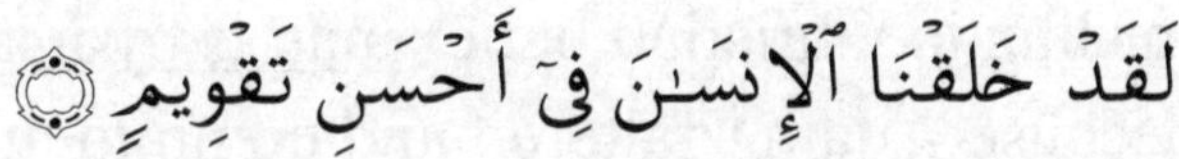

[95:5] Surely, We have created man in the best of creative plans.

Commentary

The verse may mean:

1. Man has been endowed with the best natural powers and qualities, by making use of which he can make infinite progress

2. God has endowed man with a creative power i.e., he can be a good architect and builder in both the physical and spiritual senses.

The question naturally arises: **When man has been endowed with such wonderful natural powers and**

capacities, why does he sin? Various schools have their own explanation for this baffling question.

i. According to one school man is prone to evil, though he has also been endowed with the power to correct and reform himself. This is the Buddhist conception of evil.

ii. According to Christian belief man is by nature sinful, because Adam[as] faltered and committed a sin, and his progeny inherited the taint of sin from their progenitor.

iii. The third school holds the view that man is not born with a good or bad nature. He comes into the world with some natural inclinations and instinctive impulses and it is the sort of education which he gets or the atmosphere in which he moves that make him good or bad. Some mystics hold the view that man is deprived of all freedom of will or action and is completely denied discretion or volition and that he is a helpless victim of predetermined set of conditions and circumstances which he cannot overcome.

iv. The protagonists of the theory of Transmigration of Souls are of the view that man is born to suffer

for the evil deeds he does in a former existence and goes through various forms of re-birth to cleanse himself of his sins.

All these views evidently contravene human reason and offend against his moral sense.

According to Islam, however, man is born with a pure and unsullied nature, with a natural tendency to do good, but he has also been given a large measure of freedom of will and action to mould himself as he chooses.

He has been endowed with great natural powers and qualities to make unlimited moral progress and to rise spiritually so high as to become the mirror in which Divine attributes are reflected. But if he misuses God-given powers and attributes he sinks lower than even beasts and brutes and becomes the Devil incarnate as the next verse shows.

Briefly, the verse signifies that man is blessed with great potentialities for good or evil.

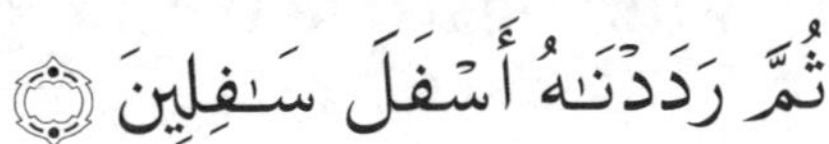

[95:6] Then We reverted him to the state of the lowest of the low.

Commentary

If “man” is taken to mean the whole mankind the verse signifies that good precedes evil. This is Islam's main difference with the protagonists of the theory of man’s moral evolution, according to whom evil precedes good.

If man is taken as an individual the verse means that God has bestowed upon man great natural faculties and powers and has revealed guidance in order that by making right use of them and following Divinely-revealed guidance he might reach the high destiny intended for him.

إِلَّا ٱلَّذِينَ ءَامَنُواْ وَعَمِلُواْ ٱلصَّـٰلِحَـٰتِ فَلَهُمْ أَجْرٌ غَيْرُ مَمْنُونٍ ۝

[95:7] Save those who believe and do good works; so for them is an unfailing reward.

فَمَا يُكَذِّبُكَ بَعْدُ بِٱلدِّينِ ۝

[95:8] Then what is there to give the lie to thee after *this* with regard to the Judgment?

أَلَيْسَ ٱللَّهُ بِأَحْكَمِ ٱلْحَٰكِمِينَ ۝

[95:9] Is not Allah the Best of judges?

Commentary

The verse purports to say that when man has been created to achieve a very high spiritual destiny and God sent his Messengers such as Adam[as], Noah[as], Moses[as] and the Holy Prophet[sa], to help him achieve his great goal and that if he does not make proper use of his natural faculties and rejects the Divine Message, opposing God's Messengers he is punished, then, who can, with reason, deny that there is a Day of Judgement in this life and in the Hereafter, and that the commandments of God Who is the Best of Judges cannot be defied with impunity and man's action will not go unrequited.

This is a simple explanation of this verse. But in view of the different significations of the word دين (Dīn), the verse may also mean:

1. How can the pagan Quraish, after having seen the evil end to which opponents of God's Messengers

always come, possibly hope that they will escape God's judgement and will not be punished and the Holy Prophet will not succeed?

2. When God has been revealing the Shari'at from time immemorial, then why do disbelievers find fault with the Holy Prophet[sa], if he has brought a new Law?

3. The disbelievers can advance no sane or solid argument against the claim of the Holy Prophet[sa]. Any charge or objection they raise against him equally applies to all Divine Messengers.

4. In view of the innumerable Signs shown in favour of the Holy Prophet[sa], no plan or argument can succeed against him or can disprove his claim.

5. No truly righteous man can reject the Holy Prophet[sa]

6. After having known the tragic end of the opponents of God's Messengers who will dare say that he can compel the Holy Prophet[sa] to give up his mission?

What is the key message of this portion of the Holy Qur'ān?

How does this message apply to your personal life?

SATURDAY

DAY	SALAT	FIRST RAK'AH	2ND RAK'AH
SATURDAY	Fajr	Sūrah al-Baqarah 1-8	Sūrah al-Baqarah 9-17
	Maghrib	Sūrah al-Falaq	Sūrah an-Nās
	'Ishā'	Sūrah al-Baqarah 256 (Āyatul-Kursī)	Sūrah al-Baqarah 287

First Rak'ah of the Saturday Fajr Prayer

First Rak'ah of the Saturday Fajr Prayer

Importance of Sūrah al-Baqarah

- al-Baqarah is the longest chapter of the Holy Qur'ān. The Holy Prophet[sa] said that everything has its peak and the peak of the Qur'ān is al-Baqarah (Tirmidhī).
- The Holy Prophet[sa] said that whosoever recites ten verses of this chapter, first four verses, Āyatul-Kursī and last three verses, Satan will not enter his house till the morning (Ibne Kathīr).
    - [1]This means that these verses embody the Islamic teachings and that satan cannot come near a person who faithfully acts on these teachings.
    - 'Till the morning' means that teachings, however excellent, if not regularly practiced cannot be fully effective and the good influences of such teachings are lost.

[1] The Holy Qur'ān with English Translation and Commentary. 3rd ed. Islām International Publications Limited; 2002. Volume 1, Page 24

- [2]In the first 4 verses a sketch is drawn for a pious life, Āyatul-Kursī has a great explanation of the attributes of God and the last three verses contain prayers that purify the heart. When these three things come together, one's heart is purified and satanic thoughts disappear.
    - To do good deeds in following the words of Allāh
    - To ponder over the attributes of Allāh the Exalted
    - To always engage in prayers and commit oneself totally to God.
- [3]The Promised Messiah[as] said that in this chapter the rights of Allāh and rights of people are described in great detail. Do's and don'ts have been explained and there is a great emphasis on patience and sacrifice.

---

[2] *Tafsīr-e-Kabīr*. Ḥaḍrat Mirzā Bashīr-ud-Dīn Maḥmūd Aḥmad[ra], Printwell Amritsar 2004. Volume 1, Page 51

[3] *Tafsīrul-Qur'ān* by The Promised Messiah[as], Ḥaḍrat Mirzā Ghulām Aḥmad of Qadian, Page 1 available on www.alislam.org

- The Khalīfatul Masīḥ III, Ḥaḍrat Mirzā Nāṣir Aḥmad[ra] enjoined Ahmadi children to memorise the first seventeen verses of Sūrah al-Baqarah.

بِسْمِ ٱللَّهِ ٱلرَّحْمَٰنِ ٱلرَّحِيمِ ﴿١﴾

الٓمٓ ﴿١﴾ ذَٰلِكَ ٱلْكِتَٰبُ لَا رَيْبَ ۛ فِيهِ ۛ هُدًى لِّلْمُتَّقِينَ ﴿٢﴾
ٱلَّذِينَ يُؤْمِنُونَ بِٱلْغَيْبِ وَيُقِيمُونَ ٱلصَّلَوٰةَ وَمِمَّا رَزَقْنَٰهُمْ
يُنفِقُونَ ﴿٣﴾ وَٱلَّذِينَ يُؤْمِنُونَ بِمَآ أُنزِلَ إِلَيْكَ وَمَآ أُنزِلَ مِن
قَبْلِكَ وَبِٱلْءَاخِرَةِ هُمْ يُوقِنُونَ ﴿٤﴾ أُو۟لَٰٓئِكَ عَلَىٰ هُدًى مِّن
رَّبِّهِمْ ۖ وَأُو۟لَٰٓئِكَ هُمُ ٱلْمُفْلِحُونَ ﴿٥﴾ إِنَّ ٱلَّذِينَ كَفَرُوا۟
سَوَآءٌ عَلَيْهِمْ ءَأَنذَرْتَهُمْ أَمْ لَمْ تُنذِرْهُمْ لَا يُؤْمِنُونَ ﴿٦﴾ خَتَمَ
ٱللَّهُ عَلَىٰ قُلُوبِهِمْ وَعَلَىٰ سَمْعِهِمْ ۖ وَعَلَىٰٓ أَبْصَٰرِهِمْ غِشَٰوَةٌ ۖ وَلَهُمْ
عَذَابٌ عَظِيمٌ ﴿٧﴾ وَمِنَ ٱلنَّاسِ مَن يَقُولُ ءَامَنَّا بِٱللَّهِ وَبِٱلْيَوْمِ
ٱلْءَاخِرِ وَمَا هُم بِمُؤْمِنِينَ ﴿٨﴾

Translation

Alif Lām Mīm. This is a perfect Book; there is no doubt in it; *it is* a guidance for the righteous, Who believe in the unseen and observe Prayer, and spend out of what We have provided for them; And who believe in that which has been revealed to thee, and that which was revealed before thee, and they have firm faith in what is *yet* to come. It is they who follow the guidance of their Lord and it is they who shall prosper. Those who have disbelieved — it is equal to them whether thou warn them or warn them not — they will not believe. Allah has set a seal on their hearts and their ears, and over their eyes is a covering; and for them is a great punishment.

الٓمٓ ۝

[2:2] Alif Lām Mīm.

[4]Commentary

Abbreviations like الم (*alif, lām mīm*) are known as المقطعات (*al-muqaṭṭa'āt*) i.e. letters used and pronounced separately. They occur in the beginning of not less than 28 Sūrahs, and are made up of one or more, to a maximum of five, letters of the Arabic alphabet. The letters out of which these abbreviations are constituted are 13 in number; *Alif, Lām, Mīm, Ṣād, Rā, Kāf, Hā, Yā, 'Ain, Ṭā, Sīn, Ḥā*, and *Qāf*. Of these *Qāf* occurs alone in the beginning of one Sūrah only, the rest occur in combinations of two or more in the beginning of certain *Sūrahs*.

Of the meanings ascribed to *Muqaṭṭa'āt* two seem to be more authentic:

---

[4] The Holy Qur'ān with English Translation and Commentary. 3rd ed. Islām International Publications Limited; 2002. Volume 1, Pages 26-31

1. That each letter has a definite numerical value. Thus ا (*Alif*) has the value of 1, ب (*Bā*) of 2, ج (*Jīm*) of 3, د (*Dāl*) of 4, ه (*Hā*) of 5, and so on (Aqrab). This system was known to the early Arabs and is mentioned in some well-known books of tradition (e.g. *Jarīr,i. 70 & 71)*. In numerical terms the letters الم (a*lif lām mīm*) would signify the length of time which the full manifestation of the inner significance of the Sūrah was meant to take.

   The letters الم (a*lif lām mīm*) have the numerical value of 71 (ا [Alif] being 1, ل [*Lām*] 30 and م [*Mīm*] 40). Thus the placing of a*lif lām mīm* in the beginning of the Sūrah would mean that the subject-matter of *Al-Baqarah* i.e. the special consolidation of early Islam would take 71 years to unfold itself completely. It is well known that this consolidation went on until the year 71 A.H., the year of the coming to power of Yazīd, son of Mu'āwiya, when the history of Islam took a different turn.
2. The second and much more important significance of the *Muqaṭṭa'āt* is that they are abbreviations for specific attributes of God and a Sūrah before which the *Muqaṭṭa'āt* are placed is, in its subject-matter,

> connected with the Divine attributes for which the *Muqaṭṭa'āt* stand. Thus, the letters الم (a*lif lām mīm*) stand for أنا الله أعلم (*anallāho A'lamo*) i.e., " I am Allah, the All Knowing"—a meaning which has the authority of Ibn-e-'Abbās, cousin of the Holy Prophet[sa] (*Jarīr*). Thus a*lif lām mīm* placed in the beginning of *Al-Baqarah* indicate that the central theme of this chapter is Divine knowledge. God proclaims, as it were, that Muslims, weak in the beginning, will soon become strong and attain to knowledge, wisdom and power.

The system of using *Muqaṭṭa'āt* was in vogue among the Arabs, who used them in their poems and conversations. In the modern West also the use of abbreviations has become very widespread. Nearly every dictionary provides a list of them along with their meaning

ذَٰلِكَ ٱلْكِتَٰبُ لَا رَيْبَ ۛ فِيهِ ۛ هُدًى لِّلْمُتَّقِينَ ۝

[2:3] This is a perfect Book; there is no doubt in it; ***it is*** **a guidance for the righteous,**

Commentary

The clause ذلک الکتاب (*zālikal-kitāb*) (this is a perfect book) placed in the beginning of the verse, is capable of several interpretations, the following two being more in harmony with the Qur'ānic text:

1. This is a complete and perfect Book, a Book which possesses all the excellences that a complete and perfect Book should possess.

2. This is that Book or this is the Book (which you prayed for, or which was promised to you).

Combined with the words لَا رَيْبَ فِيهِ (*lā raiba fīh*) the full clause ذٰلِکَ الْکِتٰبُ لَا رَيْبَ فِيهِ (*zālikal-kitābu lā raiba fīh*) would mean that this Book is perfect in all respects and contains nothing of ريب (*raib*) doubt in it, i.e., nothing that may make one's mind uneasy, nothing doubtful, nothing that may cause affliction, etc.

A Book claiming to be revealed and demanding acceptance in the presence of other Books which also claim Divine origin must at the very outset make such a claim to set at

rest the natural question as to what was the necessity of a new Book when already so many Books existed in the world. So the Qur'an, in the very beginning, asserts that of all Books it alone is perfect, satisfying human needs in a perfect manner.

The above claim of the Qur'an is capable of detailed substantiation. Briefly, however, it is founded on the comprehensiveness of its teaching.

- The Qur'ān deals clearly and adequately with all important questions such as God and His attributes, the origin, nature and purpose of man, his life here and hereafter.

- It instructs man in the regulation of his relations with God and his fellow-men in a manner unequalled by other religious Books.

- It also instructs parents and children, husbands and wives and other relatives in their duties.

- It teaches about wills and inheritance and about the rights of neighbours, employers and employees, rulers and ruled.

- Above all, it tells how man should conduct himself in relation to God and His Prophets. The other Books either do not teach about these matters at all or their treatment of them is very fragmentary.

The Qur'ān also gives a very systematic account of morals-- a subject on which the other Books say either little or nothing. In the Buddhist teaching we have a discussion of the basic instincts of man, but that discussion is very meagre compared with the account of the Qur'ān. The Qur'ān tells us about the roots of instincts, the ends which they serve and the use to which they may rightly be put. It also tells us how instincts become transformed into good or bad moral qualities, and how good qualities may be promoted and bad ones eradicated or discouraged. The Buddhist teaching inculcates the killing of desires but does not tell how bad desires arise and how they can be checked. The Qur'ān teaches about the source of sin and about the means of damming them.

Dealing with all these subjects in detail, the Qur'ān is yet a book of very small dimensions, a fact which makes the reading, understanding and remembering of it a comparatively easy task. Thousands of persons know it completely by heart. The claim of the Qur'ān that it is a

perfect Book is, therefore, based on fact, and is appropriately made in the beginning of the text.

The second meaning of ذلك الكتاب (*zālikal-kitāb*) this is the Book is that the prayer, *Guide us in the right path*, contained in *Al-Fātiḥah* meets with acceptance in this verse. Man prayed for guidance and guidance has come. "This is the Book which was promised to you".

The full meaning of ذلك الكتاب (*zalikal-kitāb*) this is a perfect Book becomes clear when we read it together with the ensuing words لَا رَيْبَ فِيهِ هُدًى لِّلْمُتَّقِينَ (*lā raiba fīhe hudal-lil-muttaqīn*) i.e. this is a perfect Book; there is nothing of doubt in it; it is a guidance for the righteous. To a new message the first natural reaction is that of fear lest it should lead one into error or evil; the second reaction is the hope that the message may prove beneficial. Both these reactions-- the first negative and the second positive—have thus been satisfied in this verse. The Qur'ān is a perfect Book, because on the one hand there is nothing in the Qur'an to cause uneasiness or to create doubt or despair, and on the other, there is everything in it which can be a guidance for the God-fearing. Elsewhere in the Qur'ān we read, *Aye! it is in the word of God (more literally, the*

remembrance of Allāh), that hearts can find comfort (13:29).

The words, *there is no doubt in it*, do not mean that nobody will ever entertain any doubt about the Qur'ān. The Qur'ān itself refers to objections that disbelievers raised against it. The words, therefore, only mean that the teaching of the Qur'ān is so rational that a right-thinking person who approaches it impartially cannot but accept it as a guide.

Moreover, the word ريب (*raib*) does not mean a doubt which helps the investigation of truth but a doubt born of unfounded suspicion. Accordingly, the words لَا رَيْبَ فِيْهِ (*lā raiba fīh*) would mean that there is nothing in the Qur'ān, which is based on doubt, i.e., everything is based on truth and certainty. The Qur'ān asserts no doctrine or principle without also giving cogent reasons for it.

The word ريب (*raib*) also means, "affliction or calamity". The Qur'ān contains nothing that may in any way cause misery or affliction to an individual or a people. It raised nations from the quagmire of moral degradation and social depravity to the highest pinnacles of worldly and spiritual glory. Little wonder they became convinced through

experience that there was not a single commandment in it by acting upon which they could come to grief.

The word ريب (*raib*) is also used in the sense of "evil opinion or false charge or calumny". In this sense the clause would mean that the Qur'an contains nothing that may, in any way, lay a false charge against anyone. Indeed, the Qur'an seeks to usurp the right of no one, and it slanders nobody-- neither God nor any revealed Book nor any Prophet.

It may seem strange, but is nevertheless true, that religious Books, such as the Vedas, the Zend-Avesta, the Old and the New Testament, ascribed to God imperfections of one kind or another. The Qur'an, on the contrary, declares Him free of all defects, the Most Perfect in Power, Majesty, and Holiness.

The word of God has also come in for much criticism. There is the school which holds the view that revelation is man's own mental response to the problems on which he reflects. Thus, certainty of faith, which comes of the spoken word of God, is denied to man, and there remains no distinction between man's own thoughts and those revealed by God. The Qur'ān exonerates the revealed

Books of different religions from the charge that they are not the spoken Word of God but only a reflection of peculiarly sensitive individuals' own thoughts (4:165). The Qur'ān accepts the divine origin of the books of other religions (3:4; 35:25).

The prophets of God-- Adam[as], Abraham[as], Moses[as], Jesus[as], Krishna[as] -- also have been calumniated unknowingly by their own followers and knowingly by others. The Qur'ān declares them all to be innocent. Belief in the sinlessness of Prophets is among the cardinal beliefs of Islam (6; 125). The Qur'ān also proclaims their innocence individually (20: 116; 53:38: 20:23; 20:88; 20:91; 2:103; 21:92; 2:88; 19:14).

To sum up, the words لَا رَيْبَ فِيهِ (*lā raiba fīh*) would mean that:

1. The Qur'ān contains nothing that may make one's mind uneasy
2. There is nothing doubtful in it; every teaching and every statement made in it is supported by arguments
3. There it contains nothing that may bring misery or affliction to an individual or a nation

4. It contains no accusation against, or low opinion about, any object of faith.

The words هدى للمتقين (*hudal-lil-muttaqīn*) guidance for the righteous bring before us the positive side of the Qur'ān. The reader is told that the Qur'ān contains not only nothing harmful but also positive good of the highest order. As explained above, guidance has three stages:

1. Showing the right path
2. Leading one up to it
3. Making one follow it till one reaches the goal

The words, *guidance for the righteous*, therefore, mean that guidance contained in the Qur'an is limitless, helping man to higher and still higher stages of perfection and making him more and more deserving of the favours of God. The ways and means by which a devotee attains to nearness to his Creator are infinite and unfold themselves one after another without end (29:70). The process of the spiritual advance of man does not stop with death but continues in the life to come (66:9).

The objection has been raised that, if the Qur'ān guides only the righteous, what about those who have not attained righteousness? The objection is groundless. The Qur'ān

abounds in verses which prove that it is a guidance not only for the righteous but for all seekers, to whatever stage they may have attained (2:22; 2:186; 3:139; 17:42; 18:55; 30:59).

ٱلَّذِينَ يُؤْمِنُونَ بِٱلْغَيْبِ وَيُقِيمُونَ ٱلصَّلَوٰةَ وَمِمَّا رَزَقْنَـٰهُمْ

يُنفِقُونَ ۝

[2:4] Who believe in the unseen and observe Prayer, and spend out of what We have provided for them;

Commentary

In this verse three important qualities of a متقى (*muttaqī*) righteous have been mentioned;

1. A believer in the unseen
2. Steadfast in Prayer
3. Spending out of what God has provided for him

Of these the first relates to faith or belief which must always come first; the other two relate to actions. Belief in the unseen does not mean blind belief or belief in things

which cannot be grasped or understood. Nothing can be farther from the spirit of the Qur'ān then to imagine that it demands from Muslims beliefs which reason and understanding do not support. The Qur'an strongly denounces such beliefs. True faith, according to it, is that which is supported by reason and argument (53:23; 46:5; 30:36; 6:149,150; 25:74).

Moreover, the word غيب (*ghaib*) used in the Qur'ān does not mean, as assumed by some hostile critic's, imaginary and unreal things, but real and verified things, though unseen (49:19; 32:7). It is, therefore, wrong to suppose, as Wherry has done in his commentary, that Islam forces upon its followers some mysteries of faith and invites them to believe in them blindly. It is Christianity which forces on its followers mysteries like Trinity in Unity and the Sonship of Jesus, completely beyond human understanding and human reason.

The word غيب (*ghaib*) as stated above, means things which, though beyond the comprehension of human senses, can nevertheless be proved by reason or experience. The supersensible need not necessarily be irrational. Nothing of 'the unseen' which a Muslim is called upon to believe is

outside the scope of reason. There are many things in the world which, though unseen, are yet proved to exist by invincible arguments, and nobody can deny their existence. God cannot be perceived by the physical senses nor, for that matter, can angels or life after death. But can the existence of God and the angels be denied because of this? Can life after death be denied because it remains unseen?

The words, *who believe in the unseen*, may also mean that the Faithful discharge their duties and perform their acts of worship without a bargaining spirit. They are above such bargaining. They suffer hardships, undergo tribulations and make sacrifices not for the sake of any visible or immediate reward, but out of a selfless desire to serve the large and, as it were, invisible cause of community or country or humanity at large. This is all believing in the unseen.

Another meaning of the word غيب (*ghaib*) is the state of being hidden from the public eye. In this sense, the expression would mean that the faith of a true believer is ever firm and steadfast, whether he is in the company of other believers or is alone. The faith that needs constant watching and exhortation is not worth much. True and real faith has roots deep in the heart of the Faithful and lives by itself. It does not fail or falter when a Muslim is deprived

of the company of other Muslims or even when surrounded by disbelievers. Such faith is described in 21:50 and 57:26.

The second quality of a متقى (*muttaqī*) relates to actions.

According to the different meanings of اقام الصلوة (*iqāmuṣ-ṣalāt*), the expression, *observe Prayer*, would mean:

1. That a Muslim should observe Prayers throughout his life, keeping constant vigil over them. In fact irregular Prayers are no prayers (70:35).
2. That he should say Prayers regularly at their appointed hours and in accordance with the rules prescribed for them (4:104).
3. That he should say his Prayers in a true spirit and not allow them to be spoiled by wandering thoughts which may disturb and distract his attention (23:3).
4. That he should say his Prayers in congregation (2:44)
5. That he should also exhort others to say their Prayers regularly and thus help to spread the habit (20:133)

Prayer is not a form of bargaining with God, in which a Muslim looks for something in return. Islam strongly

repudiates this idea and describes Prayers as a purifying agent for man himself. Through worship man attains to certainty of knowledge which dispels doubt and helps to establish a real and living contact between him and his Creator.

There is a tendency to condemn institutional worship as useless ceremonial. Worship, it is said, is an attitude of the mind and should be confined strictly to it. There is no doubt that attitudes belong to the mind and if the mind is corrupt, humility of the body can be of no avail. A person whose heart is unimpressed by the Majesty and Glory of God and who yet sings His praise is a hypocrite; but so also is the person who claims to except a certain truth, yet his body and behaviour show no signs of it. When a person is in love, his face betrays a peculiar emotion when the beloved appears before him. Parents fondle and kiss their children and friends express their affection by visible movements. These demonstrations of affection are spontaneous, not assumed. It is, therefore, impossible that a man should love God and entertain a true longing for Him, but should not seek to express this love or longing by some outward acts; and this is the secret of all worship. Worship is the outer expression of the inner relationship of man to God. Moreover, God's favours surround the body as well

as the soul. So perfect worship is only that in which body and soul both play their part. Without the two the true spirit of worship cannot be preserved, for though adoration by the heart is the substance and adoration by the body only the shell, yet the substance cannot be preserved without the shell. If the shell is destroyed, the substance is bound to meet with a similar fate.

Besides other advantages, Prayers in congregation, such as Muslim Prayers always are, foster the spirit of brotherhood. Five times a day believers, both rich and poor, have to stand unceremoniously together, shoulder to shoulder, and offer their humble supplications to God. The busiest and the biggest of them have to find the time and join in this united act of worship. Such a fellowship cannot but react wholesomely on the worshipper's hearts.

Incidentally, it may also be remarked that the outward form of the Islamic Prayer includes all the poses of the body expressive of humility, i.e. standing with the folded arms, bowing, prostrating, and sitting with folded knees, each pose being allotted a corresponding prayer. Besides the prescribed Prayers, one is free to pray in one's own words in one's own way.

The expression, ***they spend out of what we have provided for them***, includes not only spending in the cause of Allah but also spending for the welfare of the individual and the community. The words used here are used in their widest possible sense. Wealth, power, influence, physical and intellectual capacities — in short, all that one may receive from God — must be devoted, partly at least, to the well-being of others.

The application of this injunction is not confined to the poor only. All those who have claims over the belongings of a Muslim are entitled to a share in them. The injunction applies to a mother who gives suck to her child, to a father who spends upon the education and upbringing of his children, to a husband who provides for the needs of his wife, and to the children who serve their parents. The commandment is aptly explained in the famous Hadith:

> "Your self has a claim upon you, and your Lord has a claim upon you, and your guest has a claim upon you, and your family has a claim upon you. So you should give to everyone his due" (*Tirmidhi*)

The verse, in short, lays down three directions and describes three stages for the spiritual well-being of man:

1. A Muslim should believe in the truths which are hidden from his eyes and beyond his physical senses, for it is such a belief that can show him to be possessed of the right sort of تقوى (*taqwā*) or righteousness. An intelligent person does not remain satisfied with natural phenomena as he sees them, but looks deeper into their sources and origin; and it is this delving into the depths of the unknown that leads to great knowledge and great achievement. All this comes under "belief in the unseen" which has special reference to God, Who is the source of all creation.

2. When the believer reflects on the creation of the universe and the marvellous order and design which exists in it and when, as a result of this reflection, he becomes convinced of the existence of the Creator, an irresistible longing to have a real and true union with Him takes hold of him. This finds consummation in اقام الصلوة (*iqāmuṣ-ṣalāt*) or observance of prayer.
3. Lastly, when the believer succeeds in establishing a living contact with his Creator, he feels an

inward urge to serve his fellow-beings who, being the creatures of his own Lord and Master, are members of the large family to which he himself belongs. So, in order to meet their needs and requirements, he spends willingly and freely out of the wealth, knowledge or anything else which God has given him.

وَٱلَّذِينَ يُؤْمِنُونَ بِمَآ أُنزِلَ إِلَيْكَ وَمَآ أُنزِلَ مِن قَبْلِكَ وَبِٱلْآخِرَةِ هُمْ

يُوقِنُونَ ۝

[2:5] And who believe in that which has been revealed to thee, and that which was revealed before thee, and they have firm faith in what is *yet* to come.

Commentary

This verse describes three more qualities of a متقى (*muttaqī*) i.e. a righteous person. In the previous verse mention was made of faith in general. But as a true believer seeks to know the detail of تقوى (*taqwā*) righteousness in order to

perfect his faith, he is told here that for its consummation he must believe in the Holy Prophet[sa] and through him in the previous Prophets, and must at the same time believe in 'what is yet to come'. Thus belief in the Holy Prophet[sa] is the central point so far as belief in the Prophets of God is concerned, and no person can become متقی (*muttaqī*) a truly righteous person unless he believes in the Holy Prophet[sa].

From the words, that which has been revealed to thee, quite an erroneous inference is sometimes drawn to the effect that it is belief in the Qur'ān and not belief in the Holy Prophet[sa] that is enjoined. This view the Qur'ān forcefully contradicts. Besides making it clear in several places that belief in the Prophet[sa] is as essential as belief in the Book e.g. (2:286; 4:66; 4:137), the Qur'ān makes the point clear in another way also.

At one place we have, **He it is Who has sent down to you the Book clearly explained** (6:115), and at another, **and in like manner, have We sent down the Book to thee (O Prophet)** (29:48). The fact that God sometimes speaks of the Qur'ān as having been sent to the people and sometimes to the Prophet[sa] is not without point. In fact, the difference in construction is full of meaning; for where the Qur'ān is spoken of as having been sent to the people, the

intention is to point out that the Qur'ānic teaching is suitable and appropriate for them and is meant for their good; and where the Qur'ān is spoken of as having been sent to the Prophet[sa], the intention is to emphasize that he is not merely the bearer of a message, but is the person best fitted to explain the message he has brought and to become an exemplar of the teaching contained in the message.

Elsewhere God says, **Allāh knows best where to place His message** (6:125), which is a clear proof of the fact that a Prophet is not merely the bearer of a message, but is selected by God for a higher purpose, i.e., to become a model for his followers; otherwise, anybody can be sent as a bearer of a message and the question of special selection does not arise.

The words, and that which was revealed before thee, illustrate a special characteristic of Islam, i.e., it not only recognizes the truth of all previous Prophets but makes it obligatory upon its followers to believe in the Divine origin of the teachings they brought with them (see also 13:8; 35:25 of the Five Volume Commentary). But it must be remembered that Islam is a complete and final teaching which has superseded all previous teachings. Belief in them, therefore, is only in the sense of reverence for them

and not in the sense that a Muslim should act upon them. That is why in the verse under comment God mentions the earlier scriptures after the Qur'ān and not before it, as the chronological order required, so that the attention of the believers may be drawn to the fact that belief in the previous books is based on the Qur'ān and is not independent of it.

According to the Qur'ān (35:25), Prophets have appeared among all peoples and all nations and we are commanded to believe in all previous revelations, and thus an effective step has been taken to promote peace and harmony among the followers of different religions. The verse applies to no particular Book. Any earlier Book which claims divine origin and has been accepted for a long time and by a large section of mankind to be the word of God falls within the meaning of this verse.

The word الآخرة (*al-ākhirah*) what is yet to come, means either "the message or revelation which is to follow" or "the Last Abode" i.e., the next life. Of these two meanings the first is more applicable here; for it fits in with the other two parts of the verse which speak of God's revelations. In this connection it is also noteworthy that while the word

ايمان (*īmān*) faith has been used in reference to the past and present revelations, the word يقين (*yaqīn*) clear and established has been used in reference to the future one. This is because ايمان (*īmān*) faith relates to something definite and determined, and as the future revelation was not yet definite and determined at the time when the verse was revealed, so the word يقين (*yaqīn*) clear and established was used for it.

The subject of the latter part of this verse, referred to in the words, what is yet to come, finds further exposition in (62:3,4), where the Qur'ān speaks of two advents of the Holy Prophet[sa]. His first advent took place among the Arabs in the seventh century of the Christian era when the Qur'ān was revealed to him; and his second advent was to take place in the latter days of the world in the person of one of his followers who was to come in his spirit and power. This prophecy found its fulfilment in the person of Ahmad, the Promised Messiah[as] and Founder of the Ahmadiyya Movement in Islam, in whose advent have been fulfilled also the prophecies of other Prophets regarding the appearance of a World-Messenger in the Latter Days.

أُوْلَـٰٓئِكَ عَلَىٰ هُدًى مِّن رَّبِّهِمْ ۖ وَأُوْلَـٰٓئِكَ هُمُ ٱلْمُفْلِحُونَ ۝

[2:6] It is they who follow the guidance of their Lord and it is they who shall prosper.

Commentary

The verse explains that when a man has fulfilled all the conditions of تقوى (*taqwā*) righteousness in respect of both belief and actions, then he may be sure not only of being rightly guided but also of being a master of guidance whose success in this life as well as in the life to come is assured. The words عَلَىٰ هُدًى (*alā hudan*) literal meaning on guidance also hint that as the believer prayed for guidance in the opening chapter of the Qur'ān, so guidance of the highest order has been provided for him -- a guidance on which he can ride comfortably and speed on happily towards his Lord and Master.

إِنَّ ٱلَّذِينَ كَفَرُواْ سَوَآءٌ عَلَيۡهِمۡ ءَأَنذَرۡتَهُمۡ أَمۡ لَمۡ تُنذِرۡهُمۡ لَا

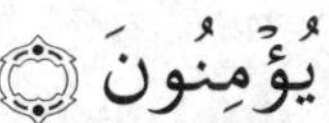

[2:7] Those who have disbelieved — it is equal to them whether thou warn them or warn them not — they will not believe.

Commentary

After speaking of the class of true believers and describing the high stage of faith, God now speaks of the extreme type of disbelievers who have become so indifferent to truth that it matters not whether they receive a warning or not. Of such disbelievers it has been declared that as long as their present condition continues, they will not believe.

The verse does not at all mean that no disbeliever will henceforward believe. The idea is not only repugnant to the teaching of the Qur'ān but is also opposed to all established facts of history; for people continued to embrace Islam even after this verse was revealed. Again, it was after this verse that the Sūrah النصر (an-Naṣr, Chapter 110) was revealed to the Holy Prophet[sa], in which God spoke to him

saying that people would soon begin to join Islam in very large numbers (110:3), and so it actually came to pass.

In short, the words, *they will not believe*, refer only to such disbelievers as turn a deaf ear to the warnings of the Prophet, and to them also the words apply only so long as they do not change their present condition. A person who turns a deaf ear to a warning today but begins to heed it tomorrow does not, indeed, cannot, come under the so-called ban.

خَتَمَ ٱللَّهُ عَلَىٰ قُلُوبِهِمْ وَعَلَىٰ سَمْعِهِمْ ۖ وَعَلَىٰٓ أَبْصَـٰرِهِمْ غِشَـٰوَةٌ ۖ

وَلَهُمْ عَذَابٌ عَظِيمٌ ۝

[2:8] Allah has set a seal on their hearts and their ears, and over their eyes is a covering; and for them is a great punishment.

Commentary

The verse refers to the disbelievers mentioned in the last verse and explains how they have reached their present woeful condition. It is common observation that organs which remain unused for a long time become dead and

useless. The eyes lose their sight and the ears their hearing if they remain out of use, and the limbs become stunted for the same reason. The disbelievers mentioned here refused to employ their hearts and ears for the comprehension of the truth, and as a result their capacities for hearing and understanding were lost. It is thus only the natural consequence of wilful indifference which is described in the clause, *Allah has set a seal on their hearts and their ears, and over their eyes is a covering*.

As all laws proceed from God, the final Controller of the universe, and every cause is followed by its natural effect under His will, so the sealing of the hearts and the ears of disbelievers is ascribed to Him. It is, therefore a mistake to take the verse to mean that as God had Himself sealed up their hearts, so the disbelievers could not believe. The Qur'ān contradicts this view and states clearly that it is the disbelievers themselves who seal their fate and God's seal follows only as a result of their action (See 4:156; 40:36; 47:25; 83:15).

Says the Holy Prophet[sa]: 'When a man commits a sin, a black spot is thereby formed on his heart. Then if he repents and gives up the sin and asks God's forgiveness, the black spot is washed off, leaving the heart clean. But if he

repents not and commits another sin, another black spot is formed on his heart and so on, until his whole heart is covered with a black covering, and that is the covering of rust to which the Qur'ān refers in Sūrah "*Tatfif*" (Jarīr).

It may also be noted that in the present verse the word 'ears' has been put before the word 'eyes'. This is in conformity with the law of nature that the ears of a new-born baby begin to function earlier than the eyes.

What is the key message of this portion of the Holy Qur'ān?

How does this message apply to your personal life?

Second Rak‘ah of the Saturday Fajr Prayer

Second Rak'ah of the Saturday Fajr Prayer

Importance of Sūrah al-Baqarah

- al-Baqarah is the longest chapter of the Holy Qur'ān. The Holy Prophet[sa] said that everything has its peak and the peak of the Qur'ān is al-Baqarah (Tirmidhī).
- The Holy Prophet[sa] said that whosoever recites ten verses of this chapter, first four verses, Āyatul-Kursī and last three verses, Satan will not enter his house till the morning (Ibne Kathīr).
    - [1]This means that these verses embody the Islamic teachings and that satan cannot come near a person who faithfully acts on these teachings.
    - 'Till the morning' means that teachings, however excellent, if not regularly practiced cannot be fully effective and the good influences of such teachings are lost.

[1] The Holy Qur'ān with English Translation and Commentary. 3rd ed. Islām International Publications Limited; 2002. Volume 1, Page 24

- [2]In the first 4 verses a sketch is drawn for a pious life, Āyatul-Kursī has a great explanation of the attributes of God and the last three verses contain prayers that purify the heart. When these three things come together, one's heart is purified and satanic thoughts disappear.
    - To do good deeds in following the words of Allāh
    - To ponder over the attributes of Allāh the Exalted
    - To always engage in prayers and commit oneself totally to God.

- [3]The Promised Messiah[as] said that in this chapter the rights of Allāh and rights of people are described in great detail. Do's and don'ts have been explained and there is a great emphasis on patience and sacrifice.

---

[2] *Tafsīr-e-Kabīr*. Ḥaḍrat Mirzā Bashīr-ud-Dīn Maḥmūd Aḥmad[ra], Printwell Amritsar 2004. Volume 1, Page 51

[3] *Tafsīrul-Qur'ān* by The Promised Messiah[as], Ḥaḍrat Mirzā Ghulām Aḥmad of Qadian, Page 1 available on www.alislam.org

- The Khalīfatul Masīḥ III, Ḥaḍrat Mirzā Nāṣir Aḥmad[ra] enjoined Ahmadi children to memorise the first seventeen verses of Sūrah al-Baqarah.

وَمِنَ ٱلنَّاسِ مَن يَقُولُ ءَامَنَّا بِٱللَّهِ وَبِٱلْيَوْمِ ٱلْأَخِرِ وَمَا هُم

بِمُؤْمِنِينَ ۝ يُخَٰدِعُونَ ٱللَّهَ وَٱلَّذِينَ ءَامَنُواْ وَمَا يَخْدَعُونَ

إِلَّآ أَنفُسَهُمْ وَمَا يَشْعُرُونَ ۝ فِى قُلُوبِهِم مَّرَضٌ فَزَادَهُمُ ٱللَّهُ

مَرَضًا ۖ وَلَهُمْ عَذَابٌ أَلِيمٌۢ بِمَا كَانُواْ يَكْذِبُونَ ۝ وَإِذَا قِيلَ

لَهُمْ لَا تُفْسِدُواْ فِى ٱلْأَرْضِ قَالُوٓاْ إِنَّمَا نَحْنُ مُصْلِحُونَ ۝

أَلَآ إِنَّهُمْ هُمُ ٱلْمُفْسِدُونَ وَلَٰكِن لَّا يَشْعُرُونَ ۝ وَإِذَا قِيلَ لَهُمْ

ءَامِنُواْ كَمَآ ءَامَنَ ٱلنَّاسُ قَالُوٓاْ أَنُؤْمِنُ كَمَآ ءَامَنَ ٱلسُّفَهَآءُ ۗ أَلَآ

إِنَّهُمْ هُمُ ٱلسُّفَهَآءُ وَلَٰكِن لَّا يَعْلَمُونَ ۝ وَإِذَا لَقُواْ ٱلَّذِينَ

ءَامَنُواْ قَالُوٓاْ ءَامَنَّا وَإِذَا خَلَوْاْ إِلَىٰ شَيَٰطِينِهِمْ قَالُوٓاْ إِنَّا مَعَكُمْ

Sūrah al-Baqarah, Verses 9-17

إِنَّمَا نَحْنُ مُسْتَهْزِءُونَ ۝ ٱللَّهُ يَسْتَهْزِئُ بِهِمْ وَيَمُدُّهُمْ فِى طُغْيَٰنِهِمْ
يَعْمَهُونَ ۝ أُو۟لَٰٓئِكَ ٱلَّذِينَ ٱشْتَرَوُا۟ ٱلضَّلَٰلَةَ بِٱلْهُدَىٰ فَمَا
رَبِحَت تِّجَٰرَتُهُمْ وَمَا كَانُوا۟ مُهْتَدِينَ ۝

Translation

And of the people there are some who say, 'We believe in Allāh and the Last Day;' while they are not believers at all. They would deceive Allah and those who believe, and they deceive none but themselves; only they perceive *it* not. In their hearts was a disease, and Allah has increased their disease to them; and for them is a grievous punishment because they used to lie. And when it is said to them: 'Create not disorder on the earth,' they say: 'We are only promoters of peace.' Beware! it is surely they who create disorder, but they do not perceive *it*. And when it is said to them, 'Believe as *other* people have believed,' they say: 'Shall we believe as the foolish have believed?' Beware! it is

surely they that are foolish, but they do not know. And when they meet those who believe, they say: 'We believe;' but when they are alone with their ringleaders, they say: 'We are certainly with you; we are only mocking.' Allah will punish their mockery and will let them continue in their transgression, wandering blindly. These are they who have taken error in exchange for guidance; but their traffic has brought them no gain, nor are they rightly guided.

وَمِنَ ٱلنَّاسِ مَن يَقُولُ ءَامَنَّا بِٱللَّهِ وَبِٱلْيَوْمِ ٱلْءَاخِرِ وَمَا هُم بِمُؤْمِنِينَ ﴿٩﴾

[2:9] And of the people there are some who say, 'We believe in Allāh and the Last Day;' while they are not believers at all.

[4]**Commentary**:

After describing the condition of believers (vv. 4-6) and that of disbelievers (vv. 7-8) the Qur'ān proceeds to describe the condition of a third group, the hypocrites. These were mixed up with the believers and posed as such.

They were divided into two classes;

(1) Disbelievers at heart but united with the believers for the sake of some material or communal advantages
(2) Believers at heart but lacking the strength of conviction necessary for thorough conversion and complete obedience.

[4] The Holy Qur'ān with English Translation and Commentary. 3rd ed. Islām International Publications Limited; 2002. Volume 1, Pages 38-47

The reference here is to the first class of hypocrites, those who mixed with the believers but did not at heart believe in the truth of Islam.

It may be noted that only God and the Last Day are mentioned here, other Islamic beliefs being left out. This has led some to think that Islam requires belief only in God and the Last Day. The truth, however, is that 'God' and the 'Last Day' are respectively the first and the last items in the Islamic formula of faith and a profession of them *ipso facto* implies profession of the other items. Elsewhere the Qur'ān clearly states how belief in the Last Day implies belief in angels as well as in the divine Books (6:93).

The omission may also be explained in another way. The hypocrites wanted to deceive the believers, so possibly they expressed themselves purposely in these words, omitting all reference to the Prophet[sa] and the Qur'ān. By mentioning God and the Last Day they would induce believers to think that they subscribed fully to the Islamic faith, but in their hearts they made a reservation as regards belief in the Qur'ān and the Prophet[sa]. This interpretation finds support in the following verse which says that the hypocrites wished to deceive the believers. The expression, *they are not believers at all*, has been used to intensify the

repudiation of the claim of the hypocrites to be believers. If a mere negation of their claim had been intended, it would have been expressed by some such expression as "they are hypocrites".

Strong denunciation of hypocrites is characteristic of the Qur'ān (3:168; 5:42 & 5:62). According to the Qur'ān, hypocrites are only disbelievers. This view of the Qur'ān furnishes a strong refutation of the criticism that Islam permits the use of force in religious matters. Conversion by force can never be sincere, while the Qur'ān insists upon sincerity in believers. A religion which makes sincerity a necessary quality of belief cannot tolerate, much less encourage, the use of force in religion.

يُخَٰدِعُونَ ٱللَّهَ وَٱلَّذِينَ ءَامَنُوا۟ وَمَا يَخْدَعُونَ إِلَّآ أَنفُسَهُمْ

وَمَا يَشْعُرُونَ ۝

[2:10] They would deceive Allah and those who believe, and they deceive none but themselves; only they perceive *it* not.

Commentary

The verse makes it clear that effective faith is based upon truth and sincerity. Faith not so based amounts to deception and God cannot be deceived. The verse has given rise to some objections:

1. How can it be possible for any man to deceive God?
2. The word يخادعون *(yukhādi'ūna)* is derived from the verb خادع (*khāda'a*) in the measure of مفاعلة (*mufā*'alah) which denotes two parties mutually engaged in the same operation. The words يخادعون الله (*yukhādi'ūnallāha*) would, therefore, mean that hypocrites and God are both engaged in deceiving each other.

In answer to the first objection

used here is خادع (*khāda'a*) and not خدع (*khada*') the former, as explained above, signifying only an attempt at deception and not actual deception. The objection is, therefore, without foundation.

The second objection also does not hold good. The measure مفاعلة (*mufā'alah*) does not always carry the sense of mutual participation. Sometimes it signifies only one of the parties so engaged. For example, in the sentence عاقبت اللص (*'āqabtul-Lisṣ*) meaning, "I punished the thief" the word عاقبت (*'āqabto*) belongs to the measure of مفاعلة (*mufā'alah*) yet here it does not denote mutual participation in the act. It only means, I punished the thief.

A note on the hypocrites will not be out of place here. Before the coming of Islam into Medinah there were in that city two pagan Arab tribes known as *Aus* and *Khazraj*, and three Jewish tribes names *Banū Quraiẓah, Banū Naḍīr* and *Banū Qainuqa'*. The two pagan tribes were superior to the Jews in numbers but inferior to them in wealth and education. The Jews thus exercised great influence over the pagans of Medinah. In order further to increase their influence, they encouraged internecine (internal) feuds among their idolatrous neighbours. A few years before the rise of Islam the pagan tribes of Medinah, realising how they had been duped, decided to organise themselves under a duly elected king. Their choice fell upon one 'Abdullah bin Ubayy', chief of the tribe of

Khazraj, and they were preparing for his coronation when news came to them of the rise of Islam in Makkah. Events suddenly began to take a different turn. The idolatrous tribes of Aus and Khazraj became attracted towards Islam and began to embrace the new faith in large numbers, believing that the solution of their difficulties lay not in electing a king but in accepting Islam. Soon after the Holy Prophet[sa] emigrated to Medīnah.

The tide of enthusiasm became irresistible; and Abdullah bin Ubayy and his party felt it wise to follow their tribesmen into the new faith. They did not realise at the time that the establishment of Islām would mean the frustration of their own hopes. When, however, the power of Islam became established, they realised that they had put an end to their hopes. This realisation destroyed any attachment they had for Islam. Instead, they developed actual hostility towards it. But as a preponderating (prevailing) majority of their tribesmen had already become zealous followers of Islam, they could not openly leave its fold. Thus came into being the hypocrites --- a party professing Islam outwardly but at heart hostile to it. Not strong enough to oppose Islam openly, they naturally thought of entering into a secret alliance with the Jews in order to injure the cause of Islam. In the beginning they

had nothing to do with the Makkans for whom they bore a long-standing tribal antipathy. After the battle of Uhud, however, at the instigation of the Jews and prompted by their own jealousy, they forgot their enmity and began secretly to conspire with the Quraish of Makkah, keeping up a show of attachment for Islam. Their leader 'Abdullah' continued to accompany the Holy Prophet[sa] in many of his expeditions.

In the Qur'ān this party of hypocrites is mentioned in several places. Their last act of hostility towards Islam was their attempt, after the fall of Makkah, to conspire with the Byzantine Christian power. The occasion was the Tabūk expedition led by the Holy Prophet[sa] in the ninth year of Hijra. The attempt met with discomfiture. It was probably the shock of its failure that caused, only two months later, the death of 'Abdullah bin Ubayy'. The party then broke up. Some of its members entered Islam sincerely; others ended their days in obscurity.

فِي قُلُوبِهِم مَّرَضٌ فَزَادَهُمُ ٱللَّهُ مَرَضًا ۖ وَلَهُمْ عَذَابٌ أَلِيمٌۢ بِمَا كَانُوا۟ يَكْذِبُونَ ﴿١٠﴾

[2:11] In their hearts was a disease, and Allah has increased their disease to them; and for them is a grievous punishment because they used to lie.

Commentary

God speaks of two diseases of the heart:

1. كفر (*kufr*) i.e. disbelief.
2. نفاق (*nifāq*) i.e. hypocrisy.

The former has already been referred to in verses 7 and 8. The present verse refers to the disease of hypocrisy and points out that those suffering from it do not act as normal, healthy persons do. The Holy Prophet[sa] has mentioned the following signs of hypocrisy. Says he: "when a hypocrite speaks, he lies; and when he makes a promise, he does not fulfil it; and when he is entrusted with anything, he acts dishonestly; and when he makes a contract, he breaks it; and when he engages in a dispute, he uses foul words" (Bukhāri).

In the verse under comment the increase of hypocrisy is attributed to God, not because God increases it but because the increase results from disregard of His commands; also because it is God who finally dispenses the good and evil consequences of human actions. The Qur'ān has only been revealed for healing diseases. Says Allāh: *O mankind! There has come to you an exhortation from your Lord and a cure for whatever disease there is in the hearts* (10: 58).

The increasing of disease also means that the expanding power of Islam was naturally increasing the disease of the hypocrites who were all the more forced to remain, against their will, in outward friendliness with the Muslims.

In the case of disbelievers the punishment mentioned is عذاب عظيم (*'azābun 'aẓīm*) great punishment whereas in the case of hypocrites it is عذاب اليم (*'azābun alīm*) grievous punishment. This is because disbelievers express their disbelief and enmity openly, while hypocrites keep their feelings of hatred and malice concealed in their hearts, thinking that they are thereby deriving twofold pleasure—one of enmity towards Islam and the other of befooling the Muslims. So the retribution in store for the hypocrites is

characterised by special pain and anguish --- a fit recompense for their false pleasure.

وَإِذَا قِيلَ لَهُمۡ لَا تُفۡسِدُواْ فِي ٱلۡأَرۡضِ قَالُوٓاْ إِنَّمَا نَحۡنُ مُصۡلِحُونَ ۝

[2:12] And when it is said to them: 'Create not disorder on the earth,' they say: 'We are only promoters of peace.'

Commentary

The hypocrites tried to create disturbance in various ways:

1. They tried to sow discord among the Muslims themselves by instigating the انصار (*anṣār*) i.e. Medinite Helpers against the مهاجرين (*muhājirīn*) i.e. Makkan Refugees (63:8, 9).
2. Sometimes they imputed motives to the Holy Prophet[sa] in the distribution of alms (9:58), or his system of gathering information (9:61).

3. Sometimes they tried to undermine the spirit of the Muslims (9:50), or to demoralise them by spreading rumours (4:84).
4. Sometimes they encouraged non-Muslims to fight against Muslims (59:12).

In the present verse reference is made to the double-dealing of the hypocrites. Confronted with this the hypocrites invariably pleaded that they were prompted by nothing but sincerity of purpose and that their intention was not to create ill-will but to establish mutual cordiality and peace. This is the typical defence of all mischief-makers.

The presence of hypocrites and malcontents is inevitable in every organised society. In a society, not properly organised, it is easy for disaffected members to leave. But in a well organised community, the malcontents find it difficult to leave. So they remain within and carry on their nefarious activities secretly. The presence of hypocrites is not a sign of weakness but rather of strength in a community. But this should not make a community neglectful about them. On the contrary, it is imperative that malcontents and hypocrites should be closely watched and properly dealt with, as and when

circumstances require. The Holy Prophet[sa] was ever watchful of this class.

أَلَآ إِنَّهُمۡ هُمُ ٱلۡمُفۡسِدُونَ وَلَـٰكِن لَّا يَشۡعُرُونَ ۝

[2:13] Beware! it is surely they who create disorder, but they do not perceive *it*.

Commentary

In the last verse the hypocrites insinuated that it was not they but the main body of Muslims who caused disorder. The reply to this insinuation is given in the present verse in the emphatic words, *Beware! It is surely they who create disorder.*

The last words of the verse signify that the hypocrites lack the faculty of insight. If, instead of fabricating a defence for their duplicity, they had tried only to study their own mind, they could have easily perceived that it was not the desire of peace or reform but cowardice and jealousy that prompted their loathsome conduct.

وَإِذَا قِيلَ لَهُمْ ءَامِنُوا۟ كَمَآ ءَامَنَ ٱلنَّاسُ قَالُوٓا۟ أَنُؤْمِنُ كَمَآ ءَامَنَ

ٱلسُّفَهَآءُ ۗ أَلَآ إِنَّهُمْ هُمُ ٱلسُّفَهَآءُ وَلَـٰكِن لَّا يَعْلَمُونَ ﴿١٣﴾

[2:14] And when it is said to them, 'Believe as *other* people have believed,' they say: 'Shall we believe as the foolish have believed?' Beware! it is surely they that are foolish, but they do not know.

Commentary

The verse means that when the believers asked the hypocrites to be sincere in their faith, the hypocrites would say that the believers were, like fools, squandering away their lives and property, a mere handful of men who had taken up the fight against the whole country.

The hypocrites called true Muslims "fools" because they thought they (the hypocrites) could protect their lives and property by maintaining friendly relations with the disbelievers, while the true Muslims, on account of their complete estrangement from disbelievers, were exposing their lives and possessions to constant danger. Muslims were also given to spending recklessly on religion. Such

allegations are contained in 5:59; 8:50, 9:79 and 63:8. God replies to them by saying: Their possessions and their children should not excite thy wonder; Allah only intends to punish them therewith in this world, that their souls may depart while they are disbelievers (9:85). The verse means that soon the hypocrites would witness the ruin of their possessions, while Muslims would prosper. Success and prosperity come, not of cowardice and stinginess, but of courage and sacrifice, and the hypocrites were hopelessly lacking in both these qualities.

In fulfilment of this prophecy 'Abdullah bin Ubayy, the hypocrite leader, lived to see the frustration of his designs against Islam and his only son became a true and zealous Muslim.

وَإِذَا لَقُوا۟ ٱلَّذِينَ ءَامَنُوا۟ قَالُوٓا۟ ءَامَنَّا وَإِذَا خَلَوْا۟ إِلَىٰ شَيَـٰطِينِهِمْ

قَالُوٓا۟ إِنَّا مَعَكُمْ إِنَّمَا نَحْنُ مُسْتَهْزِءُونَ ﴿١٤﴾

[2:15] And when they meet those who believe, they say: 'We believe;' but when they are alone with their ringleaders, they say: 'We are certainly with you; we are only mocking.'

Commentary

The context of the verse makes it clear that by شياطين(*shayāṭīn*) is here meant not evil spirits but rebellious ringleaders among the disbelievers and the hypocrites who were proud and haughty and ready to transgress all limits. Reference to such leaders has been made in 33: 68 where God says, **And they (the people of Hell) will say, *'Our Lord, we obeyed our chiefs and our great ones and they led us astray from the way'***. These were the men who egged on the hypocrites to mischief and who were ever burning with jealousy and hate at seeing the Muslims prosper and who had gone far astray from the truth.

Some Christian writers have rendered the word شياطين (*shayāṭīn*) in this verse as "satans" or "devils", and then charged the Qur'ān with reviling idolaters, Jews and Christians. The charge is groundless; for, as already explained, the word شياطين (*shayāṭīn*) does not here mean "satans" but simply proud and mischievous ringleaders. In fact, as shown above, the word شيطان (*shaiṭān*) has a very wide significance in Arabic. The Holy Prophet[sa] once said to his Companions, "A single rider is a *shaiṭān*, a pair of

riders also is a pair of *shaiṭān*, but three riders are a body of riders" (Sunan Abū Dāwūd). The meaning here is that one rider is exposed to mischief and danger and so are two riders, but three riders travelling together form a safe company.

Christian critics, ever keen on finding fault with the Qur'ān, forget the New Testament passages (Mark 8:33; 8:38 & Matt. 3:7; 23:33) where Jesus[as] calls a disciple satan and his opponents serpents and a generation of vipers, etc. This meaning of the word شياطين (*shayāṭīn*) i.e. ringleaders from among the disbelievers and hypocrites, is supported by eminent Muslim scholars like Ibn-e-'Abbās, Qatādah, Mujāhid, and 'Abdullāh bin Masūd (Jarīr).

ٱللَّهُ يَسْتَهْزِئُ بِهِمْ وَيَمُدُّهُمْ فِي طُغْيَـٰنِهِمْ يَعْمَهُونَ ۝

[2:16] Allah will punish their mockery and will let them continue in their transgression, wandering blindly.

Commentary

In this verse the word يستهزئ (*yastahzi'o*) literally meaning will mock has been used for God, and this has occasioned

the criticism that the God of the Qur'an is given to mocking. The criticism is due to the utter ignorance of Arabic idiom and usage. In Arabic, punishment for an evil is sometimes denoted by the term used for the evil itself.

Thus the expression الله يستهزئ بهم (*Allāhu yastahzi'o bihim*) does not means, Allah shall mock at them, but that Allah will punish them for their mocking. The former meaning, followed by some translators, is absolutely inconsistent with the spirit of the Qur'ān which condemns jest and ridicule as marks of ignorance (2:68). How, then, can God attribute to Himself what He declares to be a practice of the ignorant?

The clause, ***Allāh will let them continue in their transgression***, should not be understood to mean that God grants the hypocrites respite to let them increase in transgression. Such a meaning is contradicted by verses 6:111 and 35:38, where it is clearly stated that God grants the disbelievers respite with the sole object of reforming them but they unfortunately only increase in transgression.

The word يعمهون (*ya'mahūn*) wandering blindly is derived from the root عمه (*'a ma ha*) which signifies, besides other meanings, the absence of signs or marks. The meaning here

would, therefore, be that the hypocrites persist in their wickedness without care or consideration, as if the way they are travelling has lost all signs, leaving the traveller without any sense of distance or direction.

أُوْلَـٰٓئِكَ ٱلَّذِينَ ٱشْتَرَوُاْ ٱلضَّلَـٰلَةَ بِٱلْهُدَىٰ فَمَا رَبِحَت تِّجَـٰرَتُهُمْ وَمَا

كَانُواْ مُهْتَدِينَ ۝

[2:17] These are they who have taken error in exchange for guidance; but their traffic has brought them no gain, nor are they rightly guided.

Commentary:

The expression, ***who have taken error in exchange for guidance***, means that:

(1) They have given up guidance and taken error instead

(2) Both guidance and error were offered to them but they preferred error and refused guidance.

Both these meanings apply here.

According to the first, the verse would mean that originally everybody is endowed with a pure nature and the best of capacities (30:31; 95:5), but, owing to wrong training or wrongdoing, the original nature and capacities become lost. In this case "guidance" would mean the nature or capacities with which every man is endowed by God, and "exchange" would mean that through making wrong use people lose the God-given guidance, landing themselves in error instead.

According to the second meaning, the verse would signify that through His Messengers, God communicates to man only truth and guidance, whereas Satan presents to him his own evil teaching. Wrong choice by man results in his acceptance of error instead of guidance.

This traffic, however, brings the hypocrites no gain. They believe that by preferring the promptings of Satan to the guidance of God they would reap a good profit in this life. But, says God, they will reap no such profit. On the contrary, they will be the losers and suffer humiliation through their own wrong choice.

The words, ***nor are they rightly guided***, point to yet another consequence of the wrong choice of hypocrites. They will not only suffer loss and humiliation in this life, but will also suffer punishment in the life to come, for

being deprived of guidance they will not reach the goal. Thus the words, ***their traffic has brought them no gain***, refer to the benefits that accrue to one in this life, and the words, ***nor are they rightly guided***, refer to the end they will meet in the life to come.

The verse teaches an important truth. Every action of man is attended by two kinds of results, one immediate and the other deferred. A person who is detected in theft suffers punishment and humiliation in this life. This is the immediate consequence of his action. The deferred consequence is that by the same action he reduces his ability to find and accept the truth and guidance. Similarly, when a person does a good deed, the immediate result is that he is pleased with himself and rises in the estimation of others. The deferred consequence is that the he increases his power of finding and accepting the truth and guidance. It is the deferred consequences that are referred to in the expression, ***nor are they rightly guided***.

What is the key message of this portion of the Holy Qur'ān?

How does this message apply to your personal life?

First Rak‘ah of Maghrib Prayer on Saturday, Sunday, Monday, Wednesday and Thursday

First Rak'ah of Maghrib Prayer, Saturday, Sunday, Monday, Wednesday and Thursday

[1]Importance of Sūrah al-Falaq

- This and the next *Sūrah* an-Nās are so closely linked in the subject matter and may be regarded as complementary to each other.

- Both the Sūrah together are called *Mu'awwidhatān* meaning, "the two Sūrahs that afford protection," because both of them open with the expression "I seek refuge in the Lord."

- In these two Sūrahs the believers are told that they should not be afraid of any tyrant, dictator or ruler in the discharge of this sacred duty and should hold the firm belief that God is the sole Director and Controller of the whole universe. Allah has the power to protect His devotees from any harm or

[1] The Holy Qur'ān with English Translation and Commentary. 3rd ed. Islām International Publications Limited; 2002. Volume 5, Page 2912

injury which the forces of darkness might seek to do them.

- Though constituting an integral part of the Qur'ān, these two Sūrahs may be regarded as forming a sort of epilogue to it. The main body of the Qur'ān seems to end with Sūrah al-Ikhlāṣ, which recapitulates, as it were, in a nutshell, the basic Qur'ānic principles, and in these two Sūrahs believers are enjoined to seek Divine protection against deviating from the right path and against the mischiefs and evils which might adversely affect their material well-being and spiritual development.

- The Holy Prophet[sa] used to recite these two Sūrahs regularly before going to bed.

Sūrah al- Falaq, Chapter 113

بِسۡمِ ٱللَّهِ ٱلرَّحۡمَـٰنِ ٱلرَّحِيمِ ۝

قُلۡ أَعُوذُ بِرَبِّ ٱلۡفَلَقِ ۝ مِن شَرِّ مَا خَلَقَ ۝ وَمِن شَرِّ غَاسِقٍ
إِذَا وَقَبَ ۝ وَمِن شَرِّ ٱلنَّفَّـٰثَـٰتِ فِى ٱلۡعُقَدِ ۝ وَمِن شَرِّ
حَاسِدٍ إِذَا حَسَدَ ۝

<u>Translation</u>

In the name of Allah, the Gracious, the Merciful. Say, 'I seek refuge with the Lord of cleaving, 'From the evil of that which He has created, 'And from the evil of the night when it overspreads, 'And from the evil of those who blow into knots *to undo them*, 'And from the evil of the envier when he envies.'

بِسۡمِ ٱللَّهِ ٱلرَّحۡمَـٰنِ ٱلرَّحِيمِ ۝١

[113:1] In the name of Allah, the Gracious, the Merciful.

قُلۡ أَعُوذُ بِرَبِّ ٱلۡفَلَقِ ۝٢

[113:2] Say, 'I seek refuge in the Lord of cleaving,

[2]Commentary

A believer is enjoined to invoke the protection of God, the Lord of the فلق (*falaq*) dawn. In view of different meanings of the word, he is told to pray:

1. That when the night of darkness over Islam has passed away and the morning of its bright future dawns, its sun should continue to shine till it reaches the Meridian.

---

[2] The Holy Qur'ān with English Translation and Commentary. 3rd ed. Islām International Publications Limited; 2002. Volume 5, Pages 2913-2914

2. That God might protect him from the hidden and manifest evil of all that He has created, including the evils of heredity, bad environment, defective education or other corrupting influences.

3. That God should save him from the torments of Hell in this life and in the Hereafter.

4. That God should enable him to avoid extremes and to adopt the middle course in all things which is the safest course, since the idea implied in ربوبية (*rubūbiyyat*) is development by degrees and in stages.

مِن شَرِّ مَا خَلَقَ ۝

[113:3] 'From the evil of that which He has created,

وَمِن شَرِّ غَاسِقٍ إِذَا وَقَبَ ۝

[113:4] 'And from the evil of the night when it overspreads.

Commentary

The verse may refer to the evils of the time when the light of truth becomes extinguished and the darkness of sin and iniquity spreads over the entire face of the earth.

Or it may refer to the evils of the time when one is overwhelmed by distress and privation, when it is darkness all around him, and the last ray of hope disappears. See also last verse of the Sūrah.

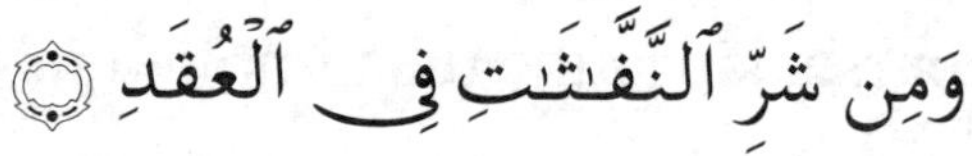

[113:5] 'And from the evil of those who blow into knots *to undo them*,

Commentary

The reference in the verse is to those whisperers of evil suggestions who cause solemn contracts and friendships to break down, and who inspire people with a spirit of defiance of established authority or with violating the oath of fealty, and thus seek to create discord and dissension in the Muslim Community and to encourage fissiparous tendencies among them.

وَمِن شَرِّ حَاسِدٍ إِذَا حَسَدَ ۝

[113:6] 'And from the evil of the envier when he envies

Commentary

The Sūrah deals with the material side of man's life as does the next Sūrah with its spiritual side.

Man is confronted with various kinds of dangers and difficulties in life. When he is engaged in an undertaking of a serious import, particularly when he takes upon himself to spread the light of Truth, forces of darkness surround him on all sides; and when he proceeds further men of evil designs bar his way and create all sorts of impediments and difficulties. When at last success dawns on him, persons of a jealous nature seek to deprive him of the fruit of his labour. As protection against all these difficulties, obstacles and perils in life, a believer is enjoined to invoke the help and assistance of the Lord of فلق (*falaq*) dawn to give him light when there is darkness all around; to protect him from the evil designs of mischief makers and the nefarious machinations of jealous persons. What a complete and comprehensive prayer!

The last two Sūrahs of the Qu'rān may also specially refer to the time of the Promised Messiah[as] and the Mahdi. Verse 4 of the present Sūrah may refer to the eclipse of the sun and the moon which, according to a well-known saying of the Holy Prophet[sa] was to take a place in the time of the Mahdi (Sunan Dar Quṭnī), and the last two verses may refer to his enemies who will create all sorts of difficulties for him and will burn with rage as they will see his mission making rapid progress.

حاسد (*ḥāsid*) the envious one may also refer to the *Dajjāl,* the Arch envier who will give the Promised Mahdī[as] an obstinate fight.

What is the key message of this portion of the Holy Qur'ān?

How does this message apply to your personal life?

Second Rak‘ah of Maghrib Prayer on Saturday, Sunday, Monday, Wednesday and Thursday

Second Rak'ah of Maghrib Prayer on Saturday, Sunday, Monday, Wednesday and Thursday

Importance of Sūrah an-Nās

- This Sūrah, the second of the *Mu'awwidhatān*, constitutes an extension of its predecessor and is in a way complementary to it, in that in Sūrah al-Falaq the believers were enjoined to seek protection from God against the hardships and privations of life, in the present Sūrah protection is sought from trials and tribulations that hamper man's spiritual development, and the protection is to be invoked not only by verbal solicitation of the commandment conveyed by the word قل (*qul*) say.

- The main message of this Sūrah is that one should seek Allāh's protection from the disorder of Dajjāl[1].

- **Dajjāl**—A term in Arabic that literally means, 'the great deceiver.' In Islamic terminology '*Dajjāl*'

[1] *Tafsīrul-Qur'ān* by The Promised Messiah, Ḥaḍrat Mirzā Ghulām Aḥmad[as] of Qadiān, Page 527 available on www.alislam.org

refers to those satanic forces that would be unleashed in the Latter Days to oppose the Promised Messiah[as] and *al-Imām al-Mahdī*. [2]A similar prophecy in the Christian faith about the appearance of the Antichrist refers to the same phenomenon, and we have therefore translated the term '*Dajjāl*' as 'Antichrist.

- The Sūrah is quite fittingly entitled الناس (*an-nās*) mankind, since protection has been solicited from the Lord, King and God of mankind الناس (*an-nās*) against the mischief of whisperers from among the Jinn and men, who whisper evil thoughts into the hearts of men الناس (*an-nās*).

- [3] In the last verse of the Holy Qur'ān Dajjāl is named Khannās. .

---

[2] Conditions of Bai'at & responsibilities of an Ahmadī, by Ḥaḍrat Mirzā Masroor Aḥmad (Khalīfatul Masīḥ V [aba], Islām International Publications Ltd. 2006 Page xiv

[3] *Tafsīrul-Qur'ān* by The Promised Messiah[as], Ḥaḍrat Mirzā Ghulām Aḥmad of Qadiān, Page 531 available on www.alislam.org

Sūrah an-Nās, Chapter 114

بِسۡمِ ٱللَّهِ ٱلرَّحۡمَٰنِ ٱلرَّحِيمِ ۝

قُلۡ أَعُوذُ بِرَبِّ ٱلنَّاسِ ۝ مَلِكِ ٱلنَّاسِ ۝ إِلَٰهِ ٱلنَّاسِ ۝
مِن شَرِّ ٱلۡوَسۡوَاسِ ٱلۡخَنَّاسِ ۝ ٱلَّذِى يُوَسۡوِسُ فِى صُدُورِ
ٱلنَّاسِ ۝ مِنَ ٱلۡجِنَّةِ وَٱلنَّاسِ ۝

Translation

In the name of Allah, the Gracious, the Merciful Say, 'I seek refuge in the Lord of mankind, 'The King of mankind, 'The God of mankind, 'From the evil of the sneaking whisperer, 'Who whispers into the hearts of men, 'From among the Jinn and mankind.'

بِسۡمِ ٱللَّهِ ٱلرَّحۡمَـٰنِ ٱلرَّحِيمِ ۝

[114:1] In the name of Allah, the Gracious, the Merciful.

قُلۡ أَعُوذُ بِرَبِّ ٱلنَّاسِ ۝

[114:2] Say, 'I seek refuge in the Lord of mankind,

Commentary[4]

In the present Sūrah *three* Divine attributes viz.,رب الناس (*Rabbun-nās*) Lord of mankind, مالک الناس (*Mālikun-nās*) King of mankind, اله الناس (*Ilahun-Nās*) God of mankind, have been invoked as against one attribute, *viz*,. رب الفلق (*Rabbul-falaq*) Lord of the dawn in the preceding *Sūrah*,

[4] The Holy Qur'ān with English Translation and Commentary. 3rd ed. Islām International Publications Limited; 2002. Volume 5, Pages 2915-2916

because this one attribute comprises all the three above-mentioned attributes. Whereas One Divine attribute, *viz.*, رب الفلق (*Rabbul-Falaq*) Lord of the dawn has been invoked against four kinds of mischief in the previous *Sūrah*, in the *Sūrah* under comment three Divine attributes have been invoked against one mischief i.e., whispering of the Evil One. This is because promptings or insinuations of Satan cover all conceivable evils.

Mention of three Divine attributes in the *Sūrah* implies that all sin proceeds from three causes, viz., when a person looks upon other men as his رب (*Rabb*) Lord or ملك (*Malik*) King or اله (*Ilah*) God, that is to say, he regards them as the main prop or support of his life or slavishly surrenders to their undue authority or makes them the object of his love and adoration.

A believer is enjoined here to look up to God alone as the real support of his life, and to render Him alone true and unconditional obedience and to make Him alone the real object of his love and adoration. Or, the believer may have been enjoined in these verses constantly to seek protection against the ravages of exploiting capitalists, tyrannical rulers and from the crafty priestly class who, taking undue

advantage of the unwary and simple-minded folk exploit them mercilessly. The reference seems particularly to be to the conditions obtaining in the Latter Days.

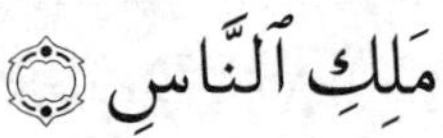
مَلِكِ ٱلنَّاسِ

[114:3] 'The King of mankind,

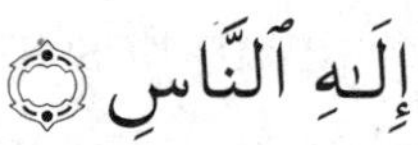
إِلَٰهِ ٱلنَّاسِ

[114:4] 'The God of mankind,

مِن شَرِّ ٱلۡوَسۡوَاسِ ٱلۡخَنَّاسِ

[114:5] 'From the evil of the sneaking whisperer,

ٱلَّذِى يُوَسۡوِسُ فِى صُدُورِ ٱلنَّاسِ

[114:6] 'Who whispers into the hearts of men,

مِنَ ٱلْجِنَّةِ وَٱلنَّاسِ ۝

[114:7] 'From among the Jinn and mankind.

The verse may mean that the Evil One whispers evil thoughts into the hearts of Jinn (big men) and common men, sparing nobody. Or it may mean that whisperers of evil are to be found both among Jinn and common men. The verse may also refer to the evils of Western Democracies and of the Communist Powers that work from behind the iron curtain.

What is the key message of this portion of the Holy Qur'ān?

How does this message apply to your personal life?

First Rak'ah of Saturday 'Ishā' Prayer

Please see Page 356
First Rak'ah of Tuesday Fajr Prayer

Second Rak'ah of Saturday 'Ishā' Prayer

Please see Page 277
First Rak'ah of Monday Fajr Prayer

SUNDAY

DAY	SALAT	FIRST RAK'AH	2ND RAK'AH
SUNDAY	Fajr	Sūrah al-Kahf 103-107	Sūrah al-Kahf 108-111
	Maghrib	Sūrah al- Falaq	Sūrah an-Nās
	'Ishā'	Sūrah Ḥā Mīm as-Sajdah 31-33	Sūrah Ḥā Mīm as-Sajdah 34-37

First Rak'ah of Sunday and Wednesday Fajr Prayer

First Rak'ah of Wednesday and Sunday Fajr Prayer

Importance of Sūrah al-Kahf

- [1], [2]It is mentioned in Ḥadīth that whoever would learn the first and the last ten verses of Sūrah al-Kahf would be protected from the evil influence of Dajjāl or antichrist (Musnad).
-
    - [3],[4]According to the Arabic lexicon, Dajjāl signifies a group of people who present themselves as trustworthy and pious, but are neither trustworthy nor pious. Rather, everything they say is full of dishonesty and deceit. This characteristic is to be found in the class of Christians known as the clergy.

---

[1] The Holy Qur'ān with English Translation and Commentary. 3rd ed. Islām International Publications Limited; 2002. Volume 3, Page 1478

[2] *Tafsīr-e-Kabīr*. Ḥaḍrat Mirzā Bashīr-ud-Dīn Maḥmūd Aḥmad[ra], Printwell Amritsar 2004. Volume 4, Pages 403-404

[3] The *Essence of Islām*. The Promised Messiah, Ḥaḍrat Mirzā Ghulām Aḥmad of Qadian[as]: First edition. Islam International Publications Limited; 2005. Volume III, Pages 279-287

[4] *Kitābul-Bariyyah, Ruḥānī Khazā'in*, vol. 13, Pages 243-244.

Another group is that of the philosophers and thinkers who are busy trying to assume control of machines, industries and the Divine scheme of things. They are the Dajjāl because they deceive God's creatures by their actions and tall claims as if they are partners in God's dominion. The clergy are arrogating to themselves the status of Prophethood because they ignore the true heavenly Gospel and spread a perverted and corrupted version as the supposed translation of the Gospel. For detailed discussion about the concept of Dajjāl, please see Essence of Islam, Volume 3)

- It is stated in the Ḥadīth when Sūrah al-Kahf was revealed, 70,000 angels descended to protect it (Manthūr Vol 4, Page 210). This is a metaphorical expression that means that in order to fulfil the Divine prophecy of the final triumph of Islam given in this Sūrah, Allāh the Exalted, in accordance with His Divine law, will appoint thousands of angels to help bring about this success.

أَفَحَسِبَ ٱلَّذِينَ كَفَرُوٓاْ أَن يَتَّخِذُواْ عِبَادِى مِن دُونِىٓ
أَوْلِيَآءَ ۚ إِنَّآ أَعْتَدْنَا جَهَنَّمَ لِلْكَٰفِرِينَ نُزُلًا ۝ قُلْ هَلْ نُنَبِّئُكُم
بِٱلْأَخْسَرِينَ أَعْمَٰلًا ۝ ٱلَّذِينَ ضَلَّ سَعْيُهُمْ فِى ٱلْحَيَوٰةِ ٱلدُّنْيَا
وَهُمْ يَحْسَبُونَ أَنَّهُمْ يُحْسِنُونَ صُنْعًا ۝ أُوْلَٰٓئِكَ ٱلَّذِينَ كَفَرُواْ
بِـَٔايَٰتِ رَبِّهِمْ وَلِقَآئِهِۦ فَحَبِطَتْ أَعْمَٰلُهُمْ فَلَا نُقِيمُ لَهُمْ يَوْمَ
ٱلْقِيَٰمَةِ وَزْنًا ۝ ذَٰلِكَ جَزَآؤُهُمْ جَهَنَّمُ بِمَا كَفَرُواْ وَٱتَّخَذُوٓاْ
ءَايَٰتِى وَرُسُلِى هُزُوًا ۝

Translation

Do the disbelievers think that they can take My servants as protectors instead of Me? Surely, We have prepared Hell as an entertainment for the disbelievers. Say, 'Shall We tell you of those who are the worst losers

with regard to their deeds? —'Those whose labour is *all* lost in *search after things pertaining to* the life of this world, and they think that they are doing good works.' Those are they who disbelieve in the Signs of their Lord and in the meeting with Him. So their works are vain, and on the Day of Resurrection We shall give them no weight. That is their reward — Hell; because they disbelieved, and made a jest of My Signs and My Messengers

أَفَحَسِبَ ٱلَّذِينَ كَفَرُوٓاْ أَن يَتَّخِذُواْ عِبَادِى مِن دُونِىٓ أَوۡلِيَآءَ ۚ
إِنَّآ أَعۡتَدۡنَا جَهَنَّمَ لِلۡكَٰفِرِينَ نُزُلًا ۝

[18:103] Do the disbelievers think that they can take My servants as protectors instead of Me? Surely, We have prepared Hell as an entertainment for the disbelievers.

[5]Commentary

The verse speaks of those people who look upon Jesus[as] as their saviour and as the son of God and to whom reference has already been made in the beginning of this Chapter. This shows that the foregoing verses also deal with the same people - Christian nations of the West.

[5] The Holy Qu'rān with English Translation and Commentary. 3rd ed. Islām International Publications Limited; 2002. Volume 3, Pages 1543-1544

قُلْ هَلْ نُنَبِّئُكُم بِٱلْأَخْسَرِينَ أَعْمَٰلًا ۝

[18:104] Say, 'Shall We tell you of those who are the worst losers with regard to their deeds? —

ٱلَّذِينَ ضَلَّ سَعْيُهُمْ فِى ٱلْحَيَوٰةِ ٱلدُّنْيَا وَهُمْ يَحْسَبُونَ أَنَّهُمْ يُحْسِنُونَ

صُنْعًا ۝

[18:105] 'Those whose labour is *all* lost in *search after things pertaining to* the life of this world, and they think that they are doing good works.'

Commentary

The verse means to say that these people look upon the acquisition of material comforts and worldly benefits and upon making new inventions and discoveries to add to those comforts as the sole aim and object of their life. They have no place for God in their hearts.

أُوْلَٰٓئِكَ ٱلَّذِينَ كَفَرُواْ بِـَٔايَٰتِ رَبِّهِمْ وَلِقَآئِهِۦ فَحَبِطَتْ أَعْمَٰلُهُمْ فَلَا نُقِيمُ لَهُمْ يَوْمَ ٱلْقِيَٰمَةِ وَزْنًا ﴿١٠٥﴾

[18:106] Those are they who disbelieve in the Signs of their Lord and in the meeting with Him. So their works are vain, and on the Day of Resurrection We shall give them no weight.

<u>Commentary</u>

As all their labour is for this life and they have completely disregarded the life to come, so no sign or trace of their works will be left in this world and on the Last Day also their deeds will prove quite futile.

ذَٰلِكَ جَزَآؤُهُمْ جَهَنَّمُ بِمَا كَفَرُواْ وَٱتَّخَذُوٓاْ ءَايَٰتِى وَرُسُلِى هُزُوًا ﴿١٠٦﴾

[18:107] That is their reward — Hell; because they disbelieved, and made a jest of My Signs and My Messengers.

Commentary

As these people turned their backs upon God and did nothing to win His pleasure, they can expect no reward in the Hereafter. On the contrary, they will burn in the fire of Hell which will be the natural consequence of their disbelief and evil deeds and of their mocking at the Signs of God and defying His Messengers.

What is the key message of this portion of the Holy Qur'ān?

How does this message apply to your personal life?

Second Rak'ah of Sunday and Wednesday Fajr Prayer

Second Rak'ah of Sunday and Wednesday Fajr Prayer

Importance of Sūrah al-Kahf

- [1], [2]It is mentioned in Ḥadīth that whoever would learn the first and the last ten verses of Sūrah al-Kahf would be protected from the evil influence of Dajjāl or antichrist (Musnad).

- [3], [4]According to the Arabic lexicon, Dajjāl signifies a group of people who present themselves as trustworthy and pious, but are neither trustworthy nor pious. Rather, everything they say is full of dishonesty and deceit. This characteristic is to be found in the class of Christians known as the clergy. Another group is that of the philosophers and

---

[1] The Holy Qur'ān with English Translation and Commentary. 3rd ed. Islām International Publications Limited; 2002. Volume 3, Page 1478

[2] *Tafsīr-e-Kabīr*. Ḥaḍrat Mirzā Bashīr-ud-Dīn Maḥmūd Aḥmad[ra], Printwell Amritsar 2004. Volume 4, Pages 403-404

[3] The *Essence of Islām*. The Promised Messiah, Ḥaḍrat Mirzā Ghulām Aḥmad of Qadian[as]: First edition. Islam International Publications Limited; 2005. Volume III, Pages 279-287

[4] *Kitabul-Bariyyah, Ruḥānī Khazā'in*, vol. 13, Pages. 243-244.

thinkers who are busy trying to assume control of machines, industries and the Divine scheme of things. They are the Dajjāl because they deceive God's creatures by their actions and tall claims as if they are partners in God's dominion. The clergy are arrogating to themselves the status of Prophethood because they ignore the true heavenly Gospel and spread a perverted and corrupted version as the supposed translation of the Gospel. For detailed discussion about the concept of Dajjāl, please see Essence of Islam, Volume 3)

- It is stated in the Ḥadīth when Sūrah al-Kahf was revealed, 70,000 angels descended to protect it (Manthūr Vol 4, Page 210). This is a metaphorical expression that means that in order to fulfil the Divine prophecy of the final triumph of Islam given in this Sūrah, Allāh the Exalted, in accordance with His Divine law, will appoint thousands of angels to help bring about this success.
    - This chapter gives the information about the challenges of Gog and Magog; huge powers of Christian nations and their attempts to misrepresent and distort the Islamic teachings.

Despite the might of Gog and Magog, weak Muslims will be helped by Allāh the Exalted to bring true the prophecy of triumph of Islam, Allāh Almighty will assign angels to help them

- ([5],[6]*Yājūj* [Gog] and *Mājūj* [Magog] are two peoples who have been mentioned in earlier scriptures. The reason why they are so called is that they make extensive use of *Ajīj* [fire], and would reign supreme on earth and dominate every height. At the same time, a great change will be ordained from heaven and will usher in days of peace and amity.

- [7]I have also proved that it is essential for the Promised Messiah to appear at the time of Gog and Magog. Since *Ajīj*, from which the words Gog and Magog are derived, means

---

[5] The *Essence of Islām*. The Promised Messiah, Ḥaḍrat Mirzā Ghulām Aḥmad of Qadian[as]: First edition. Islam International Publications Limited; 2005. Volume III, Pages 305

[6] *Lecture Siālkot, Rūḥānī Khazā'in*, vol. 20, Page. 211

[7] *Ayyāmuṣ-Ṣulḥ, Rūḥānī Khazā'in*, vol. 14, Pages. 424-425

'fire', God Almighty has disclosed to me that Gog and Magog are a people who are greater experts in the use of fire than any other people. Their very names indicate that their ships, trains and machines will be run by fire. They will fight their battles with fire. They will excel all other people in harnessing fire to their service. This is why they will be called Gog and Magog. These are the people of the West, as they are unique in their expertise in the use of fire. In Jewish scriptures too it was the people of Europe who were described as Gog and Magog. Even the name of Moscow, which is the ancient capital of Russia, is mentioned. Thus it was preordained that the Promised Messiah would appear in the time of Gog and Magog. [8]For detailed discussion about the concept of Gog and Magog, please see Essence of Islam, Volume 3).

---

[8] The *Essence of Islām*. The Promised Messiah, Ḥaḍrat Mirzā Ghulām Aḥmad of Qadian[as]: First edition. Islam International Publications Limited; 2005. Volume III, Pages 305-310

إِنَّ ٱلَّذِينَ ءَامَنُواْ وَعَمِلُواْ ٱلصَّٰلِحَٰتِ كَانَتۡ لَهُمۡ جَنَّٰتُ ٱلۡفِرۡدَوۡسِ
نُزُلًا ۝ خَٰلِدِينَ فِيهَا لَا يَبۡغُونَ عَنۡهَا حِوَلٗا ۝ قُل لَّوۡ كَانَ
ٱلۡبَحۡرُ مِدَادٗا لِّكَلِمَٰتِ رَبِّي لَنَفِدَ ٱلۡبَحۡرُ قَبۡلَ أَن تَنفَدَ كَلِمَٰتُ
رَبِّي وَلَوۡ جِئۡنَا بِمِثۡلِهِۦ مَدَدٗا ۝ قُلۡ إِنَّمَآ أَنَا۠ بَشَرٞ مِّثۡلُكُمۡ يُوحَىٰٓ
إِلَيَّ أَنَّمَآ إِلَٰهُكُمۡ إِلَٰهٞ وَٰحِدٞۖ فَمَن كَانَ يَرۡجُواْ لِقَآءَ رَبِّهِۦ
فَلۡيَعۡمَلۡ عَمَلٗا صَٰلِحٗا وَلَا يُشۡرِكۡ بِعِبَادَةِ رَبِّهِۦٓ أَحَدَۢا ۝

Translation

Surely, those who believe and do good deeds, will have Gardens of Paradise for an abode, Wherein they will abide; they will not desire any change therefrom. Say, 'If the ocean became ink for the words of my Lord, surely, the ocean would be exhausted before the words of my Lord came to an end, even though We brought

the like thereof as *further* help.' Say, 'I am only a man like yourselves; *but* I have received the revelation that your God is only One God. So let him, who hopes to meet his Lord do good deeds, and let him join no one in the worship of his Lord.

إِنَّ ٱلَّذِينَ ءَامَنُوا۟ وَعَمِلُوا۟ ٱلصَّـٰلِحَـٰتِ كَانَتْ لَهُمْ جَنَّـٰتُ ٱلْفِرْدَوْسِ نُزُلًا ۝

[18:108] Surely, those who believe and do good deeds, will have Gardens of Paradise for an abode.

خَـٰلِدِينَ فِيهَا لَا يَبْغُونَ عَنْهَا حِوَلًا ۝

[18:109] Wherein they will abide; they will not desire any change therefrom.

[9]Commentary

With the decline of Christian nations will begin the progress and advancement of Muslims and on the ashes of their departed glory will be laid the foundations of a new

[9] The Holy Qur'ān with English Translation and Commentary. 3rd ed. Islām International Publications Limited; 2002. Volume 3, Pages 1544-1545

and better world order. At last the believers will get the reward of their sacrifices and sufferings but their sacrifices in the way of their Lord will know no end. The Faithful will feel such peace of mind and happiness in their sacrifices that they will not like to change this blessed state of spiritual bliss.

قُل لَّوْ كَانَ ٱلْبَحْرُ مِدَادًا لِّكَلِمَـٰتِ رَبِّى لَنَفِدَ ٱلْبَحْرُ قَبْلَ أَن

تَنفَدَ كَلِمَـٰتُ رَبِّى وَلَوْ جِئْنَا بِمِثْلِهِۦ مَدَدًا ﴿١١٠﴾

[18:110] Say, 'If the ocean became ink for the words of my Lord, surely, the ocean would be exhausted before the words of my Lord came to an end, even though We brought the like thereof as *further* help.'

Commentary

Christian nations of the West boast of their great inventions and scientific discoveries and seem to labour under the misconception that they have succeeded in fathoming the secret of creation itself. But, says the verse, this is nothing but a vain boast.

God's secrets are so inexhaustible and He has endowed His creatures with such wonderful powers and attributes that far from fathoming the secret of creation, what these people will be able to discover after all their striving will not be even as much as a drop in the ocean.

The verse also hints that those will be the days of publicity and innumerable books on all sorts of subjects will be published but even then the vast ocean of knowledge will remain unfathomed.

قُلْ إِنَّمَآ أَنَا۠ بَشَرٌ مِّثْلُكُمْ يُوحَىٰٓ إِلَيَّ أَنَّمَآ إِلَٰهُكُمْ إِلَٰهٌ وَٰحِدٌ ۖ فَمَن
كَانَ يَرْجُوا۟ لِقَآءَ رَبِّهِۦ فَلْيَعْمَلْ عَمَلًا صَٰلِحًا وَلَا يُشْرِكْ بِعِبَادَةِ
رَبِّهِۦٓ أَحَدًۢا ۝

[18:111] Say, 'I am only a man like yourselves; *but* I have received the revelation that your God is only One God. So let him, who hopes to meet his Lord, do good deeds, and let him join no one in the worship of his Lord.

Commentary

The Holy Prophet[sa] is here commanded to say to the disbelieving Christian people that, even after having disclosed so many secrets of the unknown and having made great prophecies about the ultimate triumph of his cause and the downfall of Christian nations, he cannot claim to be a son of God or to have been endowed with divine powers. He is but a human being and his greatest merit lies in his being the bearer of the divine Message. If disbelievers too desire to be blessed with revelation, they should also give up associating false gods with Allāh. Then will God bestow His favours upon them and lay open to them the treasures of heavenly secrets.

The Holy Prophet[sa] is reported to have said that the recitation of the last ten verses of this chapter makes one secure against the spiritual onslaughts of the *Dajjāl*.

This shows that the *Dajjāl* and Gog and Magog are one and the same people--- Christian nations of the West; the *Dajjāl* representing the evil aspect of their religious propaganda and Gog and Magog their material and political predominance.

What is the key message of this portion of the Holy Qur'ān?

How does this message apply to your personal life?

First Rak'ah of Maghrib Prayer on Saturday, Sunday, Monday, Wednesday and Thursday

Please see page 183

Second Rak'ah of Maghrib Prayer on Saturday, Sunday, Monday, Wednesday and Thursday

Please see page 195

First Rak'ah of Sunday 'Ishā' Prayer

First Rak'ah of Sunday 'Ishā' Prayer

[1]Importance of Sūrah Ḥā Mīm as-Sajdah

- The main message of this Sūrah is to give glad tidings to believers of success and triumph while opponents who reject and belittle the signs of Allāh will meet a bad end.

[1] The Holy Qur'ān with English Translation and Commentary. 3rd ed. Islām International Publications Limited; 2002. Volume 4, Pages 2318-2319

إِنَّ ٱلَّذِينَ قَالُواْ رَبُّنَا ٱللَّهُ ثُمَّ ٱسْتَقَـٰمُواْ تَتَنَزَّلُ عَلَيْهِمُ
ٱلْمَلَـٰٓئِكَةُ أَلَّا تَخَافُواْ وَلَا تَحْزَنُواْ وَأَبْشِرُواْ بِٱلْجَنَّةِ ٱلَّتِى كُنتُمْ
تُوعَدُونَ ۝ نَحْنُ أَوْلِيَآؤُكُمْ فِى ٱلْحَيَوٰةِ ٱلدُّنْيَا وَفِى ٱلْـَٔاخِرَةِ ۖ
وَلَكُمْ فِيهَا مَا تَشْتَهِىٓ أَنفُسُكُمْ وَلَكُمْ فِيهَا مَا تَدَّعُونَ ۝ نُزُلًا
مِّنْ غَفُورٍ رَّحِيمٍ ۝

Translation

As for **those who say, 'Our Lord is Allah,' and then remain steadfast, the angels descend on them,** ***saying*****: 'Fear ye not, nor grieve; and rejoice in the Garden that you were promised. 'We are your friends in this life and in the Hereafter. Therein you will have all that your**

souls will desire, and therein you will have all that you will ask for —'An entertainment from the Most Forgiving, the Merciful.'

إِنَّ ٱلَّذِينَ قَالُوا۟ رَبُّنَا ٱللَّهُ ثُمَّ ٱسْتَقَـٰمُوا۟ تَتَنَزَّلُ عَلَيْهِمُ

ٱلْمَلَـٰٓئِكَةُ أَلَّا تَخَافُوا۟ وَلَا تَحْزَنُوا۟ وَأَبْشِرُوا۟ بِٱلْجَنَّةِ ٱلَّتِى كُنتُمْ

تُوعَدُونَ ۝

[41:31] ***As for*** **those who say, 'Our Lord is Allah,' and then remain steadfast, the angels descend on them,** ***saying*****: 'Fear ye not, nor grieve; and rejoice in the Garden that you were promised.**

[2]Commentary

The present and the next verse show that it is in this very life that angels descend upon the Faithful to give them consolation and comfort when they exhibit perseverance in

[2] The Holy Qur'ān with English Translation and Commentary. 3rd ed. Islām International Publications Limited; 2002. Volume 4, Pages 2329-2330

the midst of severe trials and tribulations. It is when the Faithful are beset with dangers all round, when they are threatened with loss of life, property and honour in the path of God, and whatever is consoling and comforting forsakes them, so much so, that God tries them by closing the door of heartening visions and revelations for a time; it is when they are surrounded by all these dreary conditions--- and though the last ray of hope passes away, yet they show perseverance--- that the angels of God descend upon them, giving them the message of hope and good cheer. It is then that God reveals His beautiful Face to them.

نَحْنُ أَوْلِيَآؤُكُمْ فِي ٱلْحَيَوٰةِ ٱلدُّنْيَا وَفِي ٱلْأَخِرَةِ ۖ وَلَكُمْ فِيهَا مَا

تَشْتَهِىٓ أَنفُسُكُمْ وَلَكُمْ فِيهَا مَا تَدَّعُونَ ۝

[41:32] 'We are your friends in this life and in the Hereafter. Therein you will have all that your souls will desire, and therein you will have all that you will ask for.

نُزُلًا مِّنْ غَفُورٍ رَّحِيمٍ ۝

[41:33] 'An entertainment from the Most Forgiving, the Merciful.'

Commentary

The verse means to say that it is when the Faithful show firmness under severe hardships and privations, and hold on through fiery ordeals, quite willing to suffer every disgrace in the way of God, fully submitting themselves to His will, that they attain to that stage of nearness to Him in which they become, as it were, the guests of God, for whose smallest need He has the greatest regard.

What is the key message of this portion of the Holy Qur'ān?

How does this message apply to your personal life?

Second Rak'ah of Sunday 'Ishā' Prayer

Second Rak‘ah of Sunday ‘Ishā’ Prayer

[1]Importance of Sūrah Ḥā Mīm as-Sajdah

The main message of this Sūrah is to give glad tidings to believers of success and triumph while opponents who reject and belittle the signs of Allāh will meet a bad end.

[1] The Holy Qur’ān with English Translation and Commentary. 3rd ed. Islām International Publications Limited; 2002. Volume 4, Pages 2318-2319

وَمَنْ أَحْسَنُ قَوْلًا مِّمَّن دَعَآ إِلَى ٱللَّهِ وَعَمِلَ صَٰلِحًا وَقَالَ إِنَّنِى
مِنَ ٱلْمُسْلِمِينَ ۝ وَلَا تَسْتَوِى ٱلْحَسَنَةُ وَلَا ٱلسَّيِّئَةُ ۚ ٱدْفَعْ
بِٱلَّتِى هِىَ أَحْسَنُ فَإِذَا ٱلَّذِى بَيْنَكَ وَبَيْنَهُۥ عَدَٰوَةٌ كَأَنَّهُۥ وَلِىٌّ
حَمِيمٌ ۝ وَمَا يُلَقَّىٰهَآ إِلَّا ٱلَّذِينَ صَبَرُوا۟ وَمَا يُلَقَّىٰهَآ إِلَّا ذُو
حَظٍّ عَظِيمٍ ۝ وَإِمَّا يَنزَغَنَّكَ مِنَ ٱلشَّيْطَٰنِ نَزْغٌ فَٱسْتَعِذْ بِٱللَّهِ ۖ
إِنَّهُۥ هُوَ ٱلسَّمِيعُ ٱلْعَلِيمُ ۝

Translation

And who is better in speech than he who invites *men* to Allah and does good works and says, 'I am surely of

those who submit?' And good and evil are not alike. Repel *evil* with that which is best. And lo, he between whom and thyself was enmity will become as though he were a warm friend. But none is granted that save those who are steadfast; and none is granted that except the one who possess a large share of excellence. And if an incitement from Satan incite thee, then seek refuge in Allah. Surely He is the All-Hearing, the All-Knowing.

وَمَنْ أَحْسَنُ قَوْلاً مِّمَّن دَعَآ إِلَى ٱللَّهِ وَعَمِلَ صَـٰلِحًا وَقَالَ إِنَّنِى

مِنَ ٱلْمُسْلِمِينَ ۝

[41:34] And who is better in speech than he who invites *men* to Allah and does good works and says, 'I am surely of those who submit?'

[2]Commentary

There could be no better a vocation for a person than to call men to God and to conform his own conduct to the teachings he preaches to others and to submit entirely to God's will. This is the quintessence of the teaching of Islam.

[2] The Holy Qur'ān with English Translation and Commentary. 3rd ed. Islām International Publications Limited; 2002. Volume 4, Pages 2329-2330

وَلَا تَسْتَوِى ٱلْحَسَنَةُ وَلَا ٱلسَّيِّئَةُ ۚ ٱدْفَعْ بِٱلَّتِى هِىَ أَحْسَنُ فَإِذَا ٱلَّذِى بَيْنَكَ وَبَيْنَهُۥ عَدَٰوَةٌ كَأَنَّهُۥ وَلِىٌّ حَمِيمٌ ۝

[41:35] And good and evil are not alike. Repel *evil* with that which is best. And lo, he between whom and thyself was enmity will become as though he were a warm friend.

Commentary

As the preaching of truth inevitably brings in its wake hardships for the preacher, the verse enjoins upon him to bear them patiently and with fortitude, and even to return good for the evil he receives at the hands of his persecutors.

وَمَا يُلَقَّىٰهَآ إِلَّا ٱلَّذِينَ صَبَرُوا۟ وَمَا يُلَقَّىٰهَآ إِلَّا ذُو حَظٍّ عَظِيمٍ ۝

[41:36] But none is granted that save those who are steadfast; and none is granted that except the one who possess a large share of excellence.

Commentary

The very high standard of good moral conduct referred to in the preceding verse can only be attained by putting up, without grumbling or fretting, with hardships one has to face in the way of God. And fortunate, indeed, is the person who disciplines himself to such a high standard.

وَإِمَّا يَنزَغَنَّكَ مِنَ ٱلشَّيْطَـٰنِ نَزْغٌ فَٱسْتَعِذْ بِٱللَّهِ ۖ إِنَّهُۥ هُوَ ٱلسَّمِيعُ ٱلْعَلِيمُ ۝

[41:37] And if an incitement from Satan incite thee, then seek refuge in Allah. Surely He is the All-Hearing, the All-Knowing.

Commentary

نزع (*naza*') meaning, an evil suggestion or mischief, the verse purports to say that evil-minded people always try to put obstacles in the way of the cause of truth and incite men of satanic nature against one who preaches the truth to them. It enjoins all preachers of truth to seek God's protection and pray to Him for help and succour when such an ugly situation faces them.

What is the key message of this portion of the Holy Qur'ān?

How does this message apply to your personal life?

MONDAY

DAY	SALAT	FIRST RAK'AH	2ND RAK'AH
MONDAY	Fajr	Sūrah al-Baqarah 285-287	Sūrah Āl-e-'Imrān 191-195
	Maghrib	Sūrah al- Falaq	Sūrah an-Nās
	'Ishā'	Sūrah al-Ḥashr 19-22	Sūrah al-Ḥashr 23-25

First Rak‘ah of Monday and Thursday Fajr Prayer.

Verse 287 in the second Rak‘ah of Saturday ‘Ishā’ Prayer

First Rak'ah of Monday and Thursday Fajr Prayers. Verse 287 in the second Rak'ah of Saturday 'Ishā' Prayers

Importance of Sūrah al-Baqarah

- al-Baqarah is the longest chapter of the Holy Qur'ān. The Holy Prophet[sa] said that everything has its peak and the peak of the Qur'ān is al-Baqarah (Tirmidhī).
    - The Holy Prophet[sa] said that whosoever recites ten verses of this chapter, first four verses, Āyatul-Kursī and last three verses, Satan will not enter his house till the morning (Ibne Kathīr).
    - [1]This means that these verses embody the Islamic teachings and that satan cannot come near a person who faithfully acts on these teachings.
    - 'Till the morning' means that teachings, however excellent, if not regularly practiced cannot be fully effective and the good influences of such teachings are lost.

---

[1] The Holy Qur'ān with English Translation and Commentary. 3rd ed. Islam International Publications Limited; 2002. Volume 1, Page 24

- [2]In the first 4 verses a sketch is drawn for a pious life, Āyatul-Kursī has a great explanation of the attributes of God and the last three verses contain prayers that purify the heart. When these three things come together, one's heart is purified and satanic thoughts disappear.
    - To do good deeds in following the words of Allāh
    - To ponder over the attributes of Allāh the Exalted
    - To always engage in prayers and commit oneself totally to God.

- [3]The Promised Messiah[as] said that in this chapter the rights of Allāh and rights of people are described in great detail. Do's and don'ts have been explained and there is a great emphasis on patience and sacrifice.

---

[2] *Tafsīr-e-Kabīr*. Ḥaḍrat Mirzā Bashīr-ud-Dīn Maḥmūd Aḥmad[ra], Printwell Amritsar 2004. Volume 1. Pages 51

[3] *Tafsīrul-Qur'ān* by The Promised Messiah, Ḥaḍrat Mirzā Ghulām Aḥmad[as] of Qadiān, Page 1 available on www.alislam.org

لِّلَّهِ مَا فِى ٱلسَّمَٰوَٰتِ وَمَا فِى ٱلْأَرْضِ ۗ وَإِن تُبْدُوا۟ مَا فِىٓ
أَنفُسِكُمْ أَوْ تُخْفُوهُ يُحَاسِبْكُم بِهِ ٱللَّهُ ۖ فَيَغْفِرُ لِمَن يَشَآءُ
وَيُعَذِّبُ مَن يَشَآءُ ۗ وَٱللَّهُ عَلَىٰ كُلِّ شَىْءٍ قَدِيرٌ ۝ ءَامَنَ
ٱلرَّسُولُ بِمَآ أُنزِلَ إِلَيْهِ مِن رَّبِّهِۦ وَٱلْمُؤْمِنُونَ ۚ كُلٌّ ءَامَنَ بِٱللَّهِ
وَمَلَٰٓئِكَتِهِۦ وَكُتُبِهِۦ وَرُسُلِهِۦ لَا نُفَرِّقُ بَيْنَ أَحَدٍ مِّن رُّسُلِهِۦ ۚ
وَقَالُوا۟ سَمِعْنَا وَأَطَعْنَا ۖ غُفْرَانَكَ رَبَّنَا وَإِلَيْكَ ٱلْمَصِيرُ ۝ لَا
يُكَلِّفُ ٱللَّهُ نَفْسًا إِلَّا وُسْعَهَا ۚ لَهَا مَا كَسَبَتْ وَعَلَيْهَا مَا ٱكْتَسَبَتْ ۗ
رَبَّنَا لَا تُؤَاخِذْنَآ إِن نَّسِينَآ أَوْ أَخْطَأْنَا ۚ رَبَّنَا وَلَا تَحْمِلْ عَلَيْنَآ
إِصْرًا كَمَا حَمَلْتَهُۥ عَلَى ٱلَّذِينَ مِن قَبْلِنَا ۚ رَبَّنَا وَلَا تُحَمِّلْنَا مَا

لَا طَاقَةَ لَنَا بِهِۦ ۖ وَٱعْفُ عَنَّا وَٱغْفِرْ لَنَا وَٱرْحَمْنَآ ۚ أَنتَ مَوْلَىٰنَا

فَٱنصُرْنَا عَلَى ٱلْقَوْمِ ٱلْكَٰفِرِينَ ۝

Translation:

To Allāh belongs whatever is in the heavens and whatever is in the earth; and whether you disclose what is in your minds or keep it hidden, Allāh will call you to account for it; then will He forgive whomsoever He pleases and punish whomsoever He pleases; and Allāh has the power to do all that He wills. This Messenger *of Ours* believes in that which has been revealed to him from his Lord, and *so do* the believers: all *of them* believe in Allāh, and in His angels, and in His Books, and in His Messengers, *saying*, 'We make no distinction between any of His Messengers;' and they say, 'We hear, and we obey. *We implore* Thy forgiveness, O our Lord, and to Thee is the returning.' Allāh burdens not any soul beyond its capacity. It shall

have *the reward* it earns, and it shall get *the punishment* it incurs. Our Lord, do not punish us, if we forget or fall into error; and our Lord, lay not on us a responsibility as Thou didst lay upon those before us. Our Lord, burden us not with what we have not the strength to bear; and efface our *sins*, and grant us forgiveness and have mercy on us; Thou art our Master; so help us Thou against the disbelieving people.

آمين (*Āmīn*)is said after each of the phrases "and efface our *sins*", "and grant us forgiveness" "and have mercy on us".

لِّلَّهِ مَا فِى ٱلسَّمَٰوَٰتِ وَمَا فِى ٱلْأَرْضِ ۗ وَإِن تُبْدُوا۟ مَا فِىٓ
أَنفُسِكُمْ أَوْ تُخْفُوهُ يُحَاسِبْكُم بِهِ ٱللَّهُ ۖ فَيَغْفِرُ لِمَن يَشَآءُ
وَيُعَذِّبُ مَن يَشَآءُ ۗ وَٱللَّهُ عَلَىٰ كُلِّ شَىْءٍ قَدِيرٌ ۝

[2:285] To Allāh belongs whatever is in the heavens and whatever is in the earth; and whether you disclose what is in your minds or keep it hidden, Allāh will call you to account for it; then will He forgive whomsoever He pleases and punish whomsoever He pleases; and Allāh has the power to do all that He wills.

[4]Commentary:

---

4 The Holy Qur'ān with English Translation and Commentary. 3rd ed. Islām International Publications Limited; 2002. Volume 1, Pages 352-355

In this and the following two verses, with which the present Sūrah concludes, the subject of تزكية (*tazkiyah*) or purification has been dealt with as promised in the prayer of Abraham[as](2:130). By reminding us that to Allāh belongs whatever is in the heavens and whatever is in the earth, the Qur'ān teaches us that since everything is God's, we must avoid all those things which He requires us to avoid and adopt all those which He requires us to adopt. If we obey the commandments of God, which are meant for our own good, He will cause us to thrive and prosper, for He is the controller of all causes and all effects.

The verse embodies the great secret of attaining purification. That secret is, that if you wish to become pure, you should begin with the root, *i.e.*, you should make your hearts pure. Says the Holy Prophet[sa]: "In the body of man there is a piece of flesh; if this piece of flesh is sound, the whole body becomes sound; if it is corrupt, the whole body becomes corrupt. Behold! It is the heart" (Bukhārī).

The particle بِ (bā) *for* in the Arabic clause rendered as, *Allāh will call you to account for it,* means:

(a) by means of or on the basis of
(b) for or because of.

Following the first meaning, the verse would mean "Allāh will call you to account by means of it or on the basis of it" *i.e.* your actions will be judged on the basis of that which is in your hearts. They will be weighed from the point of view of your motives. This is another way of saying, in the words of the Holy Prophet[sa] انما الاعمال بالنيات (innamal-A'mālo bin-Niyyāt) *i.e.* Surely, the actions of men will be judged by the intention or the motive with which they are performed (Bukhārī).

Following the second meaning of با (bā) the verse would mean, "Allāh will call you to account for it or because of it" *i.e.* no human thought will be lost, however hidden it may be and that it will be requited or pardoned as Allāh may will it.

In connection with the words, ***whether you keep it hidden,*** it should be remembered that God will not call man to account for passing or momentary thoughts that sometimes cross his mind, for they are beyond one's control. In 2:287 we read, "Allāh burdens not any soul beyond its capacity," and it is certainly beyond our "capacity" to check the fleeting thoughts that occasionally flash across our minds.

It is only the evil thoughts that we cherish and harbor in our minds, such as malice, envy, etc., and the evil designs that we knowingly evolve and contemplate that we shall be called to account for.

The Holy Prophet[sa] is reported to have said that God has commanded the angels saying: "If a servant of mine thinks of doing an evil deed do not write it down against him; but if he carries out his intention, then write it down. And if he intends to do a good deed, but abstains from doing it, write it down as one good act;. and if he actually does a good deed then let it be noted as ten acts of virtue" (Tirmidhi).

The expression, ***whomsoever He pleases***, does not mean that God acts, as it were, arbitrarily without law or purpose. In the Qur'ānic idiom the expression "the will or pleasure of God," rather denotes the existence of a natural law (7:157). But as in the case of Allāh it is His will which stands for His law, therefore the Qu'rān uses this expression to point out that (1) God is the final authority in the universe; and that (2) His will is the law; and that (3) His will manifests itself in a just and benevolent manner, for He is the possessor of perfect attributes (17:111).

ءَامَنَ ٱلرَّسُولُ بِمَآ أُنزِلَ إِلَيۡهِ مِن رَّبِّهِۦ وَٱلۡمُؤۡمِنُونَۚ كُلٌّ ءَامَنَ
بِٱللَّهِ وَمَلَٰٓئِكَتِهِۦ وَكُتُبِهِۦ وَرُسُلِهِۦ لَا نُفَرِّقُ بَيۡنَ أَحَدٍ مِّن
رُّسُلِهِۦۚ وَقَالُواْ سَمِعۡنَا وَأَطَعۡنَاۖ غُفۡرَانَكَ رَبَّنَا وَإِلَيۡكَ
ٱلۡمَصِيرُ ۝

[2:286] This Messenger *of Ours* believes in that which has been revealed to him from his Lord, and *so do* the believers: all *of them* believe in Allāh, and in His angels, and in His Books, and in His Messengers, *saying*, 'We make no distinction between any of His Messengers;' and they say, 'We hear, and we obey. *We implore* Thy forgiveness, O our Lord, and to Thee is the returning.'

Commentary:

The mention of the believers along with the Prophet has a special significance in the verse; the purifying influence of the Holy Prophet[sa] has brought into existence a class of men

who have become purified both in belief and in deeds, thus fulfilling the object for which the Prophet for whom Abraham[as] had prayed was to make his appearance.

Good deeds are indeed the principle means for the attainment of purification, but they have their origin in the purity of the heart, which can be attained only by holding true beliefs. Hence the verse details the fundamental points of belief which the Holy Prophet[sa] taught his followers, *i.e.*, belief in God and His angels and His Books and His Messengers, mentioned in their natural order.

Among the points of belief detailed here, one is that true believers say, ***We make no distinction between any of His Messengers.*** This means that true believers should accept all the Messengers of God, without exception, and should make no distinction between them by accepting some and rejecting others.

There is in this food for thought for those Muslims who reject the Promised Messiah[as], Founder of the Ahmadiyya Movement whom God raised in fulfillment of the prophecies of the Holy Prophet[sa] and who came to demonstrate the truth of Islam by cogent reasons and powerful Signs.

Another very important means of attaining purification is prayer. The verse represents true believers as offering prayer to God in the ennobling words, ***We hear and we obey. We implore Thy forgiveness, O our Lord, and to Thee is the returning.***

This prayer contains four basic elements of purification:

(1) Man should ever be prepared to listen to God's commandments

(2) He should be ever ready to obey His commandments, whatever the circumstances

(3) He should always be asking for God's forgiveness for his sins and shortcomings

(4) He should never forget that he will one day return to, and stand before, his Maker and will render an account of his works.

لَا يُكَلِّفُ ٱللَّهُ نَفْسًا إِلَّا وُسْعَهَا ۚ لَهَا مَا كَسَبَتْ وَعَلَيْهَا مَا
ٱكْتَسَبَتْ ۗ رَبَّنَا لَا تُؤَاخِذْنَآ إِن نَّسِينَآ أَوْ أَخْطَأْنَا ۚ رَبَّنَا وَلَا

تَحۡمِلۡ عَلَيۡنَآ إِصۡرًا كَمَا حَمَلۡتَهُۥ عَلَى ٱلَّذِينَ مِن قَبۡلِنَا ۚ رَبَّنَا

وَلَا تُحَمِّلۡنَا مَا لَا طَاقَةَ لَنَا بِهِۦ ۖ وَٱعۡفُ عَنَّا وَٱغۡفِرۡ لَنَا وَٱرۡحَمۡنَآ ۚ

أَنتَ مَوۡلَىٰنَا فَٱنصُرۡنَا عَلَى ٱلۡقَوۡمِ ٱلۡكَٰفِرِينَ ۝

[2:287] Allāh burdens not any soul beyond its capacity. It shall have *the reward* it earns, and it shall get *the punishment* it incurs. Our Lord, do not punish us, if we forget or fall into error; and our Lord, lay not on us a responsibility as Thou didst lay upon those before us. Our Lord, burden us not with what we have not the strength to bear; and efface our *sins*, and grant us forgiveness and have mercy on us; Thou art our Master; so help us Thou against the disbelieving people.

Commentary

The clause, ***Allāh burdens not any soul beyond its capacity,*** is a powerful refutation of the doctrine of Atonement. It embodies two important principles:

(1) That the commandments of God are always given with due regard for human capacities and weaknesses.

(2) That purification in this world does not necessarily signify complete freedom from all kinds of failings and shortcomings.

All that man is expected to do is sincerely to strive after good and avoid sin to the the best of his power, and the rest will be forgiven him by the Merciful God. So no Atonement is needed.

The word كسب (*kasab*) earns has been used here with regard to the doing of good deeds and اكتسب (*iktasaba*) incurs for the doing of evil deeds. They are from the same root but the latter denotes greater exertion. Thus the words hint that a man will be rewarded for good deeds even if they are done casually and without concentrated effort, while he will be punished for his evil deeds only if they are committed deliberately and with concentrated effort.

In ordinary circumstances, نسيان (*nisyān*) forgetfulness and خطاء (*khatā'*) error are not punishable, for they lack intention or motive which are necessary for punishment. But here the words denote a forgetfulness and an error which might have been avoided, if due care had been exercised.

The word اصر (*iṣr*) responsibility gives a number of meanings all of which are applicable here. Hence, the verse may also be translated as:

(a) Impose not on us a sin, *i.e.*, enable us to avoid sin and prevent us from the doing of deeds which might make us stumble

(b) Do not punish us if we commit some sin or break some covenant

(c) Taking the expression لا تحمل علينا (*lā tuḥamil ʻalainā*) to mean, as it literally does, do not make it ride us or do not mount it on us, the clause may also be rendered as, do not make a responsibility or a covenant mount on us as Thou didst mount it on those before us.

The simile is beautiful. Divine covenants are meant to help the people in their onward march; but sometimes, through abuse or breach, they become a burden, instead of a help, thus turning into a rider in place of a riding beast. Muslims are taught to pray against such an eventuality.

The words, ***lay not on us a responsibility as Thou didst lay upon those before us,*** do not mean that Muslims have been taught to wish for lighter burdens. The facts of history belie that inference. The words only mean that God may help Muslims to fulfill their responsibilities and to avoid sins as well as the consequences thereof. The previous peoples were entrusted with some responsibilities and given certain commandments which were all for their own good, but many of them failed to fulfill them and also rejected Islam to which they had been invited and thus turned a blissful guidance into a veritable means of incurring God's displeasure. Thus it was that they were virtually laid under an ***iṣr*** or a burdensome responsibility. Muslims, being the bearers of the final and universal ***Sharī'ah***, have been exhorted to set a better example and pray to God for success in their great task and in the fulfillment of their heavy responsibilities. The laying of ***burden*** or ***burdensome responsibility*** has been attributed to God just as in the Qur'ānic idiom ضلالة (Ḍhalālah) misguidance is sometimes attributed to Him for which see 2:7 .

The clause, ***lay not on us a responsibility as Thou didst lay on those before us,*** may also refer to Christians particularly

who by declaring the Law to be a curse converted a Divine mercy into an ***iṣr*** *i.e.* a burden and a punishment. Muslims are thus taught to pray that for them the ***Sharī'ah*** may always remain a mercy. In this case the verse comes as a fitting preamble to the succeeding Sūrah of which Christianity forms the special theme.

The clause, ***and efface our sins and grant us forgiveness and have mercy on us,*** comprises three important invocations placed in perfect order. They not only correspond to the preceding three prayers but also constitute a perfect manifestation of a perfect treatment on the part of a perfect Master. فاعف عنا (*fā'fo 'annā*) means that God may efface our sins and leave out no trace of them to be seen by men. اغفرلنا (*ighfirlanā*) means that He may not only efface our sins but also grant us forgiveness so that He Himself may treat them as non-existent. And ارحمنا (*irḥamnā*) means that God may not only efface our sins and forgive us but also show positive mercy to us.

The concluding clause, ***help us Thou against the disbelieving people,*** provides a fitting ending to the Sūrah. The Muslims are out for a great struggle. The entire world of كفر (*kufr*) disbelief is arrayed against them and the field

of work, as hinted in Abraham's prayer (2:130), is wide and far-stretched, extending over

(1) Heavenly Signs

(2) Laws and covenants

(3) Wisdom and philosophy

(4) Morals and spirituality

(5) General progress.

This was a stupendous task and unless God came to their help, there was little hope for that tiny Muslim community that was just emerging into existence. But God did come to their help.

What is the key message of this portion of the Holy Qur'ān?

How does this message apply to your personal life?

Second Rak'ah of Monday and Thursday Fajr Prayer

Second Rak'ah of Monday Fajr Prayer

Importance of Sūrah Āl-e-'Imrān

- [1]This Sūrah is called Āl-e-'Imrān because the Holy Prophet[sa] has been likened to the Prophet Moses[as] and Moses[as] was from the progeny of 'Imrān[as].
- This chapter is continuation of the subject matter of Sūrah al-Baqarah
- [2]This chapter deals with the rules and regulations to understand the book of Allāh and commandments regarding *munāẓarah* (religious debate) and Jihād against Jews and Christians.

---

[1] *Ḥaqā'iqul- Furqān.* Ḥaḍrat Ḥakīm Maulānā Nūr-ud-Dīn[ra], Khalīfatul Masīḥ I, Printwell Focal Point Amritsar 2005. Volume 1, Page 443

[2] *Ḥaqā'iqul- Furqān.* . Ḥaḍrat Ḥakīm Maulānā Nūr-ud-Dīn[ra], Khalīfatul Masīḥ I, Printwell Focal Point Amritsar 2005. Volume 1, Page 444

إِنَّ فِى خَلْقِ ٱلسَّمَٰوَٰتِ وَٱلْأَرْضِ وَٱخْتِلَٰفِ ٱلَّيْلِ وَٱلنَّهَارِ
لَءَايَٰتٍ لِّأُو۟لِى ٱلْأَلْبَٰبِ ۝ ٱلَّذِينَ يَذْكُرُونَ ٱللَّهَ قِيَٰمًا وَقُعُودًا
وَعَلَىٰ جُنُوبِهِمْ وَيَتَفَكَّرُونَ فِى خَلْقِ ٱلسَّمَٰوَٰتِ وَٱلْأَرْضِ
رَبَّنَا مَا خَلَقْتَ هَٰذَا بَٰطِلًا سُبْحَٰنَكَ فَقِنَا عَذَابَ ٱلنَّارِ ۝
رَبَّنَآ إِنَّكَ مَن تُدْخِلِ ٱلنَّارَ فَقَدْ أَخْزَيْتَهُۥ ۖ وَمَا لِلظَّٰلِمِينَ مِنْ
أَنصَارٍ ۝ رَّبَّنَآ إِنَّنَا سَمِعْنَا مُنَادِيًا يُنَادِى لِلْإِيمَٰنِ أَنْ
ءَامِنُوا۟ بِرَبِّكُمْ فَـَٔامَنَّا ۚ رَبَّنَا فَٱغْفِرْ لَنَا ذُنُوبَنَا وَكَفِّرْ عَنَّا
سَيِّـَٔاتِنَا وَتَوَفَّنَا مَعَ ٱلْأَبْرَارِ ۝ رَبَّنَا وَءَاتِنَا مَا وَعَدتَّنَا عَلَىٰ
رُسُلِكَ وَلَا تُخْزِنَا يَوْمَ ٱلْقِيَٰمَةِ ۗ إِنَّكَ لَا تُخْلِفُ ٱلْمِيعَادَ ۝

Translation

In the creation of the heavens and the earth and in the alternation of the night and the day there are indeed Signs for men of understanding; Those who remember Allah while standing, sitting, and *lying* on their sides, and ponder over the creation of the heavens and the earth: "Our Lord, Thou hast not created this in vain; *nay*, Holy art Thou; save us, then, from the punishment of the Fire. "Our Lord, whomsoever Thou causest to enter the Fire, him hast Thou surely disgraced. And the wrongdoers shall have no helpers. "Our Lord, we have heard a Crier calling *us* unto faith, 'Believe ye in your Lord,' and we have believed. Our Lord, forgive us, therefore, our sins and remove from us our evils, and in death join us with the righteous. "Our Lord, give us what Thou hast promised to us through Thy Messengers; and disgrace us not on the Day of Resurrection. Surely, Thou breakest not Thy promise."

إِنَّ فِي خَلْقِ ٱلسَّمَٰوَٰتِ وَٱلْأَرْضِ وَٱخْتِلَٰفِ ٱلَّيْلِ وَٱلنَّهَارِ لَأَيَٰتٍ
لِّأُوْلِي ٱلْأَلْبَٰبِ ۝

[3:191] In the creation of the heavens and the earth and in the alternation of the night and the day there are indeed Signs for men of understanding;

[3]Commentary

The lesson implied in the creation of the heavens and the earth and in the alternation of night and day is that man has been created both for spiritual and temporal progress, and that if he acts righteously, his period of darkness and affliction must needs be followed by one of sunshine and happiness.

---

[3] The Holy Qur’ān with English Translation and Commentary. 3rd ed. Islām International Publications Limited; 2002. Volume 2, Pages 483-485

ٱلَّذِينَ يَذْكُرُونَ ٱللَّهَ قِيَـٰمًا وَقُعُودًا وَعَلَىٰ جُنُوبِهِمْ وَيَتَفَكَّرُونَ فِى
خَلْقِ ٱلسَّمَـٰوَٰتِ وَٱلْأَرْضِ رَبَّنَا مَا خَلَقْتَ هَـٰذَا بَـٰطِلًا سُبْحَـٰنَكَ
فَقِنَا عَذَابَ ٱلنَّارِ ۝

[3:192] Those who remember Allah while standing, sitting, and *lying* on their sides, and ponder over the creation of the heavens and the earth: "Our Lord, Thou hast not created this in vain; *nay*, Holy art Thou; save us, then, from the punishment of the Fire.

Commentary

Such a grand system to which an allusion has been made in the previous verse could certainly not have been brought into being without a definite purpose. The phenomenon of day and night referred to in the preceding verse affords an illustration of how this purpose is served.

With the rising of the sun the whole world is illuminated, and men begin to work. Then night falls and the light of the sun is hidden from our view and men go to sleep, but even then some heavenly bodies are busy doing their allotted

work. Thus both during day and night heavenly bodies perform their appointed functions and loyally serve man. The whole universe having been created to serve man, the creation of man also must have a great purpose. Of men some are bright in themselves like the sun, and there are others who possess no intrinsic light of their own but borrow it from others. Such men as place themselves in right relation to the Sun of the spiritual realm get lighted, while those that keep away from it are left in the dark.

When man ponders over the spiritual implication of the physical phenomenon of the creation of heavens and earth, the alternation of day and night and the consummate order that pervades the universe, he is deeply impressed by the great wisdom of the Creator, and from the inmost depths of his being rises the cry: ***Our Lord, Thou hast not created this in vain***. Then apprehension takes hold of him lest he should become deprived of the light of the spiritual Sun and he cries out: ***Save us from the punishment of Fire,*** which is nothing but being overtaken by spiritual darkness and moral degradation.

رَبَّنَآ إِنَّكَ مَن تُدۡخِلِ ٱلنَّارَ فَقَدۡ أَخۡزَيۡتَهُۥ ۖ وَمَا لِلظَّٰلِمِينَ مِنۡ أَنصَارٍ ۝

[3:193] "Our Lord, whomsoever Thou causest to enter the Fire, him hast Thou surely disgraced. And the wrongdoers shall have no helpers.

Commentary

A true believer dreads nothing so much as the displeasure of God which is like fire that burns up all traces of goodness, and this fire is the heritage of the wrongdoers only, whom nothing can save from punishment.

رَبَّنَآ إِنَّنَا سَمِعۡنَا مُنَادِيًا يُنَادِي لِلۡإِيمَٰنِ أَنۡ ءَامِنُواْ بِرَبِّكُمۡ فَـَٔامَنَّا ۚ رَبَّنَا فَٱغۡفِرۡ لَنَا ذُنُوبَنَا وَكَفِّرۡ عَنَّا سَيِّـَٔاتِنَا وَتَوَفَّنَا مَعَ ٱلۡأَبۡرَارِ ۝

[3:194] "Our Lord, we have heard a Crier calling *us* unto faith, 'Believe ye in your Lord,' and we

have believed. Our Lord, forgive us, therefore, our sins and remove from us our evils, and in death join us with the righteous.

Commentary

In 3:191 above the word "*day*" in the expression, the alternation of the night and the day, is placed after the word "*night*," which points to the fact that the spiritual wayfarer, after having passed through the night of trials and sins, finally basks in the light of the spiritual Sun by accepting and following the divine Crier. But, as the present verse points out, he is afraid lest his weaknesses should retard his progress or lest the dust of his sins and the clouds of his misdeeds should intervene and hide from him the light and warmth of the spiritual Sun, so he humbly prays God to disperse the dust of his sins and drive away the clouds of his misdeeds.

The expression وتوفنا مع ابرار (*wa tawaffanā ma'al abrār*) rendered as, in *death number us with the righteous*, literally means, cause us to die with the righteous, meaning, cause us to die when we are righteous, or let not death come upon us except when we are righteous.

رَبَّنَا وَءَاتِنَا مَا وَعَدتَّنَا عَلَىٰ رُسُلِكَ وَلَا تُخۡزِنَا يَوۡمَ ٱلۡقِيَٰمَةِۗ إِنَّكَ لَا تُخۡلِفُ ٱلۡمِيعَادَ ۝

[3:195] "Our Lord, give us what Thou hast promised to us through Thy Messengers; and disgrace us not on the Day of Resurrection. Surely, Thou breakest not Thy promise."

What is the key message of this portion of the Holy Qur'ān?

How does this message apply to your personal life?

First Rak'ah of Maghrib Prayer on Saturday, Sunday, Monday, Wednesday and Thursday

Please see page 183

Second Rak'ah of Maghrib Prayer on Saturday, Sunday, Monday, Wednesday and Thursday

Please see page 195

First Rak‘ah of Monday ‘Ishā’ Prayer

Importance [illegible]

[illegible]

---

[1] *Hadhrat* [illegible]

Masjid [illegible]

[2] The Holy Qur [illegible]

Brief Explan [illegible]

Khalifatul [illegible]

First Rak'ah of 'Ishā' Prayer Monday

Importance of Sūrah Al-Ḥashr

- [1]This chapter has resolved the issues between Sunni and Shī'ah regarding the garden of *Fadak*. This explains the meaning and the permissible expenditure of the acquisition of Fai', such acquisitions cannot be passed down in inheritance.

- [2]This chapter addresses the punishment given to Israelites for their disobedience and bad deeds. This is a warning to all that those who forget Allah and the consequences of their actions and transgress are destined to have punishments.

---

[1] *Ḥaqā'iqul- Furqān*. Ḥaḍrat Ḥakīm Maulānā Nūr-ud-Dīn[ra], Khalīfatul Masīḥ I, Printwell Focal Point Amritsar 2005. Volume 4, Page 46

[2] The Holy Qur'ān with Urdu Translation, Introduction of Chapters and Brief Explanatory Notes. Translated by Ḥaḍrat Mirzā Ṭāhir Aḥmad[rt], Khalīfatul Masīḥ IV, 2ND Ed. 2005, Page 1009

- Those who do good works and are ever conscious that they will be accountable for what they do, they will have a great reward.

يَـٰٓأَيُّهَا ٱلَّذِينَ ءَامَنُوا۟ ٱتَّقُوا۟ ٱللَّهَ وَلْتَنظُرْ نَفْسٌ مَّا قَدَّمَتْ لِغَدٍ ۖ
وَٱتَّقُوا۟ ٱللَّهَ ۚ إِنَّ ٱللَّهَ خَبِيرٌۢ بِمَا تَعْمَلُونَ ۝ وَلَا تَكُونُوا۟ كَٱلَّذِينَ
نَسُوا۟ ٱللَّهَ فَأَنسَىٰهُمْ أَنفُسَهُمْ ۚ أُو۟لَـٰٓئِكَ هُمُ ٱلْفَـٰسِقُونَ ۝ لَا
يَسْتَوِىٓ أَصْحَـٰبُ ٱلنَّارِ وَأَصْحَـٰبُ ٱلْجَنَّةِ ۚ أَصْحَـٰبُ ٱلْجَنَّةِ هُمُ
ٱلْفَآئِزُونَ ۝ لَوْ أَنزَلْنَا هَـٰذَا ٱلْقُرْءَانَ عَلَىٰ جَبَلٍ لَّرَأَيْتَهُۥ
خَـٰشِعًا مُّتَصَدِّعًا مِّنْ خَشْيَةِ ٱللَّهِ ۚ وَتِلْكَ ٱلْأَمْثَـٰلُ نَضْرِبُهَا
لِلنَّاسِ لَعَلَّهُمْ يَتَفَكَّرُونَ ۝

Translation

O ye who believe! fear Allah; and let *every* soul look to what it sends forth for the morrow. And fear Allah; verily Allah is Well-Aware of what you do. And be not like those who forgot Allah, So He made them forget

themselves. It is they that are the rebellious. The inmates of the Fire and the inmates of the Garden are not equal. It is the inmates of the Garden that will triumph. If We had sent down this Qur'an on a mountain, thou wouldst certainly have seen it humbled and rent asunder for fear of Allah. And these are similitudes that We set forth for mankind that they may reflect.

يَٰٓأَيُّهَا ٱلَّذِينَ ءَامَنُوا۟ ٱتَّقُوا۟ ٱللَّهَ وَلْتَنظُرْ نَفْسٌ مَّا قَدَّمَتْ لِغَدٍ ۖ
وَٱتَّقُوا۟ ٱللَّهَ ۚ إِنَّ ٱللَّهَ خَبِيرٌۢ بِمَا تَعْمَلُونَ ۝

[59:19] O ye who believe! fear Allah; and let *every* soul look to what it sends forth for the morrow. And fear Allah; verily Allah is Well-Aware of what you do.

[3]Commentary:

The root-cause of all sin is neglect and negligence. The believers here are enjoined to take care of the morrow. And there could be no real moral or spiritual progress without a sure, sincere and true belief in God.

---

[3] The Holy Qur'ān with English Translation and Commentary. 3rd ed. Islām International Publications Limited; 2002. Volume 5, Pages 2608-2609

وَلَا تَكُونُوا۟ كَٱلَّذِينَ نَسُوا۟ ٱللَّهَ فَأَنسَىٰهُمْ أَنفُسَهُمْ ۚ أُو۟لَـٰٓئِكَ هُمُ ٱلْفَـٰسِقُونَ ۝

[59:20] And be not like those who forgot Allah, So He made them forget themselves. It is they that are the rebellious.

Commentary:

Man forgets God in three ways

1. He rejects the very belief in the existence of God.
2. He has no real, true or living belief in a Supreme Being before Whom he shall have to render an account of his deeds.
3. Forgetfulness.

The inevitable and never-failing consequence of consigning God to oblivion is that man gets involved in matters which bring about his moral degradation and spiritual downfall, ending with loss of peace of mind.

لَا يَسْتَوِىٓ أَصْحَٰبُ ٱلنَّارِ وَأَصْحَٰبُ ٱلْجَنَّةِ ۚ أَصْحَٰبُ ٱلْجَنَّةِ هُمُ

ٱلْفَآئِزُونَ ۝

[59:21] The inmates of the Fire and the inmates of the Garden are not equal. It is the inmates of the Garden that will triumph.

Commentary:

The inmates of the fire have been mentioned in the preceding verse and the inmates of the Garden in the verse before that. The present verse states that the two parties are not, and never can be, equal.

لَوْ أَنزَلْنَا هَٰذَا ٱلْقُرْءَانَ عَلَىٰ جَبَلٍ لَّرَأَيْتَهُۥ خَٰشِعًا مُّتَصَدِّعًا

مِّنْ خَشْيَةِ ٱللَّهِ ۚ وَتِلْكَ ٱلْأَمْثَٰلُ نَضْرِبُهَا لِلنَّاسِ لَعَلَّهُمْ

يَتَفَكَّرُونَ ۝

[59:22] If We had sent down this Qur'an on a mountain, thou wouldst certainly have seen it humbled

and rent asunder for fear of Allah. And these are similitudes that We set forth for mankind that they may reflect.

Commentary:

Metaphorically, the word جبل (*jabal*) signifies a big and proud man; the chief or leader of a people. In this sense of the word the verse would mean that the Qur'an contains such a sublime and powerful Message that it would make the heart of even a proud man melt. Or the verse may signify that the proud pagan Arabs whom no pre-Islamic teaching could wean from their polytheistic beliefs and idolatrous practices and who like a strong rock remained unmoved and firmly wedded to their Bedouin usages unaffected by the erosive influence of the glamour and glitter of the neighbouring Christian civilization, would be humbled before its sublime and powerful Message, and from their stony hearts would gush forth fountains of light and learning.

What is the key message of this portion of the Holy Qur'ān?

How does this message apply to your personal life?

Second Rak‘ah of Monday ‘Ishā’ Prayer

Second Rak'ah of Monday 'Isha Prayer

Importance of Sūrah Al-Ḥashr

- [1]This chapter has resolved the issues between Sunni and Shi'ah regarding the garden of *Fidak*. This explains the meaning and the permissible expenditure of the acquisition of Fai', such acquisitions cannot be passed down in inheritance.

- [2]This chapter addresses the punishment given to Israelites for their disobedience and bad deeds. This is a warning to all that those who forget Allah and the consequences of their actions and transgress are destined to have punishments.

---

[1] *Ḥaqā'iqul- Furqān*. Ḥaḍrat Ḥakīm Maulānā Nūr-ud-Dīn[ra], Khalīfatul Masīḥ I, Printwell Focal Point Amritsar 2005. Volume 4, Page 46

[2] The Holy Qur'ān with Urdu Translation, Introduction of Chapters and Brief Explanatory Notes. Translated by Ḥaḍrat Mirzā Ṭāhir Aḥmad[rt], Khalīfatul Masīḥ IV, 2ND Ed. 2005, Page 1009

Those who do good works and are ever conscious that they will be accountable for what they do, they will have a great reward.

هُوَ ٱللَّهُ ٱلَّذِى لَآ إِلَـٰهَ إِلَّا هُوَ ۖ عَـٰلِمُ ٱلْغَيْبِ وَٱلشَّهَـٰدَةِ ۖ هُوَ ٱلرَّحْمَـٰنُ
ٱلرَّحِيمُ ۝ هُوَ ٱللَّهُ ٱلَّذِى لَآ إِلَـٰهَ إِلَّا هُوَ ٱلْمَلِكُ ٱلْقُدُّوسُ
ٱلسَّلَـٰمُ ٱلْمُؤْمِنُ ٱلْمُهَيْمِنُ ٱلْعَزِيزُ ٱلْجَبَّارُ ٱلْمُتَكَبِّرُ ۚ سُبْحَـٰنَ
ٱللَّهِ عَمَّا يُشْرِكُونَ ۝ هُوَ ٱللَّهُ ٱلْخَـٰلِقُ ٱلْبَارِئُ ٱلْمُصَوِّرُ ۖ لَهُ
ٱلْأَسْمَآءُ ٱلْحُسْنَىٰ ۚ يُسَبِّحُ لَهُۥ مَا فِى ٱلسَّمَـٰوَٰتِ وَٱلْأَرْضِ ۖ وَهُوَ
ٱلْعَزِيزُ ٱلْحَكِيمُ ۝

Translation

He is Allah, and there is none worthy of worship except Him, the Knower of the unseen and the seen. He is the Gracious, the Merciful.

Sūrah al-Ḥashr, Chapter 59, Verses 23-25

He is Allah, and there is none worthy of worship except Him, the Sovereign, the Holy One, the Source of Peace, the Bestower of Security, the Protector, the Mighty, the Subduer, the Exalted. Holy is Allah *far* above that which they associate *with Him*. He is Allah, the Creator, the Maker, the Fashioner. His are the most beautiful names. All that is in the heavens and the earth glorifies Him, and He is the Mighty, the Wise.

هُوَ ٱللَّهُ ٱلَّذِى لَآ إِلَـٰهَ إِلَّا هُوَ ۖ عَـٰلِمُ ٱلْغَيْبِ وَٱلشَّهَـٰدَةِ ۖ هُوَ ٱلرَّحْمَـٰنُ ٱلرَّحِيمُ ۝

[59:23] He is Allah, and there is none worthy of worship except Him, the Knower of the unseen and the seen. He is the Gracious, the Merciful.

[3]**Commentary:**

The verse means that the Qur'ān, before whose powerful Message even tall and firm mountains would crumble and fall, has been revealed by God whose attributes are inimitable and matchless. He knows everything and nothing is hidden from Him. He provides his creatures, out of His bountiful grace and mercy, and not in return for

[3] The Holy Qur'ān with English Translation and Commentary. 3rd ed. Islām International Publications Limited; 2002. Volume 5, Page 2609

anything done by them, all the means of their development and progress even before they are born..

هُوَ ٱللَّهُ ٱلَّذِى لَآ إِلَـٰهَ إِلَّا هُوَ ٱلْمَلِكُ ٱلْقُدُّوسُ ٱلسَّلَـٰمُ ٱلْمُؤْمِنُ

ٱلْمُهَيْمِنُ ٱلْعَزِيزُ ٱلْجَبَّارُ ٱلْمُتَكَبِّرُ ۚ سُبْحَـٰنَ ٱللَّهِ عَمَّا

يُشْرِكُونَ ﴿٢٣﴾

[59:24] He is Allah, and there is none worthy of worship except Him, the Sovereign, the Holy One, the Source of Peace, the Bestower of Security, the Protector, the Mighty, the Subduer, the Exalted. Holy is Allah *far* above that which they associate *with Him*.

Commentary:

God is the King Who is free from every fault, defect, or deficiency. He is the Source of all peace, and the Granter of safety and security. He is Guardian overall, overcoming every power, the Mender of every breakage and the

Restorer of every loss; and He is above every need and is the Besought of all.

هُوَ ٱللَّهُ ٱلۡخَٰلِقُ ٱلۡبَارِئُ ٱلۡمُصَوِّرُۖ لَهُ ٱلۡأَسۡمَآءُ ٱلۡحُسۡنَىٰۚ يُسَبِّحُ
لَهُۥ مَا فِي ٱلسَّمَٰوَٰتِ وَٱلۡأَرۡضِۖ وَهُوَ ٱلۡعَزِيزُ ٱلۡحَكِيمُ ۝

[59:25] He is Allah, the Creator, the Maker, the Fashioner. His are the most beautiful names. All that is in the heavens and the earth glorifies Him, and He is the Mighty, the Wise.

Commentary:

God, as represented by the Qur'ān, is the Maker of bodies, the Creator of souls, the Fashioner i.e. the Giver of final touches to things created by Him. Such is the God of Islam, the Mighty, the Wise. To him belong all excellent titles that man can imagine. The dwellers of the heavens and the earth declare His Sanctity and Holiness. He is the Great, and the Powerful.

What is the key message of this portion of the Holy Qur’ān?

How does this message apply to your personal life?

TUESDAY

DAY	SALAT	FIRST RAK'AH	2ND RAK'AH
TUESDAY	Fajr	Sūrah al-Baqarah 255-258	Sūrah Āl-e-'Imrān 26-31
	Maghrib	Sūrah al-Kāfirūn	Sūrah an-Naṣr
	'Ishā'	Sūrah az-Zilzāl	Sūrah at- Takāthur

First Ra'kah of Tuesday Fajr Prayer

First Rak'ah of Tuesday Fajr Prayer

Importance of Sūrah al-Baqarah

- al-Baqarah is the longest chapter of the Holy Qur'ān. The Holy Prophet[sa] said that everything has its peak and the peak of the Qur'ān is al-Baqarah (Tirmidhī).
    - The Holy Prophet[sa] said that whosoever recites ten verses of this chapter, first four verses, Āyatul-Kursī and last three verses, Satan will not enter his house till the morning (Ibne Kathīr).
    - [1]This means that these verses embody the Islamic teachings and that satan cannot come near a person who faithfully acts on these teachings.
    - 'Till the morning' means that teachings, however excellent, if not regularly practiced

[1] The Holy Qur'ān with English Translation and Commentary. 3rd ed. Islām International Publications Limited; 2002. Volume 1, Page 24

cannot be fully effective and the good influences of such teachings are lost.

- [2]In the first 4 verses a sketch is drawn for a pious life, Āyatul-Kursī has a great explanation of the attributes of God and the last three verses contain prayers that purify the heart. When these three things come together, one's heart is purified and satanic thoughts disappear.
  - To do good deeds in following the words of Allāh
  - To ponder over the attributes of Allāh the Exalted
  - To always engage in prayers and commit oneself totally to God.

- [3]The Promised Messiah[as] said that in this chapter the rights of Allāh and rights of people are described in great detail. Do's and don'ts have been explained and there is a great emphasis on patience and sacrifice.

---

[2] *Tafsīr-e-Kabīr*. Ḥaḍrat Mirzā Bashīr-ud-Dīn Maḥmūd Aḥmad[ra], Printwell Amritsar 2004. Volume 1. Page 51

[3] *Tafsīrul-Qur'ān* by The Promised Messiah, Ḥaḍrat Mirzā Ghulām Aḥmad[as] of Qadiān, Page 1 available on www.alislam.org

Sūrah al-Baqarah, Verse 255-258

يَٰٓأَيُّهَا ٱلَّذِينَ ءَامَنُوٓا۟ أَنفِقُوا۟ مِمَّا رَزَقْنَٰكُم مِّن قَبْلِ أَن يَأْتِىَ يَوْمٌ لَّا بَيْعٌ فِيهِ وَلَا خُلَّةٌ
وَلَا شَفَٰعَةٌ ۗ وَٱلْكَٰفِرُونَ هُمُ ٱلظَّٰلِمُونَ ۝ ٱللَّهُ لَآ إِلَٰهَ إِلَّا هُوَ ٱلْحَىُّ ٱلْقَيُّومُ ۚ لَا
تَأْخُذُهُۥ سِنَةٌ وَلَا نَوْمٌ ۚ لَّهُۥ مَا فِى ٱلسَّمَٰوَٰتِ وَمَا فِى ٱلْأَرْضِ ۗ مَن ذَا ٱلَّذِى يَشْفَعُ
عِندَهُۥٓ إِلَّا بِإِذْنِهِۦ ۚ يَعْلَمُ مَا بَيْنَ أَيْدِيهِمْ وَمَا خَلْفَهُمْ ۖ وَلَا يُحِيطُونَ بِشَىْءٍ مِّنْ
عِلْمِهِۦٓ إِلَّا بِمَا شَآءَ ۚ وَسِعَ كُرْسِيُّهُ ٱلسَّمَٰوَٰتِ وَٱلْأَرْضَ ۖ وَلَا يَـُٔودُهُۥ حِفْظُهُمَا ۚ وَهُوَ
ٱلْعَلِىُّ ٱلْعَظِيمُ ۝ لَآ إِكْرَاهَ فِى ٱلدِّينِ ۖ قَد تَّبَيَّنَ ٱلرُّشْدُ مِنَ ٱلْغَىِّ ۚ فَمَن يَكْفُرْ
بِٱلطَّٰغُوتِ وَيُؤْمِنۢ بِٱللَّهِ فَقَدِ ٱسْتَمْسَكَ بِٱلْعُرْوَةِ ٱلْوُثْقَىٰ لَا ٱنفِصَامَ لَهَا ۗ وَٱللَّهُ
سَمِيعٌ عَلِيمٌ ۝ ٱللَّهُ وَلِىُّ ٱلَّذِينَ ءَامَنُوا۟ يُخْرِجُهُم مِّنَ ٱلظُّلُمَٰتِ إِلَى ٱلنُّورِ ۖ
وَٱلَّذِينَ كَفَرُوٓا۟ أَوْلِيَآؤُهُمُ ٱلطَّٰغُوتُ يُخْرِجُونَهُم مِّنَ ٱلنُّورِ إِلَى ٱلظُّلُمَٰتِ ۗ
أُو۟لَٰٓئِكَ أَصْحَٰبُ ٱلنَّارِ ۖ هُمْ فِيهَا خَٰلِدُونَ ۝

Translation

O ye who believe! spend out of what We have bestowed on you before the day comes wherein there shall be no buying and selling, nor friendship, nor intercession; and it is those who disbelieve that do wrong *to themselves*. Allāh — there is no God but He, the Living, the Self-Subsisting and All-Sustaining. Slumber seizes Him not, nor sleep. To Him belongs whatsoever is in the heavens and whatsoever is in the earth. Who is he that will intercede with Him except by His permission? He knows what is before them and what is behind them; and they encompass nothing of His knowledge except what He pleases. His Throne extends over the heavens and the earth; and the care of them burdens Him not; and He is the High, the Great. There should be no compulsion in religion. Surely, right has become distinct from wrong; so whosoever refuses to be led by those who transgress, and believes in Allah, has surely grasped a strong handle which knows no breaking. And

Allah is All-Hearing, All-Knowing. Allah is the friend of those who believe: He brings them out of every *kind of* darkness into light. And those who disbelieve, their friends are the transgressors who bring them out of light into every *kind of* darkness. These are the inmates of the Fire; therein shall they abide.

يَـٰٓأَيُّهَا ٱلَّذِينَ ءَامَنُوٓا۟ أَنفِقُوا۟ مِمَّا رَزَقْنَـٰكُم مِّن قَبْلِ أَن يَأْتِىَ يَوْمٌ لَّا
بَيْعٌ فِيهِ وَلَا خُلَّةٌ وَلَا شَفَـٰعَةٌ ۗ وَٱلْكَـٰفِرُونَ هُمُ ٱلظَّـٰلِمُونَ ۝

[2:255] O ye who believe! spend out of what We have bestowed on you before the day comes wherein there shall be no buying and selling, nor friendship, nor intercession; and it is those who disbelieve that do wrong *to themselves*.

[4]Commentary:

Though, the final victory of the Holy Prophet[sa] of Islam was sure, yet the path before Muslims was not strewn with roses. They had to make great sacrifices in order to reach the goal. It is to this fact that the verse under comment points. It makes particular reference to financial sacrifices.

[4] The Holy Qur'ān with English Translation and Commentary. 3rd ed. Islām International Publications Limited; 2002. Volume 1, Pages 323-326

The words, ***wherein there shall be no buying and selling***, do not mean that there will be no trade and commerce on the Day of Judgement, but that on that great day nobody will be able to buy salvation, which will depend only on one's good works coupled with God's grace. The only buying or selling that will be of avail to men on the Day of Judgement will be that which they shall have made in their present life (9:111).

The words, ***nor friendship***, signify that there will be no occasion for forming new friendships on that day. Those, however, who will have taken God as their friend in their life on this earth will certainly benefit by that friendship. It is to this fact that the Qur'ān refers when it says: ***Friends on that day shall be foes to one another, except the God-fearing*** (43:68). The righteous have God as their friend, and He will continue to be their friend on the Day of Judgement.

The concept of شفاعت (*shafā'at*) intercession has been discussed in the commentary of verse 49, chapter 2 of the

Holy Qur'ān. [5]The commentary is added below for the benefits of readers.

The verse is important. God addresses the Israelites, who claimed to be the progeny of the Prophets, saying that though it was a fact that they were descendant from holy personages and He had shown special favour to them inasmuch as He had exalted them above other peoples of the age, yet as they repeatedly broke His covenant and had begun to lead wicked lives and had finally rejected the Promised Prophet, who had made his appearance in fulfilment of the prophecies contained in the Bible, they no longer deserved His blessings, but had, on the contrary, become the object of His wrath and must be prepared to render an account of their deeds. The verse under comment calls upon the Jews to prepare themselves for the Day of Retribution when they would stand alone before God and there would be none to intercede for them or help them in any other way. The fact that they were descended from holy persons would be of no avail, nor would any substitute or ransom be accepted from them. It would indeed be a dreadful day for those who reject God's

[5] The Holy Quran with English Translation and Commentary. 3rd ed. Islām International Publications Limited; 2002. Volume 1, Pages 103-107

Messengers; for on that day nothing but one's own deeds would count.

As a criminal can count on four possible means of securing his release, God has mentioned all those means and has made it clear that none of them will avail him on the Day of Reckoning.

The first idea that comes to the mind of a culprit is to prove that the offence alleged to have been committed by him was legally not committed by him at all. It was either committed by somebody else or, if it was in fact committed by him, it was committed at the instigation of another person, or another person undertook to shoulder his burden. Thus the culprit tries to secure his release by throwing the blame or the responsibility on somebody else. In view of this plea, the Qur'ān says that (on the Day of Judgement) ***no soul shall serve as a substitute for another soul***. If a person is really sinful, the blame will surely lie on his own head and will by no means be shifted to another person. Everyone will bear his own cross and there will be no atonement in the sense of one man serving as a substitute for another.

The second possible way of escape when a criminal fails to shift the responsibility to another person, is for him either

to try to secure the intercession of an influential person in his favour or to enter a plea that he is related to some big personality and hence is entitled to special treatment. In reply to this, the Qur'ān says, ***nor shall intercession be accepted for it***. The word شفاعة (*shafā'ah)* here has a twofold significance that:

(a) No influential person shall be allowed to intercede for a culprit

(b) No culprit shall himself be allowed to put in the plea that he is related to an influential person.

The third possible means of release is for the culprit to try to secure his freedom by paying a ransom. With regard to this the Qur'ān says, nor shall ransom be taken from it.

Finally, when a criminal sees that all other means of escape have failed, he thinks of using force and getting his release by violence. With regard to this, the Qur'ān says: nor shall they be helped, i.e., they shall find no helpers against God.

The Qur'ān mentions these things not by way of threat but to make the Jews realize that they should not entertain false hopes. The only way open to them was to accept the Holy Prophet[sa] whom God had raised for their own good.

<u>Here arises a very important question</u>. What is the teaching of Islam about شفاعة *(shafā'ah)* intercession? Does Islam hold it to be quite useless and unlawful, as would appear from the verse under comment, or does it hold certain forms of شفاعة *(shafā'ah)* to be useful and lawful and others to be useless and unlawful? From the teachings of the Qur'ān and the Ḥadīth it appears that the latter view is correct and we proceed to discuss it accordingly. It should be stated at once that the word "intercession" is a very imperfect rendering of the word شفاعة *(shafā'ah)*. It conveys only a part of the meaning of شفاعة *(shafā'ah)* and that too very imperfectly.

<u>The root meaning of the word شفاعة *(shafā'ah)*</u> is to attach or connect or join a thing, or, for that matter, to connect or join oneself with another thing or person so as to form a pair or a couple on the basis of similarity. The Qur'ān uses the different derivations of this word in no less than 29 different places and in all of them the root meaning of the word is retained in one form or another. The word is used in the sense of "intercession" because the person who intercedes for somebody must have a twofold connection: -

Firstly, he must have a special connection with the being or person with whom he wishes to intercede, for without such connection none dare intercede nor can intercession be fruitful.

Secondly, he must also have a special connection with the person for whom he intercedes, because none can think of interceding for a person unless he is specially connected with the latter and is akin or similar to him.

In religious terminology شفاعة (*shafā'ah)* means intercession with God by a holy man for a sinful person. Here too the twofold connection referred to above is essential.

- The holy person who intercedes with God must have a special connection with Him, enjoying His special favour and being very near and dear to Him.
- On the other hand, he should also have a real connection with the person on whose behalf he wishes to intercede; for without such connection he cannot be properly moved to intercede nor can his intercession carry much weight with God.

In fact, the intercessor, on the essential basis of the afore-mentioned double connection, approaches God saying, as it were, "My God, I come to Thee with a special request,

knowing that Thou art well pleased with me and that I enjoy Thy special favour. Here is an erring man who is sincerely connected with me but in moments of weakness he has stumbled and faltered. But as Thou art kind and good to me, O Lord, be Thou kind also to this sinful servant of Thine and pardon him his sins." This is what may be termed the essence of شفاعة *(shafā'ah)* as taught and held lawful by Islam.

From the above significance of the word it is apparent that true شفاعة *(shafā'ah)* is governed by the following conditions: -

(1). He who intercedes must be very near and dear to God enjoying His special favour.

(2). The person for whom he wishes to intercede must have a true and real connection with him.

(3). The person in whose favour intercession is to be made must be on the whole a good man, only casually tempted to sin in moments of weakness; for it cannot be entertained for a moment that an habitually wicked man can enjoy a true connection with a holy person.

(4). Intercession must always be made with God's permission; for it is God alone who knows

a. Whether a so-called holy person really stands near and dear to Him
b. Whether the person for whom intercession is being made is truly and sincerely connected with the holy man making the intercession, for there is many a connection which looks sound and genuine from outside but is rotten from within.

(5). Each and every intercession is not necessarily lawful or fruitful. Only that intercession is lawful which fulfils all the requisite conditions.

The above view finds clear corroboration in the Islamic teachings. For instance, the Qur'ān says: ***And fear the day when no soul shall serve as a substitute for another soul at all, nor shall any ransom be accepted from it, nor any*** شفاعة ***(shafā'ah) intercession) avail it, nor shall they be helped*** (2:124). This verse is addressed to the Jews and signifies that, as they have rejected the Holy Prophet[sa] and thus failed to form the most important of spiritual connections, therefore no other connection or intercession will avail them on the Day of Judgement. This makes it

clear that شفاعة (*shafā'ah)* can avail only those who accept the Messenger of the day. It cannot avail those who, by rejecting a Messenger of God, rebel against divine authority. As such people fail to form the connection that they are called upon to form, no question of شفاعة (*shafā'ah)* arises.

Again the Qur'ān says: ***on the Day of Judgement (Shafā'ah)* شفاعة *(intercession) shall not avail any person except him for whom God grants permission and with whose word (i.e. with whose expression of faith) He is pleased*** (20: 110). This verse throws light on three very important points:

(a) That if, on one hand, there are some whom شفاعة (*shafā'ah)* (intercession) will not avail, on the other hand, there are others whom it will certainly avail.

(b) But it will avail only those for whom God grants special permission.

(c) That such permission will be granted only in the case of those sinners whose faith at least is sound, i.e. their ايمان (Īmān) faith is true and well founded; only in اعمال (A'māl) practice they sometimes show weakness.

And another place the Qur'ān says: ***Who is he that will intercede with God except by His permission? He knows what is before them and what is behind them; and they encompass nothing of His knowledge except what He pleases*** (2:256). This verse supplies the reason for the principle adduced in the verse quoted above. God's permission is necessary because His knowledge alone is perfect and it is only He Who knows whether the twofold connection essential for شفاعة (*shafā'ah)* really exists;

(1) Whether the holy person wishing to intercede really enjoys the special relation with God required for such intercession.

(2) Whether the person for of whom he wishes to intercede is truly and sincerely connected with him.

To illustrate the above point, we may well quote an incident in Noah's life. At the time of great Deluge, he saw that his son had been caught by the surging waves and was going to be drowned. Thereupon he turned to God, saying that the drowning boy was one of his family whom God had promised to save. Upon this God sharply reprimanded him, saying, ***He is surely not of thy family; he is indeed a***

man of unrighteous conduct. So ask not of Me that of which thou hast no knowledge. I advise thee lest thou become one of the ignorant (11:47). This verse beautifully illustrates the philosophy of شفاعة *(shafā'ah)* In a moment of great uneasiness of mind Noah[as] interceded for his son with God but forgot to ask for His permission, whereupon God reminded him that though the boy was his son in the physical sense, he was not one in the true spiritual sense and was therefore not entitled to شفاعة *(shafā'ah)* which has its basis in spiritual kinship.

Having briefly explained the nature and conditions of شفاعة *(shafā'ah)*, we now come to the question: How many forms of شفاعة *(shafā'ah)* are there? A study of the relevant Qur'ānic verses and of the attendant facts reveals that شفاعة *(shafā'ah)* is of three kinds: -

(1) **Firstly,** there is the verbal شفاعة *(shafā'ah)* which has been interpreted as "intercession." In this form of شفاعة *(shafā'ah)* a holy person actually prays to God on the basis of his special connection with Him that a

sinful person who is truly connected with him may be granted forgiveness or that, for that matter, a person suffering from some disease or misfortune maybe restored to health or saved from the attending misfortune. In this case "intercession" is really a form of prayer but it makes a stronger appeal and is much more efficacious. For, whereas a prayer is simply a request made to God, شفاعة (*shafā'ah)* intercession is a prayer reinforced by the twofold connection referred to above. The شفيع (*shafī'*) intercessor appeals to God in a special way because: (a) he enjoys God's special favour, and (b) the person for of whom he intercedes is truly and sincerely connected with him. This twofold connection gives intercession a strength that is lacking in an ordinary prayer. The intercessor, so to speak, says to God "My God, if Thou holdest me dear, then be Thou kind also to this sufferer who is dear to me." Such a prayer, if offered with God's permission, most forcefully moves the mercy of God and is sure of acceptance.

(2) **Secondly,** there is the form of شفاعة (*shafā'ah)* which, though verbal, yet is offered not in the form of a prayer but merely as a simple statement expressive of the relation between the intercessor

and the person for whom he intercedes. Sometimes, it happens that through fear of God or through modesty the intercessor does not make an intercession in the form of a direct request or prayer but simply expresses the relation existing between him and the person for whom he wishes to intercede, leaving the conclusion to be drawn by God Himself. A case in point is that of Noah's intercession for his son referred to above. Noah[as] did not actually pray for this son but simply drew God's attention to their relationship: ***My Lord, verily my son is of my family and surely Thy promise is true*** (11:46). These are Noah's words. It is a clear case of شفاعة (*shafā'ah)* although the actual form of prayer is wanting.

(3) **Thirdly**, there is the شفاعة (*shafā'ah)* which is neither made in the form of prayer nor expressed in words. It simply consists in the practical existence of the twofold relation necessary for شفاعة (*shafā'ah)*. In fact, in this case the relationship itself is spoken of شفاعة (*shafā'ah)*. For instance, the Qur'ān speaks of the Jews saying لا تنفعها شفاعة i.e. ***on the Day of Judgement no (Shafā'ah*** شفاعة***) shall avail them*** (2:124). Here شفاعة (*shafā'ah)* is used simply in the

sense of connection. God means to say that as the Jews have refused to connect themselves with the Holy Prophet[sa] of Islam, therefore no other connection will avail them. Their being counted among the followers of Abraham[as] or Moses[as] or David[as], etc., will be of no avail to them. In this sense a Prophet of God is a شفيع (*shafī'*) or intercessor for all his true followers without distinction. Everybody who establishes a true connection with him is saved while others perish. In this sense God also is a شفيع (*shafī'*); for those who connect themselves with Him are saved, while others who remain disconnected are ruined.

Now the question arises, why has God instituted شفاعة (*shafā'ah*) at all? The answer is as follows: -

Firstly شفاعة (*shafā'ah*) in the sense of good association is the very essence of spirituality. All spiritual progress depends on a good spiritual contact. A soul not in contact with God is lost and, for that matter, a soul not in contact with the Prophet of the day, who represents God on earth, is also lost. The Qur'ān says, ***he who forms a good connection will reap the benefit thereof and he who forms an evil connection will suffer the***

loss attached thereto (4:86). Thus the need and the usefulness of شفاعة (*shafā'ah)* in the sense of a good connection is self-evident and one need not say much about it. But when we come to شفاعة (*shafā'ah)* in the sense of intercession, an explanation seems called for. When all depends on true belief and right actions, why should the necessity of intercession arise at all? Even a cursory thought leads to the conviction that this question, which has misled many, arises from the misleading conception of the word "intercession" as ordinarily understood. Unprincipled men go about interceding for criminals with unprincipled judges, thwarting the very ends of justice. Islamic شفاعة (*shafā'ah)* is far from this. It is not a mere intercession but is adjunct of the principle of true belief and right actions. According to Islam only that person is entitled to شفاعة (*shafā'ah)* who is sincerely connected with the Prophet of the day, is true in faith and earnestly tries to live a righteous life according to the teachings of Islam. But being weak, he sometimes stumbles. There is nothing inherently wrong with his connection with the Prophet, which is pure and true; only an occasional

stumbling in practice makes him fall short of the prescribed standard. God entitles such a one to شفاعة (*shafā'ah*) and that also by his special permission; and when the Knower of all things considers one to be deserving of forgiveness, who is there to object that the case is not deserving?

The Islamic شفاعة (*shafā'ah*) is, in fact, only another form of repentance. For what is توبة (*taubah*) repentance but re-forming a broken connection or tightening up a loose one? But whereas the door of repentance is closed with death, the door of شفاعة (*shafā'ah*) remains open. Moreover, شفاعة (*shafā'ah*) is a means of the manifestation of God's mercy and God says رحمتی سبقت غضبی i.e. "My mercy is stronger than My anger" (Bukhari). Thus شفاعة (*shafā'ah*) intercession is based on the manifestation of God's mercy; and as God is not judge but مالک (Mālik) Master, there is nothing to stop Him from extending His mercy to whomsoever He pleases. Yet another reason why شفاعة (*shafā'ah*) has been allowed by Islam is that by this means God honours His

Prophets. It is indeed a great honour that He should allow a person to intercede with him.

It has been objected by some Christian critics of Islam that the doctrine of شفاعة (*shafā'ah)* is likely to encourage people to commit sins. Nothing can be farther from the truth. The شفاعة (*shafā'ah*) as allowed by Islam should encourage people to strengthen their connection with the Prophet rather than weaken it. As sin is nothing but the product of weakness in spiritual connection, شفاعة (*shafā'ah*) and sin really stand poles apart and it is sheer ignorance to suggest that doctrine of شفاعة (*shafā'ah)*, whose very conception rests on the soundness of man's connection with God and His Prophet, encourages one to sin. On the contrary, it is the Christian doctrine of Atonement which throws open the floodgates of sin; for, unlike Islamic شفاعة (*shafā'ah)* the doctrine of Atonement is based on the unnatural conception that one man can bear the sins of another.

Now we come to the last question in this connection i.e., who will be شفيع (*shafī'*) intercessor on the Day of

Judgement? This question has given rise to much controversy and consequently much misunderstanding. Let it be said at once that Islam does not confine شفاعة (intercession) to one person only; for according to the Islamic conception of (Shafā'ah شفاعة) every holy person whose connection can materially influence the spiritual condition of a man is virtually a شفيع (*shafi'*) for him. All Prophets are therefore شفيع (*shafi'*) but they are شفيع (*shafi'*) only in their own respective spheres. Abraham is a شفيع (*shafi'*) for those who followed him and Moses is a شفيع (*shafi'*) for those who followed him and so on. But with the advent of the Holy Prophet[sa] of Islam all other connections have come to an end; for the message of Holy Prophet[sa] is for all time and all mankind. Even the present-day followers of Moses[as] or Jesus[as] cannot turn to these Prophets for شفاعة, because spiritually they are now under the regime of the Holy Prophet of Islam, the regimes of the previous Prophets having come to an end. As a matter of fact, as explained by the Quran itself, the real شفيع (*shafi'*) is God alone. Says the Quran:

There is no helper nor شفيع (*shafī'*) intercession for you accept Allāh; will you not then ponder? (32:5) Now as God alone is the real شفيع (*shafī'*) i.e. He is the One connection with Whom really matters, the Prophets of God become شفيع (*shafī'*) in a secondary way only. Whosoever among the Prophets represents God on earth at a particular time and in a particular place becomes a شفيع (*shafī'*) for the people of that time and that place. From this it follows that the Prophets of God who passed before Islam were شفيع (*shafī'*) for their own followers and in their own time only; with the advent of Islam the period of their شفاعة (*shafā'ah*) came to an end. Now the Prophet of Islam is the only شفيع (*shafī'*) for all times and all peoples. Being a perfect image of God he is (1) the perfect شفيع (*shafī'*) and, having a universal mission he is (2) the universal شفيع (*shafī'*); and, having cancelled all previous connections he is now (3) the only شفيع (*shafī'*) (peace and blessings of God be on him!). For proof of the fact that the Holy Prophet[sa] has

himself put forward the above claim, the reader is referred to a Ḥadīth where the aforesaid distinction of the Prophet on the Day of Judgement is most vividly set forth (Muslim ch. on Iman).

ٱللَّهُ لَآ إِلَٰهَ إِلَّا هُوَ ٱلۡحَيُّ ٱلۡقَيُّومُۚ لَا تَأۡخُذُهُۥ سِنَةٞ وَلَا نَوۡمٞۚ لَّهُۥ مَا
فِي ٱلسَّمَٰوَٰتِ وَمَا فِي ٱلۡأَرۡضِۗ مَن ذَا ٱلَّذِي يَشۡفَعُ عِندَهُۥٓ إِلَّا
بِإِذۡنِهِۦۚ يَعۡلَمُ مَا بَيۡنَ أَيۡدِيهِمۡ وَمَا خَلۡفَهُمۡۖ وَلَا يُحِيطُونَ بِشَيۡءٖ
مِّنۡ عِلۡمِهِۦٓ إِلَّا بِمَا شَآءَۚ وَسِعَ كُرۡسِيُّهُ ٱلسَّمَٰوَٰتِ وَٱلۡأَرۡضَۖ وَلَا
يَـُٔودُهُۥ حِفۡظُهُمَاۚ وَهُوَ ٱلۡعَلِيُّ ٱلۡعَظِيمُ ۝

[2:256] Allah — there is no God but He, the Living, the Self-Subsisting and All-Sustaining. Slumber seizes Him not, nor sleep. To Him belongs whatsoever is in the heavens and whatsoever is in the earth. Who is he that will intercede with Him except by His permission? He

knows what is before them and what is behind them; and they encompass nothing of His knowledge except what He pleases. His Throne extends over the heavens and the earth; and the care of them burdens Him not; and He is the High, the Great.

Commentary:

This verse is known as آيت الكرسى (*Āyatul-Kursī*) and is considered to be one of the most important verses, beautifully describing the unity of God and his great attributes. The Holy Prophet[sa] is reported to have said that the *Āyatul-Kursī* was the loftiest verse in the Qur'ān (Muslim). The verse supplies an answer to an implied question. Even if Muslims made the sacrifices required of them in 2: 255, the task before them was so great that, based on worldly calculations, there appeared no hope of success for them.

How then is the promised victory to come? The verse under comment provides a telling answer. The world was not without a Master. The destinies of its people were controlled by a Being Whose power was limitless, Whose knowledge knew no bounds, Who was ever vigilant, ever watchful, in Whose hands were the entire resources of the

earth and the heavens. If such a being willed the triumph of a party, who was there to thwart His way? The promised victory must come.

The detailed description of subject of intercession is given above. The reason why no one shall be allowed to intercede for any person except with the permission of God is that nobody knows what is in the minds of men and consequently none is in a position to intercede for another. God alone knows the secret of men's heart and hence there can be no intercession except by His permission, for He alone knows who is deserving of it. The clause, they encompass nothing of His knowledge, means that God's knowledge is unlimited; while the knowledge of others, whoever they may be, is limited; even Prophets know no more than what is apparent of the spiritual condition of their followers.

The word كرسى (*kursī*) knowledge may signify either knowledge or power; both give equally good meanings and are almost equally applicable. Allah's knowledge is as extensive as His power. Knowledge and power are indeed the two great pillars on which throne of God and, for that matter, the controlling power of everyone in authority rests.

لَآ إِكۡرَاهَ فِي ٱلدِّينِۖ قَد تَّبَيَّنَ ٱلرُّشۡدُ مِنَ ٱلۡغَيِّۚ فَمَن يَكۡفُرۡ
بِٱلطَّٰغُوتِ وَيُؤۡمِنۢ بِٱللَّهِ فَقَدِ ٱسۡتَمۡسَكَ بِٱلۡعُرۡوَةِ ٱلۡوُثۡقَىٰ لَا
ٱنفِصَامَ لَهَاۗ وَٱللَّهُ سَمِيعٌ عَلِيمٌ

[2:257] There should be no compulsion in religion. Surely, right has become distinct from wrong; so whosoever refuses to be led by those who transgress, and believes in Allah, has surely grasped a strong handle which knows no breaking. And Allah is All-Hearing, All-Knowing.

Commentary

The injunction to make special sacrifices in the cause of religion and to fight the enemies of Islam who had transgressed against the Faithful was likely to cause the misunderstanding that Allāh desired Muslims to use force for propagating their religion. The verse under comment removes this misunderstanding. The object for which Muslims have been commanded to take up arms against the disbelievers is not to force them to accept Islam, but only to check mischief and put a stop to persecution. The verse

enjoins Muslims in the clearest and strongest of words not to resort to force for converting non-Muslims to Islam. In the face of this teaching embodied in the words, ***There should be no compulsion in religion***, it is the height of injustice to accuse Islam of countenancing the use of force for the propagation of its teaching.

The verse not only gives the commandment that in no case is force to be resorted to for the purpose of converting non-Muslims to Islam, but also gives the reason why it should not be used, saying: ***Surely, right has become distinct from wrong,*** i.e., the true path has become distinct from the wrong one and therefore there is no justification for using force. Islam is a manifest truth. Anyone who sincerely desires to see this truth can easily see it; but if there is a person who does not desire to see it, no force can possibly make him do so. All that we have to do is to point out its beauties to non-Muslim; it rests with them to accept it or reject it as they like. إیمان (Īmān) or faith as defined by Islam consists in believing in a thing with the heart or the mind and expressing that belief with the tongue. No force on earth can bring about that change.

The person who sticks to true faith and shuns false ones is here represented as laying hold of a strong عروہ (*'urwah*)

which word, as shown above, gives a number of meanings. Taking it in the first-mentioned sense i.e., the handle of a mug, etc. the Qur'ān compares Islam to the pure life-giving liquid which is put into a mug, and the believer is represented as taking fast hold of the handle thereof. Taking the word in the second sense, i.e., anything which is grasped and clung to for support, the true faith is represented as something on which complete reliance can be placed in all circumstances. If one adheres to it, there is no fear of one's stumbling or falling down. Following the third significance, i.e., a pasture that remains green even in the time of draught, Islam has been likened to a grazing ground the herbage of which is everlasting. There can be no spiritual famine in Islam. Following the last-mentioned meaning of عروه (*'urwah*) Islam is represented as storehouse of spiritual treasures that are without equal.

ٱللَّهُ وَلِىُّ ٱلَّذِينَ ءَامَنُوا۟ يُخْرِجُهُم مِّنَ ٱلظُّلُمَٰتِ إِلَى ٱلنُّورِ ۖ
وَٱلَّذِينَ كَفَرُوٓا۟ أَوْلِيَآؤُهُمُ ٱلطَّٰغُوتُ يُخْرِجُونَهُم مِّنَ ٱلنُّورِ إِلَى
ٱلظُّلُمَٰتِ ۗ أُو۟لَٰٓئِكَ أَصْحَٰبُ ٱلنَّارِ ۖ هُمْ فِيهَا خَٰلِدُونَ ۝

[2:258] Allah is the friend of those who believe: He brings them out of every *kind of* darkness into light. And those who disbelieve, their friends are the transgressors who bring them out of light into every *kind of* darkness. These are the inmates of the Fire; therein shall they abide.

Commentary

The preceding verse spoke of "truth" and "error" as resulting from belief in Allāh and belief in طاغوت (*ṭāghūt*) those who transgress respectively. The present verse further develops the idea. The Word in طاغوت *(ṭāghūt)*, here mainly refers to such mischievous leaders as turn people away from the right path. Through them disbelievers are being led to failure and grief and are also gradually losing whatever light of faith they possessed before the advent of

the Holy Prophet[sa]. Their rejection of him has also led them to disown many truths which they acknowledged before. Add to this their deprivation of the light of the New Faith and the darkness becomes complete. On the contrary, Islam is not only bringing new light to its adherents but is also bringing them success and happiness.

What is the key message of this portion of the Holy Qur'ān?

How does this message apply to your personal life?

Second Rak‘ah of Tuesday Fajr Prayer

Second Rak'ah of Tuesday Fajr Prayer

Importance of Sūrah Āl-e-'Imrān

- [1]This Sūrah is called Āl-e-'Imrān because the Holy Prophet[sa] has been likened to the Prophet Moses[as] and Moses[as] was from the progeny of 'Imrān[as].
- This chapter is continuation of the subject matter of Sūrah al-Baqarah
- [2]This chapter deals with the rules and regulations to understand the book of Allāh and commandments regarding *munāẓarah* (religious debate) and Jihād against Jews and Christians.

---

[1] *Ḥaqā'iqul- Furqān.* Ḥaḍrat Ḥakīm Maulānā Nūr-ud-Dīn[ra], Khalīfatul Masīḥ I, Printwell Focal Point Amritsar 2005. Volume 1, Page 443

[2] *Ḥaqā'iqul- Furqān.* Ḥaḍrat Ḥakīm Maulānā Nūr-ud-Dīn[ra], Khalīfatul Masīḥ I, Printwell Focal Point Amritsar 2005. Volume 1, Page 444

فَكَيْفَ إِذَا جَمَعْنَٰهُمْ لِيَوْمٍ لَّا رَيْبَ فِيهِ وَوُفِّيَتْ كُلُّ نَفْسٍ مَّا
كَسَبَتْ وَهُمْ لَا يُظْلَمُونَ ۝ قُلِ ٱللَّهُمَّ مَٰلِكَ ٱلْمُلْكِ تُؤْتِى
ٱلْمُلْكَ مَن تَشَآءُ وَتَنزِعُ ٱلْمُلْكَ مِمَّن تَشَآءُ وَتُعِزُّ مَن تَشَآءُ وَتُذِلُّ
مَن تَشَآءُ ۖ بِيَدِكَ ٱلْخَيْرُ ۖ إِنَّكَ عَلَىٰ كُلِّ شَىْءٍ قَدِيرٌ ۝ تُولِجُ ٱلَّيْلَ فِى
ٱلنَّهَارِ وَتُولِجُ ٱلنَّهَارَ فِى ٱلَّيْلِ ۖ وَتُخْرِجُ ٱلْحَىَّ مِنَ ٱلْمَيِّتِ وَتُخْرِجُ
ٱلْمَيِّتَ مِنَ ٱلْحَىِّ ۖ وَتَرْزُقُ مَن تَشَآءُ بِغَيْرِ حِسَابٍ ۝ لَّا يَتَّخِذِ
ٱلْمُؤْمِنُونَ ٱلْكَٰفِرِينَ أَوْلِيَآءَ مِن دُونِ ٱلْمُؤْمِنِينَ ۖ وَمَن يَفْعَلْ ذَٰلِكَ
فَلَيْسَ مِنَ ٱللَّهِ فِى شَىْءٍ إِلَّآ أَن تَتَّقُوا۟ مِنْهُمْ تُقَىٰةً ۗ وَيُحَذِّرُكُمُ ٱللَّهُ
نَفْسَهُۥ ۗ وَإِلَى ٱللَّهِ ٱلْمَصِيرُ ۝ قُلْ إِن تُخْفُوا۟ مَا فِى صُدُورِكُمْ أَوْ
تُبْدُوهُ يَعْلَمْهُ ٱللَّهُ ۗ وَيَعْلَمُ مَا فِى ٱلسَّمَٰوَٰتِ وَمَا فِى ٱلْأَرْضِ ۗ وَٱللَّهُ عَلَىٰ
كُلِّ شَىْءٍ قَدِيرٌ ۝ يَوْمَ تَجِدُ كُلُّ نَفْسٍ مَّا عَمِلَتْ مِنْ خَيْرٍ
مُّحْضَرًا وَمَا عَمِلَتْ مِن سُوٓءٍ تَوَدُّ لَوْ أَنَّ بَيْنَهَا وَبَيْنَهُۥٓ أَمَدًۢا بَعِيدًا ۗ
وَيُحَذِّرُكُمُ ٱللَّهُ نَفْسَهُۥ ۗ وَٱللَّهُ رَءُوفٌۢ بِٱلْعِبَادِ ۝

Translation:

How *will they fare* when We will gather them together on the Day about which there is no doubt; and when every soul shall be paid in full what it has earned, and they shall not be wronged? Say, 'O Allah, Lord of sovereignty, Thou givest sovereignty to whomsoever Thou pleasest; and Thou takest away sovereignty from whomsoever Thou pleasest. Thou exaltest whomsoever Thou pleasest and Thou abasest whomsoever Thou pleasest. In Thy hand is all good. Thou surely hast power to do all things. 'Thou makest the night pass into the day and makest the day pass into the night. And Thou bringest forth the living from the dead and bringest forth the dead from the living. And Thou givest to whomsoever Thou pleasest without measure.' Let not the believers take disbelievers for friends in preference to believers — and whoever does that has no connection with Allah — except that you cautiously guard against them. And Allah cautions you against His punishment; and to Allah is the returning. Say, 'Whether you conceal what is in your breasts or reveal it, Allah knows it; and He knows whatever is in the heavens and whatever is in the earth. And Allah has

power to do all things.' *Beware of* the Day when every soul shall find itself confronted with *all* the good it has done and *all* the evil it has done. It will wish there were a great distance between it and that *evil*. And Allah cautions you against His punishment. And Allah is Most Compassionate to *His* servants

فَكَيْفَ إِذَا جَمَعْنَٰهُمْ لِيَوْمٍ لَّا رَيْبَ فِيهِ وَوُفِّيَتْ كُلُّ نَفْسٍ مَّا كَسَبَتْ وَهُمْ لَا يُظْلَمُونَ ۝

[3:26] How *will they fare* when We will gather them together on the Day about which there is no doubt; and when every soul shall be paid in full what it has earned, and they shall not be wronged?

[3]Commentary

The People of the Book are here called upon to imagine how they will fare when they will have to render an account of their deeds before God on the Day of Judgement and will find to their mortification that the fact of their being descendants of God's Prophets or their belief in the crucifixion of Jesus[as] will not save them from the punishment of Hell.

[3] The Holy Qur'ān with English Translation and Commentary. 3rd ed. Islām International Publications Limited; 2002. Volume 2, Pages 379-382

The clause, *When every soul shall be paid in full what it has earned,* shows that the reference to forgers of lies mentioned in the previous verse is particularly to Christians. This verse is an emphatic contradiction of the doctrine that the blood of any one, and not one's own good works, can be a means of salvation.

قُلِ ٱللَّهُمَّ مَـٰلِكَ ٱلْمُلْكِ تُؤْتِى ٱلْمُلْكَ مَن تَشَآءُ وَتَنزِعُ ٱلْمُلْكَ مِمَّن تَشَآءُ وَتُعِزُّ مَن

تَشَآءُ وَتُذِلُّ مَن تَشَآءُ ۖ بِيَدِكَ ٱلْخَيْرُ ۖ إِنَّكَ عَلَىٰ كُلِّ شَىْءٍ قَدِيرٌ ۝

[3:27] Say, 'O Allah, Lord of sovereignty, Thou givest sovereignty to whomsoever Thou pleasest; and Thou takest away sovereignty from whomsoever Thou pleasest. Thou exaltest whomsoever Thou pleasest and Thou abasest whomsoever Thou pleasest. In Thy hand is all good. Thou surely hast power to do all things.

تُولِجُ ٱلَّيۡلَ فِى ٱلنَّهَارِ وَتُولِجُ ٱلنَّهَارَ فِى ٱلَّيۡلِ‌ۖ وَتُخۡرِجُ ٱلۡحَىَّ مِنَ ٱلۡمَيِّتِ وَتُخۡرِجُ
ٱلۡمَيِّتَ مِنَ ٱلۡحَىِّ‌ۖ وَتَرۡزُقُ مَن تَشَآءُ بِغَيۡرِ حِسَابٍ ۝

[3:28] 'Thou makest the night pass into the day and makest the day pass into the night. And Thou bringest forth the living from the dead and bringest forth the dead from the living. And Thou givest to whomsoever Thou pleasest without measure.'

Commentary

This and the preceding verse point to the immutable divine law that nations rise and fall as they conform to, or defy, the will of God, Who is the source of all power and glory. They also refer to the fulfilment of a great prophecy.

A nation which had enjoyed temporal and spiritual sovereignty for a long time was going to be abased, because it had persistently violated the divine law and had become spiritually dead; and in place of it another nation, till now very low in the scale of humanity, was going to be raised to the highest pinnacle of temporal and spiritual power. The sovereignty or kingdom mentioned in the preceding verse refers to both the temporal and spiritual kingdom which was promised to the progeny of Abraham[as]

and which the Israelites had enjoyed for a long time. That kingdom was now going to be transferred to the House of Ishmael to find its completest manifestation in Islam. A living nation had suffered death and another, as good as dead, had arisen into life.

The word النهار (*an-Nahār*) day represents prosperity and power, and اليل (*al-Lail*) night signifies the loss of power combined with decline and decadence. By using this simile, the Qur'ān draws attention to the fact that a people who wish that the night of woes and miseries should never overtake them and that they should ever continue to enjoy the day of prosperity and glory, should so place themselves in front of the Divine Sun as to continue to be illuminated by its ever-effulgent light. In this connection it may also be noted that the Qur'ānic expression, ***Thou makest the night pass into the day and makest the day pass into the night***, does not merely signify alternate ending and beginning of day and night but also the conversion of part of the day into night and *vice versa*, thus hinting at the lengthening of the one at the cost of the other.

The clause, **And Thou *givest to whomsoever thou pleasest without measure***, holds out a promise to Muslims that the glory of Islam will be unparalleled and will last for ever. Islam will never be displaced as a religion and Muslims will always continue to be one of the most exalted peoples of the earth till the end of time.

The appearance of Ahmad[as], the Promised Messiah, at a time when the temporal power of Islam was at its lowest ebb and Muslims had also become morally and spiritually degenerate, was in fulfilment of this very promise. Through him Islam has found a new life. It will now bloom and blossom till whole nations shall come under its spiritual sway, and Muslims shall regain their pristine glory and shall become the most dominant people on the face of the earth.

لَّا يَتَّخِذِ ٱلْمُؤْمِنُونَ ٱلْكَٰفِرِينَ أَوْلِيَآءَ مِن دُونِ ٱلْمُؤْمِنِينَ ۖ وَمَن يَفْعَلْ ذَٰلِكَ فَلَيْسَ
مِنَ ٱللَّهِ فِى شَىْءٍ إِلَّآ أَن تَتَّقُوا۟ مِنْهُمْ تُقَىٰةً ۗ وَيُحَذِّرُكُمُ ٱللَّهُ نَفْسَهُۥ ۗ وَإِلَى ٱللَّهِ
ٱلْمَصِيرُ ۝

[3:29] Let not the believers take disbelievers for friends in preference to believers — and whoever does

that has no connection with Allāh — except that you cautiously guard against them. And Allah cautions you against His punishment; and to Allāh is the returning.

Commentary

With the advent of political power to Islam, as promised in the preceding verses, the contracting of political alliances became necessary for the Muslim State. The verse under comment embodies the guiding principle that no Muslim State should enter into any treaty or alliance with a non-Muslim State which should in anyway injure, or conflict with, the interests of other Muslim States. The interests of Islam should transcend all other interests.

The phrase, ***in preference to believers***, means that:

(1) Muslims should not form friendly relations with disbelievers in preference to believers, shunning the latter and seeking the former.

(2) Muslims should not form any connection with disbelievers in a way that may harm the interests of Muslims.

They are, however, free to contract friendly relations with such non-Muslims as are friendly to them, according to the exigencies of time and circumstances (60:9,10).

The verse also instructs Muslims to be on their guard against the plots and machinations of disbelievers. The expression, ***except that you cautiously guard against them***, refers not to the power of the enemy but to his cunning against which Muslims should always be on their guard.

وَيُحَذِّرُكُمُ اللّٰهُ نَفْسَهٗ The clause (*wa yuḥadhdhirokumullāho nafsahū)* rendered as, ***And Allah cautions you against His punishment***, may also be translated as "and Allah cautions or warns you concerning Himself", meaning that if you do not faithfully accept the guidance of God, and make friends with disbelievers in preference to believers, you will lose God, Who will in that case have no connection with you.

قُلْ إِن تُخْفُوا۟ مَا فِى صُدُورِكُمْ أَوْ تُبْدُوهُ يَعْلَمْهُ ٱللَّهُ ۗ وَيَعْلَمُ مَا فِى ٱلسَّمَٰوَٰتِ وَمَا
فِى ٱلْأَرْضِ ۗ وَٱللَّهُ عَلَىٰ كُلِّ شَىْءٍ قَدِيرٌ ۝

[3:30] Say, 'Whether you conceal what is in your breasts or reveal it, Allah knows it; and He knows whatever is in the heavens and whatever is in the earth. And Allah has power to do all things.'

Commentary

This and the succeeding verse are addressed to the enemies of Islam. They are warned that all their open or secret machinations against Islam shall come to naught, for the obvious reason that the Almighty and the All-Knowing God had promised to protect it.

يَوْمَ تَجِدُ كُلُّ نَفْسٍ مَّا عَمِلَتْ مِنْ خَيْرٍ مُّحْضَرًا وَمَا عَمِلَتْ مِن سُوٓءٍ تَوَدُّ لَوْ أَنَّ
بَيْنَهَا وَبَيْنَهُۥٓ أَمَدًۢا بَعِيدًا ۗ وَيُحَذِّرُكُمُ ٱللَّهُ نَفْسَهُۥ ۗ وَٱللَّهُ رَءُوفٌۢ بِٱلْعِبَادِ ۝

[3:31] *Beware of* the Day when every soul shall find itself confronted with *all* the good it has done and *all* the evil it has done. It will wish there were a great distance between it and that *evil*. And Allāh cautions you against His punishment. And Allāh is Most Compassionate to *His* servants

Commentary

For the meaning of the clause, ***And Allah cautions you against his punishment***, see 3:29 above.

What is the key message of this portion of the Holy Qur'ān?

How does this message apply to your personal life?

First Rak'ah of Tuesday Maghrib Prayer

First Rak‘ah of Tuesday Maghrib Prayer

Importance of Sūrah al-Kāfirūn

- The Holy Prophet[sa] advised that this Sūrah should be recited frequently.
- The Holy Prophet[sa] is reported to have said that that Sūrah al-Ikhlāṣ was equal to 1/3rd of the Holy Qur'ān and Sūrah al-Kāfirūn was equal to a ¼ Qur'ān, and whoever will recite these Sūras frequently and reflects on their subject matter, will command great respect and prestige (Ibne Marduwaih).
    - [1]This Hādith means that al-Ikhlāṣ deals with the main principle of Islam that is Divine Unity and in the present Sūrah believers are enjoined to stick courageously to their faith in a hostile environment and adverse circumstances.

---

[1] The Holy Quran with English Translation and Commentary. 3rd ed. Islām International Publications Limited; 2002. Volume 5, Page 2899

- o Anyone who will recognize and comprehends the importance of these Sūrahs, will necessarily command great respect.

- The Holy Prophet[sa] used to recite Sūrah al-Kāfirūn in the second Rak'ah of Vitr Prayers (Musnad Ḥakam).

- The Holy Prophet[sa] advised one of his Companions to recite Sūrah al-Kāfirūn at night and go to sleep saying its last verses as they contain rejection of *Shirk* (associating partners with Allah the Exalted).

- [2]The Promised Messiah[as] explained that Sūrah al-Kāfirūn is recited in the first Rak'ah of Prayer of *Istikhārah* (a special Prayer to seek Allah's guidance in making this important decision).

  - o Islam does not allow omen and premonition, it advises on prayers to seek guidance from Allah for a particular matter. In Salat, God's help is sought admitting that he is the knowledge of all sources.

---

[2] *Tafsīrul-Qur'ān* by The Promised Messiah, Ḥaḍrat Mirzā Ghulām Aḥmad[as] of Qadian, page 499 available on www.alislam.org

- [3]A Companion was advised by the Holy Prophet[sa] to recite Sūrah al- Kāfirūn and the following five Sūrahs, when travelling.
  - These Sūrahs refute other religious beliefs, draw attention to overcome one's weaknesses, recommend perseverance in the face of adversary and prohibit in-fighting.
  - One who deliberates over these qualities, ends up adopting them by realising their importance.
  - Such a person gains respect in the eyes of others and becomes a source of unity of his own people.

---

[3] *Tafsīr-e-Kabīr*. Ḥaḍrat Mirzā Bashīr-ud-Dīn Maḥmūd Aḥmad[ra], Printwell Amritsar 2004. Volume 10, Pages 385-388

بِسۡمِ ٱللَّهِ ٱلرَّحۡمَٰنِ ٱلرَّحِيمِ ۝

قُلۡ يَٰٓأَيُّهَا ٱلۡكَٰفِرُونَ ۝ لَآ أَعۡبُدُ مَا تَعۡبُدُونَ ۝ وَلَآ
أَنتُمۡ عَٰبِدُونَ مَآ أَعۡبُدُ ۝ وَلَآ أَنَا۠ عَابِدٞ مَّا عَبَدتُّمۡ ۝ وَلَآ
أَنتُمۡ عَٰبِدُونَ مَآ أَعۡبُدُ ۝ لَكُمۡ دِينُكُمۡ وَلِيَ دِينِ ۝

Translation

In the name of Allah, the Gracious, the Merciful. Say, 'O ye disbelievers! 'I worship not that which you worship; Nor worship you what I worship. 'And I am not *going* to worship that which you worship; 'Nor will you worship what I worship. 'For you your religion, and for me my religion.

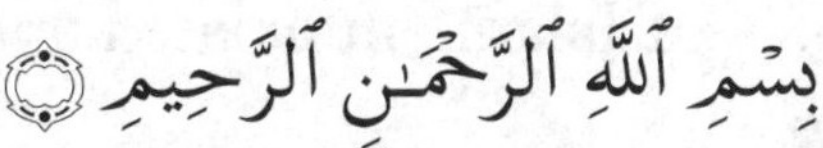

[109:1] In the name of Allah, the Gracious, the Merciful.

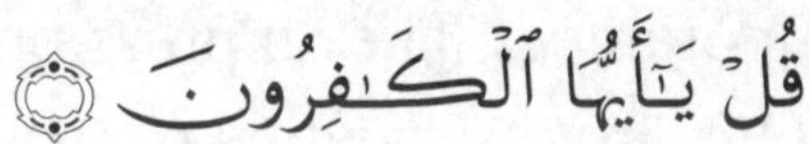

[109:2] Say, 'O ye disbelievers!

[4]Commentary

The Divine command expressed by قل (qul) say applies, besides the Holy Prophet[sa], to every Muslim. Besides the present *Sūrah*, this word is placed at the beginning of Chapters 72, 112, 113 and 114, and is used in about 306 verses of the Qur'ān, and wherever it is used it emphasizes the importance of the subject governed by it. Thus believers are enjoined to proclaim loudly and repeatedly,

---

[4] The Holy Quran with English Translation and Commentary. 3rd ed. Islām International Publications Limited; 2002. Volume 5, Pages 2900-2901

and to convey to disbelievers in clear and definite terms, the great principles of Islam enunciated and emphasized in the present *Sūrah.*

The use of word ايها (*ayyuhā*) O Ye is intended to draw pointed attention to the subject-matter of the *Sūrah* and to emphasize its importance. The expression has frequently been used in the Qur'ān to serve this purpose.

The word الكافرون (*al-Kāfirūn*) the disbelievers has a general application, or it may refer to those confirmed disbelievers who by their persistent and defiant rejection of Truth rule out all possibility of accepting it and disbelief becomes, as it were, a part of their being.

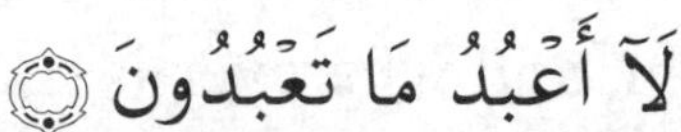

[109:3] 'I worship not that which you worship;

Commentary

Various explanations have been given to the present and the next three verses by Commentators. Some say that as

the pagan Makkans had put their question in two forms, therefore two forms have been adopted in answer to their question. Others say that the repetition is for the sake of emphasis."

وَلَآ أَنتُمْ عَـٰبِدُونَ مَآ أَعْبُدُ ۝

[109:4] 'Nor worship you what I worship.

وَلَآ أَنَا۠ عَابِدٌ مَّا عَبَدتُّمْ ۝

[109:5] 'And I am not *going* to worship that which you worship;

وَلَآ أَنتُمْ عَـٰبِدُونَ مَآ أَعْبُدُ ۝

[109:6] 'Nor will you worship what I worship.

لَكُمْ دِينُكُمْ وَلِىَ دِينِ ۝

[109:7] 'For you your religion, and for me my religion.

Commentary

According to different meanings of دين (*dīn*), the verse signifies; "as there is absolutely no meeting ground between your way of life and mine and as we are in

complete disagreement not only with regard to the basic concepts of religion but also with regard to its details and other aspects, therefore, there can possibly be no compromise between us.

What is the key message of this portion of the Holy Qur'ān?

How does this message apply to your personal life?

Second Rak'ah of Tuesday Maghrib Prayer

Second Rak'ah of Tuesday Maghrib Prayer

Importance of Sūrah an-Naṣr Chapter 110

- [1]This Sūrah is revealed close to the time of demise of the Holy Prophet[sa], with a clear and strong message of victory, support for Islam and achievement of objectives of the religion.

- [2]This Sūrah is revealed after the time of Farewell Hajj giving glad tidings of success based on powerful arguments and evidence.
- [3]In continuation with chapter 119, it is argued that the truthfulness of Islam is based on powerful evidence and there is no need to compromise with disbelievers.

---

[1] Tafsīrul-Qur'ān by The Promised Messiah, Ḥaḍrat Mirzā Ghulām Aḥmad[as] of Qadiān, Page 504 available on www.alislam.org

[2] *Tafsīr-e-Kabīr*. Ḥaḍrat Mirzā Bashīr-ud-Dīn Maḥmūd Aḥmad[ra], Printwell Amritsar 2004. Volume 10, Page 466

[3] *Tafsīr-e-Kabīr*. Ḥaḍrat Mirzā Bashīr-ud-Dīn Maḥmūd Aḥmad[ra], Printwell Amritsar 2004. Volume 10, Pages 474-475

بِسْمِ ٱللَّهِ ٱلرَّحْمَـٰنِ ٱلرَّحِيمِ ۝

إِذَا جَآءَ نَصْرُ ٱللَّهِ وَٱلْفَتْحُ ۝ وَرَأَيْتَ ٱلنَّاسَ يَدْخُلُونَ فِى
دِينِ ٱللَّهِ أَفْوَاجًا ۝ فَسَبِّحْ بِحَمْدِ رَبِّكَ وَٱسْتَغْفِرْهُ ۚ إِنَّهُۥ كَانَ
تَوَّابًۢا ۝

Translation

In the name of Allah, the Gracious, the Merciful. When the help of Allah comes, and the victory, And thou seest men entering the religion of Allah in troops, Glorify thy Lord, with *His* praise, and seek forgiveness of Him. Surely He is Oft-Returning *with compassion*.

بِسۡمِ ٱللَّهِ ٱلرَّحۡمَـٰنِ ٱلرَّحِيمِ ۝

[110:1] In the name of Allah, the Gracious, the Merciful.

إِذَا جَآءَ نَصۡرُ ٱللَّهِ وَٱلۡفَتۡحُ ۝

[110:2] When the help of Allah comes, and the victory,

[4]**Commentary**

الۡفَتۡحُ (*al-Fatḥ*) means, the promised victory.

وَرَأَيۡتَ ٱلنَّاسَ يَدۡخُلُونَ فِى دِينِ ٱللَّهِ أَفۡوَاجًا ۝

[110:3] And thou seest men entering the religion of Allah in troops,

[4] The Holy Quran with English Translation and Commentary. 3rd ed. Islām International Publications Limited; 2002. Volume 5, Pages 2902-2903

فَسَبِّحْ بِحَمْدِ رَبِّكَ وَٱسْتَغْفِرْهُ ۚ إِنَّهُۥ كَانَ تَوَّابًۢا ۝

[110:4] Glorify thy Lord, with *His* praise, and seek forgiveness of Him. Surely He is Oft-Returning *with compassion*.

Commentary

The Holy Prophet[sa] is here enjoined that since God's promise has been fulfilled and large masses of people have begun to enter the fold of Islam, he should give thanks to his Lord for fulfilling His promise about victory, sing His praises and seek His protection and forgiveness.

The expression استغفره (*istaghfirho*) has a very wide significance. The Holy Prophet[sa] is here told that since victory has come to him and Islam has become predominant in the land and his erstwhile enemies have become his devoted servants, he should ask God to forgive them the grave wrongs they had done to him in the past. This seems to be the meaning and significance of the injunction to the Holy Prophet[sa] to seek God's forgiveness.

Or the Holy Prophet[sa] might have been enjoined to ask God's protection against weaknesses and shortcomings that

might find their way into the Muslim Community on account of lack of adequate training or education for the new converts.

It is significant that whenever mention is made in the Qur'ān of a destined victory or some great success falling to the Holy Prophet[sa], he is generally told to ask God's forgiveness and to seek His protection. This clearly shows that he is enjoined here to ask for God's forgiveness and to seek His protection not for himself but for others; he is asked to pray that whenever there was any danger of his followers deviating from Islamic principles or precepts, God may save them from such a crisis. Thus there is no question here of the Prophet's[sa] asking forgiveness for any of his own actions.

According to the Qur'ān, he enjoyed complete immunity from every moral lapse or deviation from the right course (53: 3). For a detailed treatment, however, of the word استغفار(*istighfār*) see 40: 56 & 48: 3.

The expression, "He is Oft-Returning with compassion," holds a message of hope to the Holy Prophet[sa]. He is told that whenever there was any danger of his followers deviating from the path of Islam and falling victims to moral

decay on a large scale, God will return to them with compassion and will raise from among them a Reformer who will lead them to the right path.

What is the key message of this portion of the Holy Qur'ān?

How does this message apply to your personal life?

First Rak‘ah of Tuesday ‘Ishā’ Prayers

First Rak'ah of Tuesday 'Ishā' Prayers

[1]Importance of Surāh Az-Zilzāl

- It is mentioned in the Ḥadīth that reading this Sūrah of the Holy Qur'ān gives on reward as much as reading half the Holy Qur'ān. The Holy Prophet[sa] has been reported to have said this at three different occasions.

    - It is reported that this was said to people who have difficulty in learning the Holy Qur'ān; an old man with tongue problems, an uneducated woman with poor memory and a non-Arab with limited knowledge of Arabic language.

    - Thus the Islamic philosophy of reward has been clarified by this Ḥadīth; it is not the quantity of good deed that determines the

[1] Tafsīrul-Qur'ān by The Promised Messiah, Ḥaḍrat Mirzā Ghulām Aḥmad[as] of Qadiān, Pages 396-402 available on www.alislam.org

reward. The highest rewards are for those who do their best given their abilities and potential.

- Hence someone with limited ability to read the Holy Qur'ān will be judged according to their abilities.

- This was said because almost half the subject matter of the Holy Qur'ān is covered in this chapter.

بِسۡمِ ٱللَّهِ ٱلرَّحۡمَٰنِ ٱلرَّحِيمِ ۝

إِذَا زُلۡزِلَتِ ٱلۡأَرۡضُ زِلۡزَالَهَا ۝ وَأَخۡرَجَتِ ٱلۡأَرۡضُ أَثۡقَالَهَا ۝
وَقَالَ ٱلۡإِنسَٰنُ مَا لَهَا ۝ يَوۡمَئِذٖ تُحَدِّثُ أَخۡبَارَهَا ۝ بِأَنَّ
رَبَّكَ أَوۡحَىٰ لَهَا ۝ يَوۡمَئِذٖ يَصۡدُرُ ٱلنَّاسُ أَشۡتَاتٗا لِّيُرَوۡاْ
أَعۡمَٰلَهُمۡ ۝ فَمَن يَعۡمَلۡ مِثۡقَالَ ذَرَّةٍ خَيۡرٗا يَرَهُۥ ۝ وَمَن
يَعۡمَلۡ مِثۡقَالَ ذَرَّةٖ شَرّٗا يَرَهُۥ ۝

Translation

In the name of Allah, the Gracious, the Merciful. When the earth is shaken with her *violent* shaking, And the earth brings forth her burdens, And man says, 'What is the matter with her?' That day will she tell her news, It

will be because your Lord would have so revealed to her. On that day will men come forth in scattered groups that they may be shown *the results of* their works. Then whoso does an atom's weight of good will see it, And whoso does an atom's weight of evil will *also* see it.

Surāh az-Zilzāl, Chapter 99

بِسۡمِ ٱللَّهِ ٱلرَّحۡمَـٰنِ ٱلرَّحِيمِ ۝

[99:1] In the name of Allah, the Gracious, the Merciful.

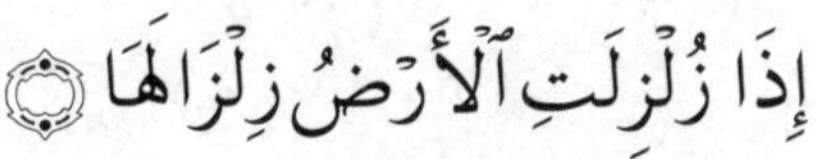

[99:2] When the earth is shaken with her *violent* shaking,

[2]Commentary

The expression زُلۡزِلَتِ الۡاَرۡضُ زِلۡزَالَهَا (*zulzilatil-arḍo zilzālahā*) means that the whole earth will experience all manner of internal as well as external commotion and upheavals. In our time not only has the earth been constantly shaken by most destructive earthquakes, wars and other calamities and catastrophes at frequent intervals, but also its dwellers have been subjected to violent and virulent agitation in every walk of life. Man has

---

[2] The Holy Qur'ān with English Translation and Commentary. 3rd ed. Islām International Publications Limited; 2002. Volume 5, Pages 2866-2868

experienced catastrophic changes never witnessed by him before.

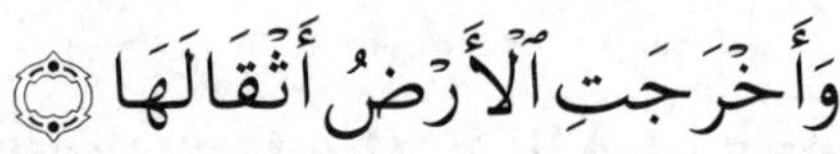

[99:3] And the earth brings forth her burdens,

<u>Commentary</u>

The verse may have one of the following interpretations:

1. The bowels of the earth will be ripped open and it will throw up its treasures of mineral wealth.
2. There will be a vast release and upsurge of knowledge of all kinds, relating to physical as well as spiritual sciences, especially in the sciences of geology and archaeology.
3. People will throw off the yoke of their rulers and religious leaders and will revolt against oppression, throwing the yoke of subjection off their shoulders.

وَقَالَ ٱلۡإِنسَٰنُ مَا لَهَا ۝

[99:4] And man says, 'What is the matter with her?'

Commentary

The changes will be so many and so far reaching and the discoveries made so great that one will exclaim in wonder and bewilderment: "What is the matter with the earth!"

يَوۡمَئِذٖ تُحَدِّثُ أَخۡبَارَهَا ۝

[99:5] That day will she tell her news,

Commentary

All prophecies concerning the present age will be fulfilled and all that had hitherto remained obscure will become manifest. The verse may also mean that the science of geology will make great strides. When asked about the meaning of the verse, the Holy Prophet[sa] is reported to have said that every action done in secret will come to light (Tirmidhī).

بِأَنَّ رَبَّكَ أَوْحَىٰ لَهَا ۝

[99:6] It will be because your Lord would have so revealed to her.

Commentary

The verse means that the earth will throw out its treasures because it is commanded by God to do so.

يَوْمَئِذٍ يَصْدُرُ ٱلنَّاسُ أَشْتَاتًا لِّيُرَوْا۟ أَعْمَـٰلَهُمْ ۝

[99:7] On that day will men come forth in scattered groups that they may be shown *the results of* their works.

Commentary

The verse means that in the time of the Promised Messiah[as], in order to protect and safeguard the political, social and economic interests, people will form themselves into parties, companies and groups. There will be political

parties and parties formed on economic basis; and powerful guilds, cartels and syndicates will also come into existence.

The words "**that they may be shown the results of their works**" signify that individuals will pool their resources, and collective effort will take the place of individual effort in order that they might make their weight felt and their labours might lead to some result.

فَمَن يَعۡمَلۡ مِثۡقَالَ ذَرَّةٍ خَيۡرًا يَرَهُۥ ۝

[99:8] Then whoso does an atom's weight of good will see it,

وَمَن يَعۡمَلۡ مِثۡقَالَ ذَرَّةٍ شَرًّا يَرَهُۥ ۝

[99:9] And whoso does an atom's weight of evil will *also* see it.

Commentary

The principle that no action of man, good or bad, is wasted and must produce some result, has been explained, variously in the Qur'an. These two verses contain at once a

message of solace and comfort for the righteous, and a warning for evil-doers, that they shall reap the consequences of their actions.

What is the key message of this portion of the Holy Qur'ān?

How does this message apply to your personal life?

Second Rak‘ah of Tuesday ‘Ishā’ Prayers

Importance of Sūrah At-Takāthur, Chapter 102

Introduction:

- [1]The Holy Prophet[sa] often used to recite the Sūrah; he is reported to have said that the Sūrah was equal in weight and worth to a thousand verses (Bayān, Baihaqī & Dailamī). The phrase 'equal to thousand verses', means that this Sūrah has a huge importance in terms of its message.

- The Sūrah deals with a very common and deadly spiritual disease, *viz.,* vying with one another in amassing worldly goods and taking pride in their abundance. This Sūrah deals with the factors which engender in man an inclination to, or a liking for, disbelief and which divert his attention away from God and Truth.

- Affluence can make a society but at times affluence can be the cause of decline of nations as well. The Ḥadīth of the Holy Prophet[sa] purports to say that by understanding and acting on the meaning of this

---

[1] Tafsīrul-Qur'ān by The Promised Messiah, Ḥaḍrat Mirzā Ghulām Aḥmad[as] of Qadiān, Pages 523-524 available on www.alislam.org

Sūrah, one can safeguard the nation against decline that comes with affluence.

- The Promised Messiah[as] has stressed that the true purpose of the advent of prophets is to help people forge a true bond with God and to lower the love of this world. This Sūrah explains the true purpose of the advents of prophets. One can achieve high moral status by comprehending and acting on the message of this sūrah.

- Once after reciting Sūrah at-Takāṭhur, the Holy Prophet[sa] is reported to have said "The son of Adam says, "My money, my money!' Yet, what is your money except that which you eat and use up, wear and tear, and spend in charity and thus keep (in your record). Other than that, it will go away and will be left for the people (the inheritors)."

بِسۡمِ ٱللَّهِ ٱلرَّحۡمَٰنِ ٱلرَّحِيمِ ۝

أَلۡهَىٰكُمُ ٱلتَّكَاثُرُ ۝ حَتَّىٰ زُرۡتُمُ ٱلۡمَقَابِرَ ۝ كَلَّا سَوۡفَ
تَعۡلَمُونَ ۝ ثُمَّ كَلَّا سَوۡفَ تَعۡلَمُونَ ۝ كَلَّا لَوۡ تَعۡلَمُونَ
عِلۡمَ ٱلۡيَقِينِ ۝ لَتَرَوُنَّ ٱلۡجَحِيمَ ۝ ثُمَّ لَتَرَوُنَّهَا عَيۡنَ
ٱلۡيَقِينِ ۝ ثُمَّ لَتُسۡـَٔلُنَّ يَوۡمَئِذٍ عَنِ ٱلنَّعِيمِ ۝

Translation:

In the name of Allah, the Gracious, the Merciful. Vying with each other for amassing wealth had made you oblivious, Even you reached the graveyards.,. Nay! you will soon come to know. Nay again! you will soon come to know.] Nay, were you to know the certain knowledge You will surely see Hell *in this very life*. Aye, you will

surely see it with the eye of certainty. Then, on that day you shall be called to account about the *worldly* favours

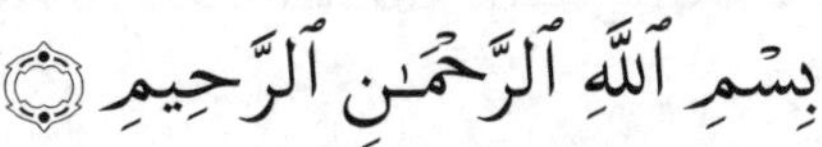

[102:1] In the name of Allah, the Gracious, the Merciful.

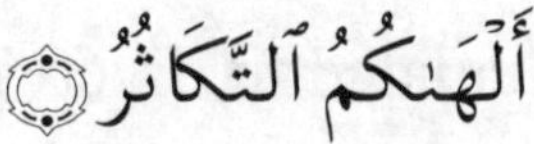

[102:2] Vying with each other for amassing wealth had made you oblivious,

[2]**Commentary**

Acquisitiveness and man's inordinate desire to outstrip others in wealth, position and prestige lies at the root of all human troubles and of neglect of higher values of life. It is man's great misfortune that his passion for acquiring worldly things knows no limit and leaves him no time to

[2] The Holy Quran with English Translation and Commentary. 3rd ed. Islām International Publications Limited; 2002. Volume 5, Pages 2876-2878

think of God or the Hereafter. He remains entirely engrossed in these things till death comes upon him.

Against general practice, the verb الها (*alhā*) has not been followed by the preposition عن (*'an*) in this verse. This enlarges the meaning of the verb, covering, as it does, all the things that are calculated to divert man's attention from God and not from any particular thing or object.

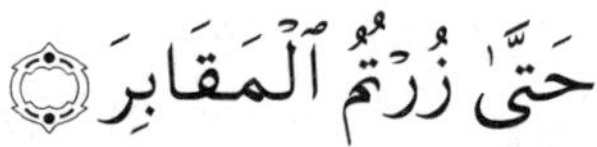

[102:3] Even you reached the graveyards.

<u>Commentary</u>

Man remains engrossed in acquiring worldly goods till death comes upon him and then he finds that he had wasted all his precious life. The verse also signifies that competition for superiority in wealth, position and numbers has led to the undoing of individuals and even of nations. Moral rather than physical death is meant here, because physical death comes uninvited, but man himself brings

about his moral death. So it is not unqualified rivalry and vying with one another that is condemned here. On the contrary, believers have been exhorted in the Qur'an to endeavour to outstrip one another in doing good (2: 149 & 35: 32). It is the blind craze for worldly things, to the detriment of higher values, to which exception has been taken in this verse.

كَلَّا سَوْفَ تَعْلَمُونَ ۝

[102:4] Nay! you will soon come to know.

ثُمَّ كَلَّا سَوْفَ تَعْلَمُونَ ۝

[102:5] Nay again! you will soon come to know.

Commentary

Repetition of the verse is intended to add emphasis to and render more effective the warning contained in the *Sūrah*. Or the *Sūrah* may refer to the Nemesis that will come in the wake of blind engrossment in the acquisition of worldly things in this life and in the Hereafter.

كَلَّا لَوْ تَعْلَمُونَ عِلْمَ ٱلْيَقِينِ ۝

[102:6] Nay! if you only knew with certain knowledge,

لَتَرَوُنَّ ٱلْجَحِيمَ ۝

[102:7] You will surely see Hell *in this very life.*

ثُمَّ لَتَرَوُنَّهَا عَيْنَ ٱلْيَقِينِ ۝

[102:8] Aye, you will surely see it with the eye of certainty.

Commentary

The verse administers a severe rebuke to disbelievers. It seems to say to them: "Why can't you understand the simple thing, that the wages of sin is death and that no spiritual life is left in you. Had you used common sense and what little amount of knowledge you possess, you would have seen a veritable Hell yawning before your eyes in this very life i.e., you would have realised that your engrossment in the pursuit of pomp, circumstance and the material advantages of this temporary existence will cause

your total ruin. But you give no thought to these stark realities of life. You do not believe that such a thing will ever happen, but the time is fast approaching when you will see Divine punishment overtaking you in the form of diverse calamities."

It may be stated here that there are three stages of certainty, viz.,

1. علم اليقين (*'ilmul-yaqīn*) i.e., "certainty by inference
2. عين اليقين (*'ainul-yaqīn*) i.e. "certainty by sight"
3. حق اليقين (*ḥaqqul-yaqīn*) "certainty by realisation."

In the first stage a thing itself is not visible but from its visible effects a man can conclude that it exists.

In the second stage not only the effects of a thing but the thing itself is visible, though its nature is not completely comprehended.

In the third stage which is the stage of perfect realisation or personal experience a man both through observation of the effects of a thing on others and through realisation of its

effect on himself, can have as complete an understanding of the nature of a thing as it is possible for him to have.

These are also the stages of human knowledge with regard to Hell. A man can, by inference, attain certainty about the existence of Hell in this very life but it is after death that he will see it with his own eyes, though it is on the Day of Resurrection that a sinful man will have full realisation of it by personally experiencing it.

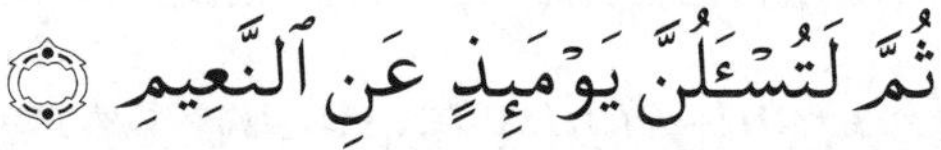

[102:9] Then, on that day you shall be called to account about the *worldly* favours.

Commentary

When disbelievers will be brought face to face to Hell, they will be told that God had bestowed upon them all kinds of favours, especially His greatest favour--- the Holy Prophet[sa]--- but they rejected and opposed him.

What is the key message of this portion of the Holy Qur'ān?

How does this message apply to your personal life?

WEDNESDAY

DAY	SALAT	FIRST RAK'AH	2ND RAK'AH
WEDNESDAY	Fajr	Sūrah al-Kahf 103-107	Sūrah al-Kahf 108-111
	Maghrib	Sūrah al- Falaq	Sūrah an-Nās
	'Ishā'	Sūrah ash-Shams	Sūrah aḍ-Ḍuḥā

First Rak'ah of Wednesday and Sunday Fajr Prayer

Please see Page 213

Second Rak‘ah of Sunday and Wednesday Fajr Prayer

Please see Page 225

First Rak'ah of Saturday, Sunday, Monday, Wednesday and Thursday Maghrib Prayer

Please see Page 183

Second Rak'ah of Saturday, Sunday, Monday, Wednesday and Thursday Maghrib Prayer

Please see Page 195

Second [illegible] of

Saturday, Sunday, Monday

Wednesday and Thursday

[illegible] Prayer

[illegible]

First Rak‘ah of Wednesday ‘Ishā’ Prayer

First Rak'ah of Wednesday 'Ishā' Prayer

[1]Importance of Sūrah Ash-Shams

- The Holy Prophet[sa] had directed that small chapters like ash-Shams or ad-Ḍūḥa should be recited in the Ẓuhr Prayers as these chapters have a special relevance to Ẓuhr (Fat ḥul-Bayān).

- The five *Sūrahs* (89-93) possess a striking similarity in subject-matter. In all of them great stress has been laid on the development of good morals, especially those good qualities that intimately concern and affect the progress and prosperity of a community.

- Muslims have been exhorted to create an atmosphere and an environment which should help to raise the standing and stature of the poor, depressed and suppressed section of their community and should enable them to take their proper share in its activities.

---

[1] The Holy Qur'ān with English Translation and Commentary. 3rd ed. Islām International Publications Limited; 2002. Volume 5, Page 2829

بِسْمِ ٱللَّهِ ٱلرَّحْمَٰنِ ٱلرَّحِيمِ ۝

وَٱلشَّمْسِ وَضُحَىٰهَا ۝ وَٱلْقَمَرِ إِذَا تَلَىٰهَا ۝ وَٱلنَّهَارِ إِذَا
جَلَّىٰهَا ۝ وَٱلَّيْلِ إِذَا يَغْشَىٰهَا ۝ وَٱلسَّمَآءِ وَمَا بَنَىٰهَا ۝
وَٱلْأَرْضِ وَمَا طَحَىٰهَا ۝ وَنَفْسٍ وَمَا سَوَّىٰهَا ۝ فَأَلْهَمَهَا
فُجُورَهَا وَتَقْوَىٰهَا ۝ قَدْ أَفْلَحَ مَن زَكَّىٰهَا ۝ وَقَدْ خَابَ
مَن دَسَّىٰهَا ۝ كَذَّبَتْ ثَمُودُ بِطَغْوَىٰهَآ ۝ إِذِ ٱنۢبَعَثَ
أَشْقَىٰهَا ۝ فَقَالَ لَهُمْ رَسُولُ ٱللَّهِ نَاقَةَ ٱللَّهِ وَسُقْيَٰهَا ۝١٣
فَكَذَّبُوهُ فَعَقَرُوهَا فَدَمْدَمَ عَلَيْهِمْ رَبُّهُم بِذَنۢبِهِمْ فَسَوَّىٰهَا ۝
وَلَا يَخَافُ عُقْبَٰهَا ۝

Translation

In the name of Allah, the Gracious, the Merciful.] By the sun and the time when it begins to radiate, And *by* the moon when it follows it (the sun), And *by* the day when it reveals its glory, And *by* the night when it draws a veil over it, And *by* the heaven and its making, And *by* the earth and its spreading out, And *by* the soul and its perfection — And He revealed to it what is wrong for it and what is right for it — Surely, he prospers who augments it, And he who corrupts it is ruined. The tribe of Thamud denied the truth because of their rebelliousness. When the most wretched among them got up, Then the Messenger of Allah said, 'Leave alone the she-camel of Allah, and let her drink.' But they rejected him and hamstrung her, so their Lord destroyed them completely because of their sin, and levelled them to the ground. And He cared not for the consequences thereof.

بِسۡمِ ٱللَّهِ ٱلرَّحۡمَـٰنِ ٱلرَّحِيمِ

[91:1] In the name of Allah, the Gracious, the Merciful.

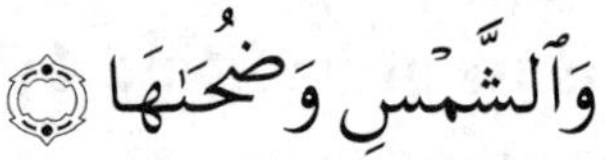

[91:2] By the sun and the time when it begins to radiate,

[2]Commentary

God's swearing by His creatures is a method adopted by the Qur'ān. The Qur'ānic oaths have deep meaning underlying them. In ordinary transactions when a person takes an oath, his object is to supply the deficiency of insufficient testimony.

The object and meaning of God's oaths must, however, be distinguished from those of the oaths of mortals. Divine laws reveal two aspects of the works of God., *viz.,* the obvious and the inferential. The *former are easily*

[2] The Holy Qur'ān with English Translation and Commentary. 3rd ed. Islām International Publications Limited; 2002. Volume 5, Pages 2829-2833

comprehensible; in the comprehension of the latter there is room for error. In the taking of oaths God has called attention to what may be inferred from what is obvious.

Taking the Oaths mentioned in the following verses, we see that the sun and the moon, the day and the night, heavens and earth belong to the "obvious", their properties as referred to in these verses are universally known and acknowledged. But the same properties found in man's soul are not obvious. To lead to an inference of the existence of these properties in the soul of man God has called to witness His obvious works.

"The sun" in the verse may refer to the sun of the spiritual universe- the Holy Prophet[sa]-who is the source of all light and who will continue to enlighten the world till the end of time.

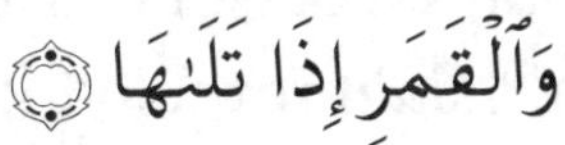

[91:3] And *by* the moon when it follows it (the sun),

<u>Commentary</u>

"The moon" may be taken as referring to the Holy Prophet[sa], who like the moon, draws his light from God and transmits it

to the spiritually dark world. Or it may refer to those religious Divines and Reformers---particularly the Promised Messiah[as]---who borrow the light of truth from the Holy Prophet[sa] and transmit it to the world to remove the darkness of moral and spiritual turpitude.

وَٱلنَّهَارِ إِذَا جَلَّىٰهَا ۝

[91:4] And *by* the day when it reveals its glory,

Commentary:

"The day" may signify the time during which the Message of Islam and the truth of its Founder was further fortified and foundations were laid for the universal propagation of the vital doctrines of the new Faith. The reference in the verse may particularly be to the time of the rightly-guided Caliphs—the first four successors of the Holy Prophet[sa]. In their time the light of Islam revealed its glory and splendour to the world.

وَٱلَّيْلِ إِذَا يَغْشَىٰهَا ۝

[91:5] And *by* the night when it draws a veil over it,

Commentary:

"The night" may refer to the period of decline and decadence of Muslims when the light of Islam had become veiled from the eyes of the world. These four verses (2-5) refer to four periods in the eventful career of Islam, *viz*.,

1. The time of the Holy Prophet[sa] himself when the spiritual sun (the Holy Prophet[sa]) was shining in full splendour in the spiritual heaven
2. The time of the Promised Messiah[as] when the light derived from the Holy Prophet[sa] was being reflected on to a dark world
3. The time of the Holy Prophet's[sa] immediate Successors when the light of Islam was still shining and
4. The period when spiritual darkness had spread over the world after the first three centuries of Islam which was its most glorious period.

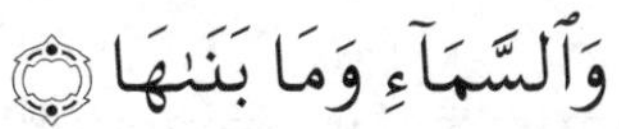

[91:6] And *by* the heaven and its making,

Commentary

In these verses attention has been focussed on the great Designer and Architect of the universe, and on the

perfection and complete freedom from flaw or defect in the design and creation of man and the universe.

وَٱلْأَرْضِ وَمَا طَحَىٰهَا ۝

[91:7] And *by* the earth and its spreading out,

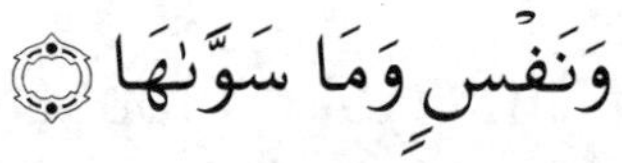

[91:8] And *by* the soul and its perfection —

Commentary

The verse means that all the properties and forces which the great heavenly bodies such as the sun and the moon, etc., devote to the service of God's creatures and to which reference has been made in the following verses bear witness to man having been endowed with similar qualities in a high degree.

In fact, man is a universe in miniature and in his soul is represented, on a small scale, all that exists in the external universe. Like the sun he sheds his lustre over the world and enlightens it with the light of wisdom and knowledge. Like the moon he transmits to those who are in the dark the light of vision, inspiration and revelation which he borrows

from the Great Original Source. He is bright like the day, and shows the ways of truth and virtue. Like the night he draws the veil over the faults and misdeeds of others, lightens their burdens and gives rest to the tired and the weary. Like the heavens he takes every distressed soul under his shelter and revives the lifeless earth with salubrious rain. Like the earth he submits in all humility and lowliness to be trampled under the feet by others as a trial for them, and from his purified soul various sorts of trees of knowledge and truth grow up in abundance, and with their shade, flowers and fruits, he regales the world.

Such are the great Divines and Heavenly Reformers, of whom the greatest and the most perfect was the Holy Prophet[sa].

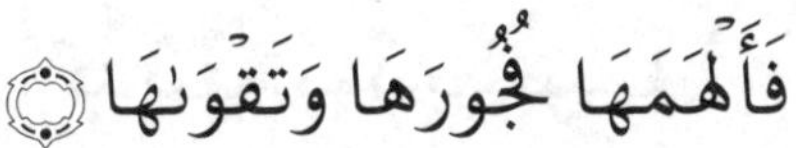

[91:9] And He revealed to it what is wrong for it and what is right for it

Commentary

The verse means that after creating the celestial and the terrestrial systems, and bringing into existence man--- the

acme and apex of the whole creation--- and endowing him with great natural potentialities and qualities, God did not leave him alone. He implanted in his nature a feeling or sense of what is good or bad.

Or the verse may mean that God reveals to man that he could achieve spiritual perfection by eschewing what is bad and wrong and adopting what is right and good because it is through Divine revelation that man could achieve it.

قَدْ أَفْلَحَ مَن زَكَّىٰهَا ۝

[91:10] Surely, he prospers who augments it,

وَقَدْ خَابَ مَن دَسَّىٰهَا ۝

[91:11] And he who corrupts it is ruined.

كَذَّبَتْ ثَمُودُ بِطَغْوَىٰهَآ ۝

[91:12] The tribe of Thamūd denied the truth because of their rebelliousness.

Commentary

In this and the next four verses is cited the example of the tribe of Thamūd who defied Divine guidance and opposed their Prophet working out thereby their own ruin.

إِذِ ٱنۢبَعَثَ أَشۡقَىٰهَا ﴿١٢﴾

[91:13] When the most wretched among them got up,

فَقَالَ لَهُمۡ رَسُولُ ٱللَّهِ نَاقَةَ ٱللَّهِ وَسُقۡيَٰهَا ﴿١٣﴾

[91:14] Then the Messenger of Allāh said, 'Leave alone the she-camel of Allāh, and let her drink.'

Commentary

The Prophet Salih[as] kept the she-camel for travels. He rode on it from place to place to preach the Divine Message. Putting obstacles in the way of its free movements was tantamount to placing impediments in the way of Salih[as] himself and preventing him from discharging the sacred duty entrusted to him. In fact, every Divine Reformer is نَاقَةُ اللهِ (*nāqatullāh*) ; God's she-camel).

فَكَذَّبُوهُ فَعَقَرُوهَا فَدَمۡدَمَ عَلَيۡهِمۡ رَبُّهُم بِذَنۢبِهِمۡ فَسَوَّىٰهَا ﴿١٤﴾

[91:15] But they rejected him and hamstrung her, so their Lord destroyed them completely because of their

sin, and levelled them to the ground.

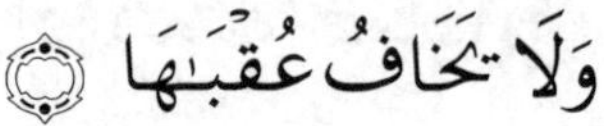

[91:16] And He cared not for the consequences thereof.

Commentary

When a people incur Divine punishment and are thus destroyed, God does not care for those who survive the destruction or for the utterly miserable state to which they are reduced. The verse may also be taken as containing a warning to the Makkans that if they behaved like the Thamūd, they will be punished like them.

What is the key message of this portion of the Holy Qur'ān?

How does this message apply to your personal life?

First Rak'ah of Friday, Second Rak'ah of Wednesday and First Rak'ah of Thursday 'Ishā' Prayer

Please see Page 77

THURSDAY

DAY	SALAT	FIRST RAK'AH	2ND RAK'AH
THURSDAY	Fajr	Sūrah al-Baqarah 285-287	Sūrah Āl-e-'Imrān 191-195
	Maghrib	Sūrah al- Falaq	Sūrah an-Nās
	'Ishā'	Sūrah aḍ-Ḍuḥā	Sūrah al-Inshirāḥ

First Rak'ah of Monday and Thursday Fajr Prayers.

Verse 287 in the second Rak'ah of Saturday 'Ishā' Prayers

Please see Page 263

Second Rak'ah of Monday and Thursday Fajr Prayer

Please see Page 285

First Rak'ah of Saturday, Sunday, Monday, Wednesday and Thursday Maghrib Prayer

Please see page 181

First Rak'ah of Sunday

Saturday, Monday

Wednesday and Thursday

Maghrib Prayer

Continues page 131

Second Rak‘ah of Saturday, Sunday, Monday, Wednesday and Thursday Maghrib Prayer

Please see page 193

First Rak'ah of Friday, Second Rak'ah of Wednesday and First Rak'ah of Thursday 'Ishā' Prayer

Please see Page 77

Second Ra‘kah of Thursday ‘Ishā’ Prayer

Second Ra'kah of Thursday 'Ishā' Prayer

Importance of Sūrah al-Inshirāḥ Chapter 94

- [1]When a person demonstrate patience in the face of extreme hardship and difficulties, which raises his status to angels. This is why Prophets are most favoured by God and they face the hardest persecution in the cause of Allah.

- [2]Sūrah ad-Dhuha deals with the physical and obvious blessings that will be bestowed on the Holy Prophet[sa], and this Sūrah gives the glad tidings of the spiritual blessings of Allāh.

---

[1] *Tafsīrul-Qur'ān* by The Promised Messiah, Ḥaḍrat Mirzā Ghulām Aḥmad[as] of Qadiān, Page 441 available on www.alislam.org

[2] *Ḥaqā'iqul- Furqān*. Ḥaḍrat Ḥakīm Maulānā Nūr-ud-Dīn[ra], Khalīfatul Masīḥ I, Printwell Focal Point Amritsar 2005. Volume 4, page 407

- [3]It is the Sunnah of the Prophets that along with obvious effort and hard work they resort to prayers and attention to God to carry out their mission. Hard work and effort are incomplete without prayer and prayers remains inadequate without endeavour.

---

[3] *Ḥaqā'iqul- Furqān*. Ḥaḍrat Ḥakīm Maulānā Nūr-ud-Dīn[ra], Khalīfatul Masīḥ I, Printwell Focal Point Amritsar 2005. Volume 4, page 409

بِسۡمِ ٱللَّهِ ٱلرَّحۡمَٰنِ ٱلرَّحِيمِ ۝

أَلَمۡ نَشۡرَحۡ لَكَ صَدۡرَكَ ۝ وَوَضَعۡنَا عَنكَ وِزۡرَكَ ۝ ٱلَّذِىٓ
أَنقَضَ ظَهۡرَكَ ۝ وَرَفَعۡنَا لَكَ ذِكۡرَكَ ۝ فَإِنَّ مَعَ ٱلۡعُسۡرِ يُسۡرًا ۝
إِنَّ مَعَ ٱلۡعُسۡرِ يُسۡرًا ۝ فَإِذَا فَرَغۡتَ فَٱنصَبۡ ۝ وَإِلَىٰ رَبِّكَ
فَٱرۡغَب ۝

Translation

In the name of Allah, the Gracious, the Merciful. Have We not opened for thee thy bosom, And removed from thee thy burden. Which had *well nigh* broken thy back, And We exalted thy name? Surely there is ease after hardship. *Aye*, surely there is ease after hardship. So when thou art free, strive hard, And to thy Lord do you turn seeking Him eagerly.

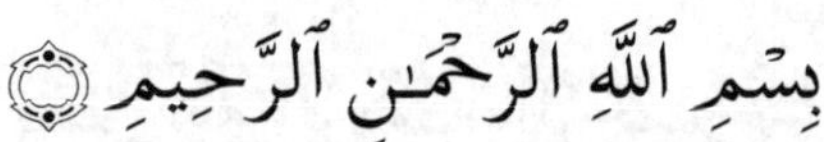

[94:1] In the name of Allah, the Gracious, the Merciful.

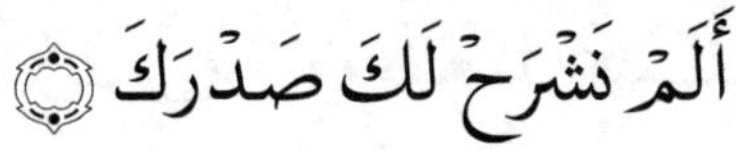

[94:2] Have We not opened for thee thy bosom,

[4]Commentary

In view of different meanings of the word شرح (*sharaḥ*), the verse may have one or all of the following interpretations:

1. God had protected the heart of the Holy Prophet[sa] from all harmful influences. It was impossible for evil to enter it.
2. God was the Prophet's own Preceptor and Teacher and besides temporal knowledge He had opened his breast to comprehend the Divine mysteries.

---

[4] The Holy Qur'ān with English Translation and Commentary. 3rd ed. Islām International Publications Limited; 2002. Volume 5, Pages 2845-2846

3. The Prophet[sa] never suffered from straitness of the heart and was endowed with patience and fortitude to such a degree that even the hardest tribulation could not disturb his peace of mind.

وَوَضَعۡنَا عَنكَ وِزۡرَكَ ۝

[94:3] And removed from thee thy burden

ٱلَّذِىٓ أَنقَضَ ظَهۡرَكَ ۝

[94:4] Which had *well nigh* broken thy back,

Commentary

The Holy Prophet[sa] had been saddled with such a nerve-racking and back-breaking task as had never been entrusted to a human being, i.e., first to raise a degenerate people from the depths of moral turpitude to the peaks of spiritual excellence and, then through them to cleanse and purify the whole of mankind of the dross of iniquity, ignorance and superstition.

This was indeed a very heavy responsibility, which had almost crushed the Prophet[sa] under its weight, but God lightened his burden in that He gave him devoted and

sincere Companions who shared his burden and helped him in the discharge of his manifold and hard duties.

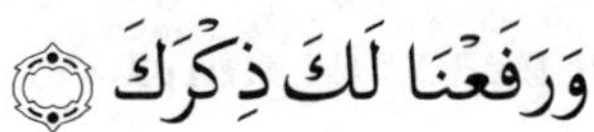

[94:5] And We exalted thy name?

Commentary

The Sūrah was revealed in the second or third year of the Call, at a time when the Prophet[sa] was hardly known outside his immediate neighbourhood, but very soon he rose to be the best-known and most respected and successful of all religious Teachers. No leader, religious or temporal, has so commanded the love and respect of his followers as has the Holy Prophet[sa].

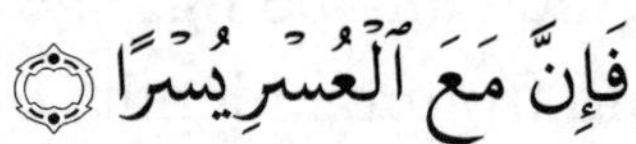

[94:6] Surely there is ease after hardship.

Commentary

The verse holds a message of hope and good cheer for the Holy Prophet[sa]. He is comforted with the assurance

that whenever Islam would be in difficulty, God would raise a Reformer from among his followers who would restore to it its former glory and greatness. Pointing out the fact that one has to face difficulties and hardships in this life the Prophet[sa] is assured that his tribulation would prove to be of short duration and would soon be followed by increasing ease, success and prosperity.

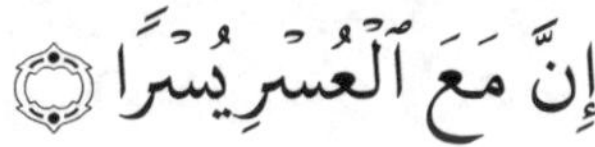

[94:7] *Aye*, surely there is ease after hardship.

Commentary

Repetition of the words, "Surely, there is ease after hardship", signifies that Islam will have to pass through very hard times but on two occasions it will have to face a challenge to its very existence, first at its birth and then in the Latter Days,--- and on both these occasions it will emerge from the ordeal with renewed strength.

These verses also indicate that the hardships with which the Holy Prophet[sa] and Muslims are faced are temporary, but his successes would be permanent and ever-expanding.

فَإِذَا فَرَغْتَ فَٱنصَبْ ۝

[94:8] So when thou art free, strive hard,

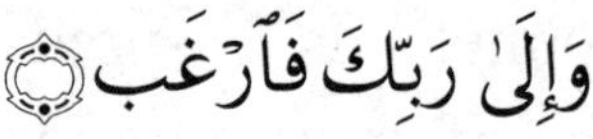

[94:9] And to thy Lord do you turn seeking Him eagerly.

<u>Commentary</u>

The Holy Prophet[sa] is told here that as endless vistas of spiritual progress lie before him, after he has conquered the difficulties that bar his way, he should not rest satisfied with his success, but having scaled one peak he should strive to climb the next, and his attention should be wholly directed towards regenerating of fallen humanity and towards establishing God's Kingdom on earth.

The verse may also signify that when the Prophet[sa] has finished his day's work of teaching and training his followers and other temporal affairs, he should turn to God as ever with all his heart, for his spiritual journey knows no end.

What is the key message of this portion of the Holy Qur'ān?

How does this message apply to your personal life?

JUMU'AH AND EID PRAYERS

DAY	SALAT	FIRST RAK'AH	2ND RAK'AH
	JUMU'AH AND EID PRAYERS	Sūrah al-A'lā	Sūrah al-Ghāshiyah

First Rak‘ah of the Friday Prayer and Eid Prayer

First Rak'ah of the Friday Prayer, Eid Prayer

Importance of Sūrah al-A'lā

- The Holy Prophet[sa] used to recite this Sūrah in the first Rak'ah of Eid and Friday Prayer as well as first Rak'ah of Witr Prayer.
- [1]It is reported in Musnad Aḥmad that the Prophet[sa] was very fond of this Sūrah.
- In accordance with the Sunnah, Ḥaḍrat Khalīfatul Masīḥ V (may Allah strengthen him with His mighty help) recites this Sūrah in the first Rak'ah_of Eid and Friday Prayer.
- [2]Ḥaḍrat Khalīfatul Masīḥ V (may Allāh strengthen him with His mighty help) gave the following discourse on verses 2-4 of Sūrah al-A'lā in his Friday sermon on May 14, 2010:

---

[1]*Tafsīr-e-Kabīr*. Ḥaḍrat Mirzā Bashīr-ud-Dīn Maḥmūd Aḥmad[ra], Printwell Amritsar 2004. Volume 8, Pages 385.

[2] Ḥaḍhrat Mirzā Masroor Aḥmad[(aba)], Khalīfatul Masīḥ V, Friday Sermon, Baitul- Futuh Mosque London UK, 14th January 2010.

- According to Ḥaḍrat Muṣleḥ-e-Mau'ūd[ra], in the second verse we have been commanded to glorify the name of God and the perfect example in this regard was set for us by the Holy Prophet[sa] who surpassed everyone in his remembrance and praise of his Lord.

- Among the many ways which the Holy Prophet[sa] taught his followers of praising and remembering Allāh, was that they should use words that comprehend all His attributes. They should ponder over these attributes and bring to mind all of Allāh's bounties as well as His Greatness and Majesty.

- Do not depend upon worldly means for your sustenance, your success, your progress or your victory; instead concentrate on your praise for God, Who is the Lord of the worlds and free from every imperfection.

- This verse also means that you should spread the name of your Lord throughout the world. In this also we find that the Holy Prophet[sa] did full justice to his mission of calling mankind

towards God. This was the quality he instilled in his Companions as well.

- In the third verse, it is said that God is the One Who creates and perfects. This means that God has invested man with all the faculties necessary for his advancement and has placed in him the seed of progress. With the proper use of his spiritual and mental faculties, man can become a reflection of God's attributes.

- Allāh the Exalted has not only provided mankind with cure for physical diseases but also for their spiritual maladies. He sent the Holy Prophet[sa] with the perfect teaching in the form of the Holy Qur'ān at a time when mankind became ridden with all spiritual maladies and the sins of all the ages had become prevalent. Ḥuḍūr[aba] said: The Promised Messiah[as] was sent by God to dig pearls of knowledge and wisdom from the Holy Book and to cure our spiritual weaknesses. These cures benefit those who reflect upon the Holy Qur'ān in the light of the

Promised Messiah's[as] teachings and commentaries.

- Regarding the fourth verse, Ḥaḍrat Muṣleḥ-e-Mau'ūd[ra] said that having given man the ability to progress and having endowed him with tremendous faculties, Allāh has also provided for him the means for limitless progress. The other meaning is that whenever man goes astray, God sends His teachings to meet his needs.

- May Allāh help us to truly live by His teachings, to praise Him, worship Him and spread His message to the whole world.

بِسۡمِ ٱللَّهِ ٱلرَّحۡمَٰنِ ٱلرَّحِيمِ ۝

سَبِّحِ ٱسۡمَ رَبِّكَ ٱلۡأَعۡلَى ۝ ٱلَّذِى خَلَقَ فَسَوَّىٰ ۝ وَٱلَّذِى
قَدَّرَ فَهَدَىٰ ۝ وَٱلَّذِىٓ أَخۡرَجَ ٱلۡمَرۡعَىٰ ۝ فَجَعَلَهُۥ غُثَآءً
أَحۡوَىٰ ۝ سَنُقۡرِئُكَ فَلَا تَنسَىٰٓ ۝ إِلَّا مَا شَآءَ ٱللَّهُۚ إِنَّهُۥ
يَعۡلَمُ ٱلۡجَهۡرَ وَمَا يَخۡفَىٰ ۝ وَنُيَسِّرُكَ لِلۡيُسۡرَىٰ ۝ فَذَكِّرۡ إِن
نَّفَعَتِ ٱلذِّكۡرَىٰ ۝ سَيَذَّكَّرُ مَن يَخۡشَىٰ ۝ وَيَتَجَنَّبُهَا
ٱلۡأَشۡقَى ۝ ٱلَّذِى يَصۡلَى ٱلنَّارَ ٱلۡكُبۡرَىٰ ۝ ثُمَّ لَا يَمُوتُ
فِيهَا وَلَا يَحۡيَىٰ ۝ قَدۡ أَفۡلَحَ مَن تَزَكَّىٰ ۝ وَذَكَرَ ٱسۡمَ رَبِّهِۦ
فَصَلَّىٰ ۝ بَلۡ تُؤۡثِرُونَ ٱلۡحَيَوٰةَ ٱلدُّنۡيَا ۝ وَٱلۡأٓخِرَةُ خَيۡرٞ
وَأَبۡقَىٰٓ ۝ إِنَّ هَٰذَا لَفِى ٱلصُّحُفِ ٱلۡأُولَىٰ ۝ صُحُفِ إِبۡرَٰهِيمَ
وَمُوسَىٰ ۝

Translation

In the name of Allāh, the Gracious, the Merciful. Glorify the name of thy Lord, the Most High, Who creates and perfects, And Who designs and guides, And Who brings forth the pasturage, Then turns it black, rotten rubbish. We shall teach thee *the Qur'ān*, and thou shalt forget *it* not, Except as Allāh wills. Surely, He knows *what is* open and what is hidden. And We shall facilitate for thee *every* facility. So go on reminding; surely; reminding is profitable. He who fears will soon heed; But the reprobate will turn aside from it, He who is to enter the great Fire. Then he will neither die therein nor live. Verily, he *truly* prospers who purifies himself, And remembers the name of his Lord and offers Prayers. But you prefer the life of this world, Whereas the Hereafter is better and more lasting. This indeed is *what is taught* in the former Scriptures -- The Scriptures of Abraham and Moses.

بِسۡمِ ٱللَّهِ ٱلرَّحۡمَـٰنِ ٱلرَّحِيمِ ۝١

[87:1] In the name of Allāh, the Gracious, the Merciful.

سَبِّحِ ٱسۡمَ رَبِّكَ ٱلۡأَعۡلَى ۝٢

[87:2] Glorify the name of thy Lord, the Most High,

[3]**Commentary**

The verse may be interpreted as:

a. glorify the name of thy Lord, the Most High
b. glorify the most high name of thy Lord.

The words رَبِّكَ الْأَعْلَى (*Rabbikal-A'lā*) the Most High Lord signify that as God has created man for unlimited progress, therefore, He has endowed him with great natural powers

[3] The Holy Quran with English Translation and Commentary. 3rd ed. Islām International Publications Limited; 2002. Volume 5, Pages 2807-2810

and faculties that he may fulfil his high destiny; only his development is to be progressive and in stages.

Incidentally, the Divine attribute رَبّ (*Rabb*) The Lord Who makes things grow and develop by stages disposes of the objection, *viz.*, why the perfect Law was not revealed in the beginning of creation? The word implies that perfect Law could only have been revealed after man's intellect and reason had attained their highest development which happened after a long and gradual process of evolution.

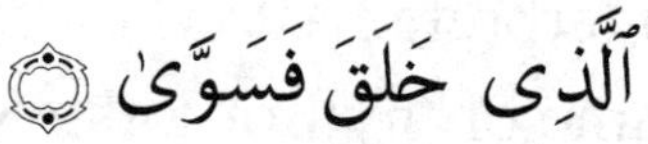

[87:3] Who creates and perfects,

Commentary

The verse shows that a high destiny awaits man and that for the fulfilment of it God has endowed him with the highest natural faculties and capacities. He can attain the highest spiritual stature; can reflect in his person Divine attributes so as to become the mirror of his Creator. This implies that the Creator Himself is perfect and is completely free from all conceivable defects and weaknesses.

وَٱلَّذِى قَدَّرَ فَهَدَىٰ ۝

[87:4] And Who designs and guides,

Commentary

This and the preceding verse give four reasons for the glorification of God, *viz*:

1. God brought us into being
2. He endowed us with all the faculties and capacities that are needed for our spiritual and intellectual development.
3. He determined man's physical and spiritual needs
4. For the fulfilment of those needs He revealed guidance that man might attain the object of his creation.

[87:5] And Who brings forth the pasturage,

فَجَعَلَهُۥ غُثَآءً أَحۡوَىٰ ۝

[87:6] Then turns it black, rotten rubbish.

Commentary

The verse constitutes a subtle answer to the objection: why God first revealed incomplete Laws, suited only to the needs of the peoples and the periods in which they were revealed, and then revealed the last and most perfect Shari'at in the form of the Qur'ān which was meant to guide mankind for all time? It purports to say that God has created two kinds of things:

1. Those that like herbage and pasture satisfy man's temporary needs and thus have a limited tenure of life. The former Scriptures, like these things, fulfilled man's temporary needs and therefore, were subject to decay and death.

2. Those things such as the sun, the moon, the earth etc., which are of permanent use for man. They will last with the universe. Like the latter the Qur'ān is meant to be man's unerring guide till the end of time;

hence it is immune to change, replacement and the wasting effect of time.

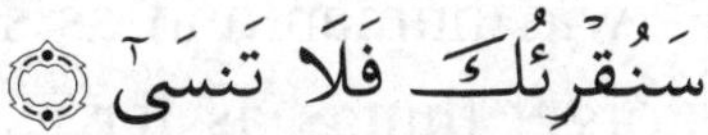

[87:7] We shall teach thee *the Qur'ān*, and thou shalt forget *it* not,

Commentary

The verse develops the argument implied in the preceding one. It purports to say that the Qur'ān being God's last Message for mankind has been granted Divine protection against interference, distortion or interpolation. The promise of protection has been given in emphatic and clear terms, *viz*: **"Verily, We Ourself have sent down the Reminder, and most surely We will be its Guardian** (15;10)". The last fourteen centuries have witnessed the fulfilment of this mighty prophecy, in that the Qur'ān has become a part of the thought and life of the Muslims as a whole, so much, that at all times there is found in the world a section of Muslims who proclaim and uphold its true teachings and learn its text by heart. The Qur'ān that we have with us today is the same, without the change of a

word or letter, which was given to the world by the Holy Prophet[sa].

The Holy Prophet[sa] was human and as such he was apt to forget and he did forget things as far as the affairs of life were concerned. But God, in His infallible wisdom, had so arranged that despite the fact that the Prophet[sa] was not literate and sometimes long Sūrāḥs were revealed to him in one piece, the revelation remained so indelibly imprinted on his mind that he was never found to forget or falter in reciting the revealed portions. It is marvellous indeed that very long Sūrāḥs such as al-Baqarah, āl-e-'Imrān or an-Nisā', were revealed piecemeal, and a period of several years had intervened between the revelation of different parts of each of those Sūrāḥs and yet the Prophet[sa] never for a moment fumbled or faltered in putting the revealed verses in their proper places.

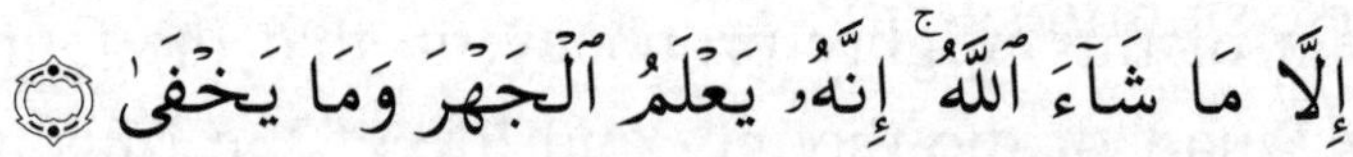

[87:8] Except as Allāh wills. Surely, He knows *what is* open and what is hidden.

Commentary

The expression "as God Wills", pertains only to matters of ordinary every-day life.

The words, "he knows what is manifest and what is hidden", mean that as God knew all the needs of man, of which man himself was unconscious and which he was incapable of knowing, God provided those needs in the Qur'ān, and so there could be no possibility of the Holy Prophet[sa] forgetting what was revealed to him.

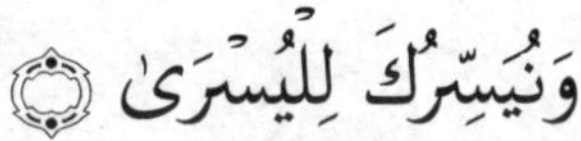

[87:9] And We shall facilitate for thee *every* facility.

Commentary

The verse signifies that:

a. It is easy to commit the Qur'ān to memory
b. Its teachings possess an adaptability all their own, which makes them conform to, and meet, the exigencies of changing conditions and circumstances

and the needs and requirements of men of different temperaments and dispositions

c. The Qur'ānic injunctions are not arbitrary but wise and rational. These factors combined together make the Qur'ān a Book easy to learn and to act upon.

These, among others, are some of the means which God has provided for the eternal protection and preservation of the Qur'ānic text and its meaning.

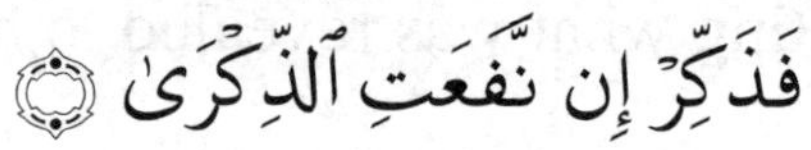

[87:10] So go on reminding; surely, reminding is profitable

Commentary

The verse means that only those people profit by admonition who have fear of God in their hearts. But as it is not given to one to know when admonition would be beneficial to a man, no opportunity should be lost to preach truth and righteousness.

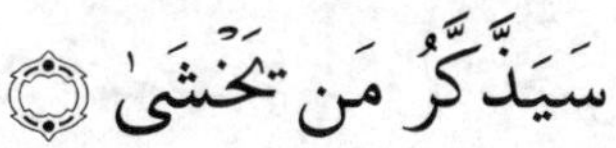

[87:11] He who fears will soon heed;

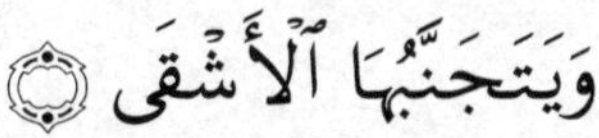

[87:12] But the reprobate will turn aside from it,

Commentary

The verse signifies that for those people who, on account of their persistent defiance and rejection of Truth and blind opposition to God's Messengers, incur punishment, a Divine decree comes into operation that they will not benefit by admonition.

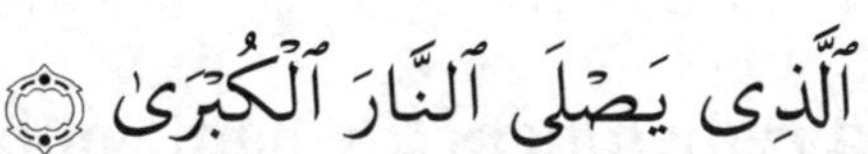

[87:13] He who is to enter the great Fire.

ثُمَّ لَا يَمُوتُ فِيهَا وَلَا يَحْيَىٰ ۝

[87:14] Then he will neither die therein nor live.

Commentary

The unfortunate disbelievers will burn in grievous torment of an abiding character and death will not be allowed to end it; on the other hand, "death will come to him from every quarter but he will not die (14:18)".

قَدْ أَفْلَحَ مَن تَزَكَّىٰ ۝

[87:15] Verily, he *truly* prospers who purifies himself,

وَذَكَرَ ٱسْمَ رَبِّهِۦ فَصَلَّىٰ ۝

[87:16] And remembers the name of his Lord and offers Prayers.

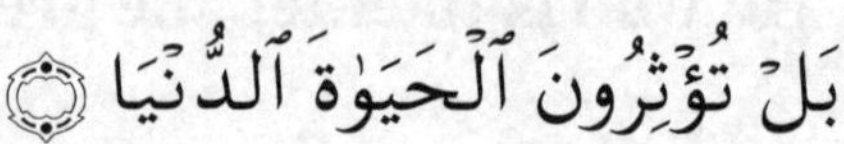

[87:17] But you prefer the life of this world,

وَٱلۡأٓخِرَةُ خَيۡرٞ وَأَبۡقَىٰٓ ۝

[87:18] Whereas the Hereafter is better and more lasting.

إِنَّ هَٰذَا لَفِي ٱلصُّحُفِ ٱلۡأُولَىٰ ۝

[87:19] This indeed is *what is taught* in the former Scriptures —

صُحُفِ إِبۡرَٰهِيمَ وَمُوسَىٰ ۝

[7:20] The Scriptures of Abraham and Moses

<u>Commentary</u>

Because the essential principles of all religions are basically identical, the teachings mentioned in the foregoing verses are also found in the Scriptures of Moses[as] and Abraham[as]. The verse may also signify that the

prophecy about the appearance of a great Prophet, who was to give to the world the last Divine Message and the most perfect Teaching, is found in the Scriptures of Moses[as] (Deut. 18: 18-19 & 33:2) and Abraham[as].

What is the key message of this portion of the Holy Qur’ān?

How does this message apply to your personal life?

Second Rak'ah of Friday and Eid Prayer

Second Rak'ah of Friday and Eid Prayer

[1]Importance of Sūrah al-Ghāshiyah

- The Holy Prophet[sa] used to recite Sūrah al-Ghāshiyah during the second Rak'ah of Eid and Friday.
- Sūrah al-Ghāshiyah has a subject matter that deals with the collective life of Muslims.
- The Promised Messiah[as] explained that the example of camels in this chapter is most pertinent regarding communal life of Muslims.

    - It is an accepted fact that camels by nature are an obedient species. The followership and obedience is in their nature, they instinctively go behind their leader, who is more experienced and knowledgeable about the tracks and pathways.

    - The Promised Messiah[as] explained that to maintain a united and moral state of a community, a leader is essential.

---

[1] *Tafsīrul-Qur'ān* by The Promised Messiah, Ḥaḍrat Mirzā Ghulām Aḥmad[as] of Qadian, Pages 356-357 available on www.alislam.org

- Along with followership the camel also has the qualities of hard work, patience and fortitude; virtues absolutely mandatory for community life.

- To adopt the followership of a leader has to be the way of life of Muslims. There are many benefits in this.

بِسْمِ ٱللَّهِ ٱلرَّحْمَٰنِ ٱلرَّحِيمِ ۝

هَلْ أَتَىٰكَ حَدِيثُ ٱلْغَٰشِيَةِ ۝ وُجُوهٌ يَوْمَئِذٍ خَٰشِعَةٌ ۝ عَامِلَةٌ
نَّاصِبَةٌ ۝ تَصْلَىٰ نَارًا حَامِيَةً ۝ تُسْقَىٰ مِنْ عَيْنٍ ءَانِيَةٍ ۝ لَّيْسَ
لَهُمْ طَعَامٌ إِلَّا مِن ضَرِيعٍ ۝ لَّا يُسْمِنُ وَلَا يُغْنِى مِن جُوعٍ ۝
وُجُوهٌ يَوْمَئِذٍ نَّاعِمَةٌ ۝ لِّسَعْيِهَا رَاضِيَةٌ ۝ فِى جَنَّةٍ عَالِيَةٍ ۝ لَّا
تَسْمَعُ فِيهَا لَٰغِيَةً ۝ فِيهَا عَيْنٌ جَارِيَةٌ ۝ فِيهَا سُرُرٌ مَّرْفُوعَةٌ ۝
وَأَكْوَابٌ مَّوْضُوعَةٌ ۝ وَنَمَارِقُ مَصْفُوفَةٌ ۝ وَزَرَابِىُّ مَبْثُوثَةٌ ۝
أَفَلَا يَنظُرُونَ إِلَى ٱلْإِبِلِ كَيْفَ خُلِقَتْ ۝ وَإِلَى ٱلسَّمَآءِ
كَيْفَ رُفِعَتْ ۝ وَإِلَى ٱلْجِبَالِ كَيْفَ نُصِبَتْ ۝ وَإِلَى

ٱلۡأَرۡضِ كَيۡفَ سُطِحَتۡ ۝ فَذَكِّرۡ إِنَّمَآ أَنتَ مُذَكِّرٞ ۝ لَّسۡتَ
عَلَيۡهِم بِمُصَيۡطِرٍ ۝ إِلَّا مَن تَوَلَّىٰ وَكَفَرَ ۝ فَيُعَذِّبُهُ ٱللَّهُ ٱلۡعَذَابَ
ٱلۡأَكۡبَرَ ۝ إِنَّ إِلَيۡنَآ إِيَابَهُمۡ ۝ ثُمَّ إِنَّ عَلَيۡنَا حِسَابَهُم ۝

Translation

In the name of Allah, the Gracious, the Merciful. Has there come to thee the news of the overwhelming *calamity*? *Some* faces on that day will be downcast; Toiling, weary. *They* shall enter a burning Fire; *And* will be made to drink from a boiling spring; They will have no food save that of dry, bitter and thorny herbage, Which will neither fatten, nor satisfy hunger. *And some* faces on that day will be joyful, Well pleased with their labour, In a lofty Garden, Wherein thou wilt hear no idle talk; Therein is a running spring, Therein are raised couches, And goblets properly placed, And cushions *beautifully* ranged, And carpets *tastefully* spread. Do they not then look at the camel, how it is created? And at the heaven, how it is

raised high? And at the mountains, how they are firmly rooted? And at the earth, how it is spread out? Admonish, therefore, for thou art but an admonisher; You are not a warden over them. But whoever turns away and disbelieves, Allah will punish him with the greatest punishment. Unto Us surely is their return, Then, surely, it is for Us to call them to account.

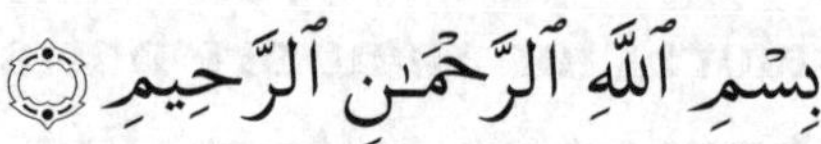

[88:1] In the name of Allah, the Gracious, the Merciful.

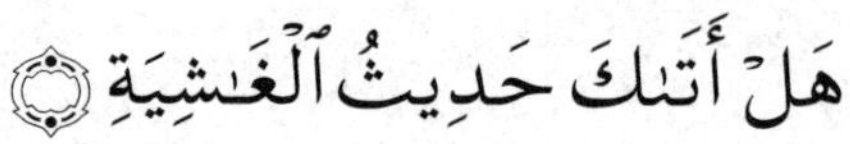

[88:2] Has there come to thee the news of the overwhelming *calamity*?

[2]**Commentary**

The reference in the verse may be to the Judgement Day or to a terrific calamity that overtakes a people in this life, on account of their misdeeds. The severe famine that held Makkah in its grip for about seven years in the time of the Holy Prophet[sa] has also been referred to in the Qur'an as

[2] The Holy Quran with English Translation and Commentary. 3rd ed. Islām International Publications Limited; 2002. Volume 5, Pages 2812-2815

غاشيه (*ghashiyah*) (44: 11-12). It was indeed a terrific calamity for the Makkans.

وُجُوهٌ يَوْمَئِذٍ خَاشِعَةٌ ۝

[88:3] ***Some*** **faces on that day will be downcast;**

Commentary

وجوه (*wujūh*) Meaning 'chiefs' or 'leaders of men; the verse signifies that on the Day of Reckoning the great leaders of disbelief will be debased and humiliation will be writ large on their faces.

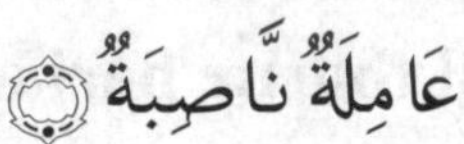

[88:4] Toiling, weary.

Commentary

The verse means to say that all the endeavours of the leaders of disbelief against Islam will be wasted as they will fail to arrest or retard its progress.

تَصۡلَىٰ نَارًا حَامِيَةً ۝

[88:5] ***They*** **shall enter a burning Fire;**

تُسۡقَىٰ مِنۡ عَيۡنٍ ءَانِيَةٍ ۝

[88:6] ***And*** **will be made to drink from a boiling spring;**

لَّيۡسَ لَهُمۡ طَعَامٌ إِلَّا مِن ضَرِيعٍ ۝

[88:7] They will have no food save that of dry, bitter and thorny herbage,

لَّا يُسۡمِنُ وَلَا يُغۡنِي مِن جُوعٍ ۝

[88:8] Which will neither fatten, nor satisfy hunger.

Commentary

Verses 3---8 signify that the enemies of Islam will try hard to check its progress. But all their efforts will prove

abortive. Before their very eyes its tender plant will grow into a mighty tree and their own power and glory will depart. Their sons and grandsons will enter the fold of Islam, and they will be consumed with rage and will burn in the fire of envy at seeing it spread fast; utter humiliation and ignominy will be their lot; they will be given hot water to drink and ضريع *(ḍarī')* to eat which, instead of giving them nourishment or slaking their thirst and satisfying their hunger, will add to their weakness and hasten the withering away of their bodies—they will be utterly deprived of peace of mind, and calamities will overwhelm them in varying forms.

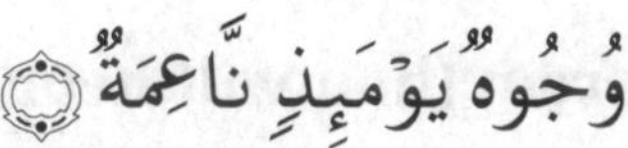

[88:9] And some faces on that day will be joyful,

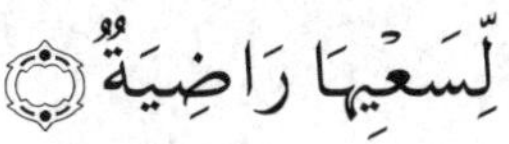

[88:10] Well pleased with their labour

Commentary

The righteous believers will be well pleased with the marvellous results of the sacrifices they had made for the cause of Islam.

فِي جَنَّةٍ عَالِيَةٍ ۝

[88:11] In a lofty Garden,

لَّا تَسْمَعُ فِيهَا لَاغِيَةً ۝

[88:12] Wherein thou wilt hear no idle talk;

فِيهَا عَيْنٌ جَارِيَةٌ ۝

[88:13] Therein is a running spring,

Commentary

Like a running spring their beneficence and goodness will flow unceasingly.

فِيهَا سُرُرٌ مَّرْفُوعَةٌ ۝

[88:14] Therein are raised couches,

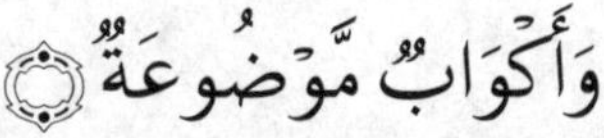

[88:15] And goblets properly placed,

وَنَمَارِقُ مَصْفُوفَةٌ ۝

[88:16] And cushions *beautifully* ranged,

وَزَرَابِيُّ مَبْثُوثَةٌ ۝

[88:17] And carpets *tastefully* spread.

Commentary

The Sūrah contains a contrast between the heavenly rewards that the righteous will receive and the severe punishment which will be meted out to the sinful for

rejecting the Divine Message. The construction of this and the preceding eight verses shows that Muslims collectively will share in the gifts and rewards mentioned in them.

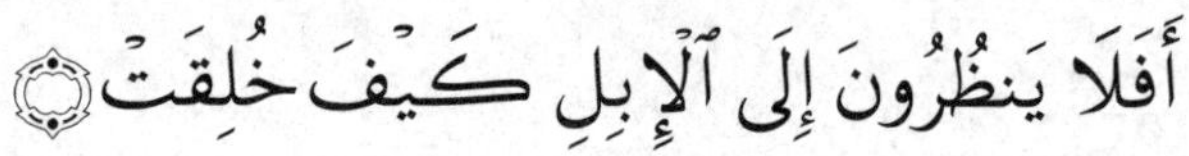

[88:18] Do they not then look at the camel, how it is created?

Commentary

The verse means that believers, like camels, going straight in a line all behind the one that leads them, give unquestioning obedience to their leader.

Or like camels which can go on for days without water in the hot sandy desert of Arabia, the believers have infinite patience under trials and go on their spiritual journey without complaining.

ابل (*ibil*) as meaning clouds, the verse would signify that God will spread the teachings of the Qur'ān which is spiritual water over the whole of the earth.

وَإِلَى ٱلسَّمَآءِ كَيۡفَ رُفِعَتۡ

[88:19] And at the heaven, how it is raised high?

Commentary:

And just as the heaven has been raised high, so will the Holy Prophet[sa], the spiritual heaven, be exalted. Or the verse may mean that just as God has placed the sun, the moon, the stars and planets in the physical heaven and through them He sustains the physical world, so will the spiritual sun (the Holy Prophet[sa]), the spiritual moon (the Promised Messiah[as]), the spiritual planets and stars (Muslims divines) sustain the spiritual world.

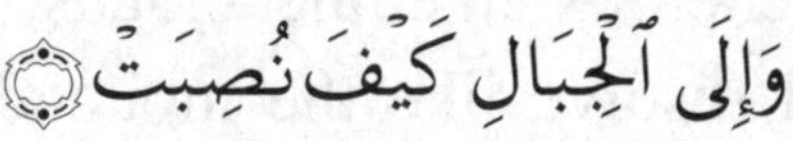

[88:20] And at the mountains, how they are firmly rooted?

Commentary

The verse may signify that like mountains the believers are firm in their faith. Or like mountains which secure the earth against earthquakes and violent commotions and render it

stable, the righteous servants of God are the cause of the stability of the spiritual world. But for them the violent earthquakes of disbelief and sin should shake the spiritual earth to its foundations and cause great havoc in it.

[88:21] And at the earth, how it is spread out?

Commentary

The verse purports to say that the earth has been spread out for the Companions of the Holy Prophet[sa] that they might carry the Message of Islam far and wide. The four verses (vv. 18-21) teach a Muslim the supreme moral lesson that he should be generous like the clouds, exalted like the heaven, of fixed resolve like the mountains, and soft and humble like the earth.

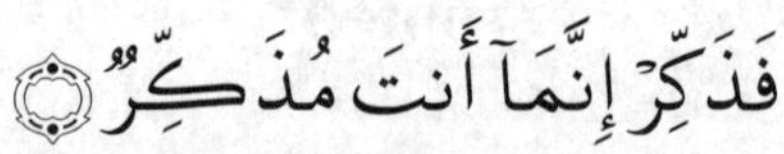

[88:22] Admonish, therefore, for thou art but an admonisher;

لَّسْتَ عَلَيْهِم بِمُصَيْطِرٍ

[88:23] You are not a warden over them

Commentary

The verse constitutes a wonderful commentary on the Divine origin of the Qur'ān. The Sūrah was revealed at Makkah in the early years of the Call when only a handful of weak and poor persons had accepted Islam and yet the verse hints that a time would come when the Holy Prophet[sa] would be given power and authority, and he is enjoined in advance that when he should have power he should not use it for imposing his opinions on others.

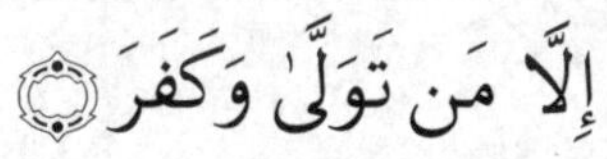

[88:24] But whoever turns away and disbelieves,

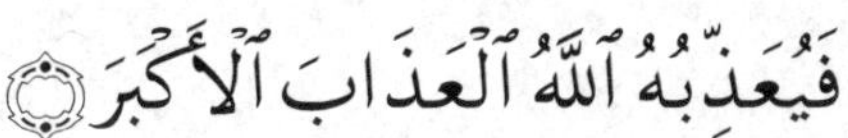

[88:25] Allah will punish him with the greatest punishment.

إِنَّ إِلَيْنَآ إِيَابَهُمْ ۝

[88:26] Unto Us surely is their return,

Commentary

These last two verses show that the subject which had commenced in Sūrah al-A'lā has come to an end here and disbelievers are told that they shall return to God to render account of their deeds and actions.

ثُمَّ إِنَّ عَلَيْنَا حِسَابَهُم ۝

[88:27] Then, surely, it is for Us to call them to account

What is the key message of this portion of the Holy Qur'ān?

How does this message apply to your personal life?

Ṣalāt Tilāwat Schedule of Ḥaḍrat Khalīfatul Masīḥ V[ABA]

DAY	SALAT	FIRST RAK'AH	2ND RAK'AH
FRIDAY	Fajr	Sūrah Banī Isrā'īl 17:79-85	Sūrah al-Kahf 18:1-11
	Maghrib	Sūrah al-Fīl Ch:105	Sūrah Quraish Ch:106
	'Ishā'	Sūrah aḍ-Ḍuḥā Ch:93	Sūrah at-Tīn Ch:95
SATURDAY	Fajr	Sūrah al-Baqarah 2:1-8	Sūrah al-Baqarah 2:9-17
	Maghrib	Sūrah al-Falaq Ch:113	Sūrah an-Nās Ch:114
	'Ishā'	Sūrah al-Baqarah 2:256 (Āyatul-Kursī)	Sūrah al -Baqarah 2:287
SUNDAY	Fajr	Sūrah al-Kahf 18:103-107	Sūrah al-Kahf 18:108-111
	Maghrib	Sūrah al-Falaq Ch:113	Sūrah an-Nās Ch:114
	'Ishā'	Sūrah Ḥā Mīm as-Sajdah 41:31-33	Sūrah Ḥā Mīm as-Sajdah 41:34-37
MONDAY	Fajr	Sūrah al-Baqarah 2:285-287	Sūrah Āl-e-'Imrān 3:191-195
	Maghrib	Sūrah al-Falaq Ch:113	Sūrah an-Nās Ch:114
	'Ishā'	Sūrah al-Ḥashr 59:19-22	Sūrah al-Ḥashr 59:23-25
TUESDAY	Fajr	Sūrah al-Baqarah 2:255-258	Sūrah Āl-e-'Imrān 3:26-31
	Maghrib	Sūrah al-Kāfirūn Ch:109	Sūrah an-Naṣr Ch:110
	'Ishā'	Sūrah az-Zilzāl Ch:99	Sūrah at-Takāthur Ch:102
WEDNESDAY	Fajr	Sūrah al-Kahf 18:103-107	Sūrah al-Kahf 18:108-111
	Maghrib	Sūrah al-Falaq Ch:113	Sūrah an-Nās Ch:114
	'Ishā'	Sūrah ash-Shams Ch:91	Sūrah aḍ-Ḍuḥā Ch:93
THURSDAY	Fajr	Sūrah al-Baqarah 2:285-287	Sūrah Āl-e-'Imrān 3:191-195
	Maghrib	Sūrah al-Falaq Ch:113	Sūrah an-Nās Ch:114
	'Ishā'	Sūrah aḍ-Ḍuḥā Ch:93	Sūrah al-Inshirāḥ Ch:94
JUMU'AH AND EID PRAYERS		Sūrah al-A'lā Ch:87	al-Ghāshiyah Ch:88

اَعُوْذُ بِاللّٰهِ مِنَ الشَّيْطٰنِ الرَّجِيْمِ

بِسْمِ اللّٰهِ الرَّحْمٰنِ الرَّحِيْمِ

Friday	Fajr	Rak‘ah	First	Sūrah Banī Isrā’īl 17:79-85

اَقِمِ الصَّلٰوةَ لِدُلُوْكِ الشَّمْسِ اِلٰى غَسَقِ الَّيْلِ وَ قُرْاٰنَ الْفَجْرِ ؕ اِنَّ قُرْاٰنَ
الْفَجْرِ كَانَ مَشْهُوْدًا ﴿۷۹﴾ وَ مِنَ الَّيْلِ فَتَهَجَّدْ بِهٖ نَافِلَةً لَّكَ ۖۗ عَسٰۤى اَنْ
يَّبْعَثَكَ رَبُّكَ مَقَامًا مَّحْمُوْدًا ﴿۸۰﴾ وَ قُلْ رَّبِّ اَدْخِلْنِیْ مُدْخَلَ صِدْقٍ وَّ
اَخْرِجْنِیْ مُخْرَجَ صِدْقٍ وَّ اجْعَلْ لِّیْ مِنْ لَّدُنْكَ سُلْطٰنًا نَّصِيْرًا ﴿۸۱﴾ وَ قُلْ
جَآءَ الْحَقُّ وَ زَهَقَ الْبَاطِلُ ؕ اِنَّ الْبَاطِلَ كَانَ زَهُوْقًا ﴿۸۲﴾ وَنُنَزِّلُ مِنَ
الْقُرْاٰنِ مَا هُوَ شِفَآءٌ وَّ رَحْمَةٌ لِّلْمُؤْمِنِيْنَ ۙ وَ لَا يَزِيْدُ الظّٰلِمِيْنَ اِلَّا
خَسَارًا ﴿۸۳﴾ وَ اِذَاۤ اَنْعَمْنَا عَلَى الْاِنْسَانِ اَعْرَضَ وَ نَاٰبِجَانِبِهٖ ۚ وَ اِذَا مَسَّهُ
الشَّرُّ كَانَ يَـُٔوْسًا ﴿۸۳﴾ قُلْ كُلٌّ يَّعْمَلُ عَلٰى شَاكِلَتِهٖ ؕ فَرَبُّكُمْ اَعْلَمُ
بِمَنْ هُوَ اَهْدٰى سَبِيْلًا ﴿۸۵﴾ ع

Friday	Fajr	Rak‘ah	Second	Sūrah al-Kahf 18:1-11

بِسۡمِ اللّٰهِ الرَّحۡمٰنِ الرَّحِيۡمِ ۝١

اَلۡحَمۡدُ لِلّٰهِ الَّذِىۡۤ اَنۡزَلَ عَلٰى عَبۡدِهِ الۡكِتٰبَ وَلَمۡ يَجۡعَلۡ لَّهٗ عِوَجًا ۝٢ قَيِّمًا
لِّيُنۡذِرَ بَاۡسًا شَدِيۡدًا مِّنۡ لَّدُنۡهُ وَ يُبَشِّرَ الۡمُؤۡمِنِيۡنَ الَّذِيۡنَ يَعۡمَلُوۡنَ
الصّٰلِحٰتِ اَنَّ لَهُمۡ اَجۡرًا حَسَنًا ۝٣ مَّاكِثِيۡنَ فِيۡهِ اَبَدًا ۝٣ وَّ يُنۡذِرَ الَّذِيۡنَ
قَالُوا اتَّخَذَ اللّٰهُ وَلَدًا ۝٥ مَا لَهُمۡ بِهٖ مِنۡ عِلۡمٍ وَّ لَا لِاٰبَآئِهِمۡ ؕ كَبُرَتۡ
كَلِمَةً تَخۡرُجُ مِنۡ اَفۡوَاهِهِمۡ ؕ اِنۡ يَّقُوۡلُوۡنَ اِلَّا كَذِبًا ۝٦ فَلَعَلَّكَ بَاخِعٌ
نَّفۡسَكَ عَلٰٓى اٰثَارِهِمۡ اِنۡ لَّمۡ يُؤۡمِنُوۡا بِهٰذَا الۡحَدِيۡثِ اَسَفًا ۝٧ اِنَّا جَعَلۡنَا
مَا عَلَى الۡاَرۡضِ زِيۡنَةً لَّهَا لِنَبۡلُوَهُمۡ اَيُّهُمۡ اَحۡسَنُ عَمَلًا ۝٨ وَ اِنَّا
لَجٰعِلُوۡنَ مَا عَلَيۡهَا صَعِيۡدًا جُرُزًا ۝٩ اَمۡ حَسِبۡتَ اَنَّ اَصۡحٰبَ الۡكَهۡفِ وَ
الرَّقِيۡمِ ۙ كَانُوۡا مِنۡ اٰيٰتِنَا عَجَبًا ۝١٠ اِذۡ اَوَى الۡفِتۡيَةُ اِلَى الۡكَهۡفِ فَقَالُوۡا
رَبَّنَاۤ اٰتِنَا مِنۡ لَّدُنۡكَ رَحۡمَةً وَّهَيِّئۡ لَنَا مِنۡ اَمۡرِنَا رَشَدًا ۝١١

Friday	Maghrib	Rak'ah	First	Sūrah al-Fīl Ch.105

بِسْمِ اللّٰهِ الرَّحْمٰنِ الرَّحِيْمِ ﴿١﴾

اَلَمْ تَرَ كَيْفَ فَعَلَ رَبُّكَ بِاَصْحٰبِ الْفِيْلِ ﴿٢﴾ اَلَمْ يَجْعَلْ كَيْدَهُمْ فِيْ
تَضْلِيْلٍ ﴿٣﴾ وَّ اَرْسَلَ عَلَيْهِمْ طَيْرًا اَبَابِيْلَ ﴿٣﴾ تَرْمِيْهِمْ بِحِجَارَةٍ مِّنْ
سِجِّيْلٍ ﴿٥﴾ فَجَعَلَهُمْ كَعَصْفٍ مَّاْكُوْلٍ ﴿٦﴾

Friday	Maghrib	Rak'ah	Second	Sūrah Quraish Ch. 106

بِسْمِ اللّٰهِ الرَّحْمٰنِ الرَّحِيْمِ ﴿١﴾

لِاِيْلٰفِ قُرَيْشٍ ﴿٢﴾ اِلٰفِهِمْ رِحْلَةَ الشِّتَآءِ وَ الصَّيْفِ ﴿٣﴾ فَلْيَعْبُدُوْا رَبَّ
هٰذَا الْبَيْتِ ﴿٣﴾ الَّذِيْٓ اَطْعَمَهُمْ مِّنْ جُوْعٍ ۵ وَّ اٰمَنَهُمْ مِّنْ خَوْفٍ ﴿٥﴾

Friday	'Ishā'	Rak'ah	First	Sūrah ad-Ḍuḥā Ch.93

بِسۡمِ اللّٰهِ الرَّحۡمٰنِ الرَّحِيۡمِ ﴿۱﴾

وَ الضُّحٰى ﴿۲﴾ وَ الَّيۡلِ اِذَا سَجٰى ﴿۳﴾ مَا وَدَّعَكَ رَبُّكَ وَ مَا قَلٰى ﴿۴﴾ وَ
لَلۡاٰخِرَةُ خَيۡرٌ لَّكَ مِنَ الۡاُوۡلٰى ﴿۵﴾ وَ لَسَوۡفَ يُعۡطِيۡكَ رَبُّكَ فَتَرۡضٰى ﴿۶﴾ اَلَمۡ
يَجِدۡكَ يَتِيۡمًا فَاٰوٰى ﴿۷﴾ وَ وَجَدَكَ ضَآلًّا فَهَدٰى ﴿۸﴾ وَ وَجَدَكَ عَآئِلًا
فَاَغۡنٰى ﴿۹﴾ فَاَمَّا الۡيَتِيۡمَ فَلَا تَقۡهَرۡ ﴿۱۰﴾ وَ اَمَّا السَّآئِلَ فَلَا تَنۡهَرۡ ﴿۱۱﴾ وَ
اَمَّا بِنِعۡمَةِ رَبِّكَ فَحَدِّثۡ ﴿۱۲﴾

Friday	'Ishā'	Rak'ah	Second	Sūrah at-Tīn Ch.95

بِسۡمِ اللّٰهِ الرَّحۡمٰنِ الرَّحِيۡمِ ﴿۱﴾

وَالتِّيۡنِ وَ الزَّيۡتُوۡنِ ﴿۲﴾ وَ طُوۡرِ سِيۡنِيۡنَ ﴿۳﴾ وَهٰذَا الۡبَلَدِ الۡاَمِيۡنِ ﴿۴﴾ لَقَدۡ
خَلَقۡنَا الۡاِنۡسَانَ فِيۡۤ اَحۡسَنِ تَقۡوِيۡمٍ ﴿۵﴾ ثُمَّ رَدَدۡنٰهُ اَسۡفَلَ سٰفِلِيۡنَ ﴿۶﴾ اِلَّا
الَّذِيۡنَ اٰمَنُوۡا وَ عَمِلُوا الصّٰلِحٰتِ فَلَهُمۡ اَجۡرٌ غَيۡرُ مَمۡنُوۡنٍ ﴿۷﴾ فَمَا
يُكَذِّبُكَ بَعۡدُ بِالدِّيۡنِ ﴿۸﴾ اَلَيۡسَ اللّٰهُ بِاَحۡكَمِ الۡحٰكِمِيۡنَ ﴿۹﴾

Saturday	Fajr	Rak'ah	First	Sūrah al-Baqarah 2:1-8

بِسۡمِ اللّٰهِ الرَّحۡمٰنِ الرَّحِيۡمِ ﴿١﴾

الٓمّٓ ﴿٢﴾ ذٰلِكَ الۡكِتٰبُ لَا رَيۡبَ ۛۚ فِيۡهِ ۛۚ هُدًى لِّلۡمُتَّقِيۡنَ ﴿٣﴾ الَّذِيۡنَ يُؤۡمِنُوۡنَ

بِالۡغَيۡبِ وَيُقِيۡمُوۡنَ الصَّلٰوةَ وَمِمَّا رَزَقۡنٰهُمۡ يُنۡفِقُوۡنَ ﴿٣﴾ وَالَّذِيۡنَ

يُؤۡمِنُوۡنَ بِمَآ اُنۡزِلَ اِلَيۡكَ وَمَآ اُنۡزِلَ مِنۡ قَبۡلِكَ ۚ وَ بِالۡاٰخِرَةِ هُمۡ

يُوۡقِنُوۡنَ ﴿٥﴾ اُولٰٓئِكَ عَلٰى هُدًى مِّنۡ رَّبِّهِمۡ ۖ وَ اُولٰٓئِكَ هُمُ الۡمُفۡلِحُوۡنَ ﴿٦﴾ اِنَّ

الَّذِيۡنَ كَفَرُوۡا سَوَآءٌ عَلَيۡهِمۡ ءَاَنۡذَرۡتَهُمۡ اَمۡ لَمۡ تُنۡذِرۡهُمۡ لَا يُؤۡمِنُوۡنَ ﴿٧﴾

خَتَمَ اللّٰهُ عَلٰى قُلُوۡبِهِمۡ وَعَلٰى سَمۡعِهِمۡ ؕ وَعَلٰٓى اَبۡصَارِهِمۡ غِشَاوَةٌ ۫ وَّلَهُمۡ

عَذَابٌ عَظِيۡمٌ ﴿٨﴾

Saturday	Fajr	Rak‘ah	Second	Sūrah al-Baqarah 2:9-17

وَمِنَ النَّاسِ مَنْ يَّقُوْلُ اٰمَنَّا بِاللّٰهِ وَ بِالْيَوْمِ الْاٰخِرِ وَمَا هُمْ بِمُؤْمِنِيْنَ ﴿٩﴾
يُخٰدِعُوْنَ اللّٰهَ وَالَّذِيْنَ اٰمَنُوْا ۚ وَمَا يَخْدَعُوْنَ اِلَّاۤ اَنْفُسَهُمْ وَمَا
يَشْعُرُوْنَ ﴿١٠﴾ ؕ فِيْ قُلُوْبِهِمْ مَّرَضٌ ۙ فَزَادَهُمُ اللّٰهُ مَرَضًا ۚ وَلَهُمْ عَذَابٌ
اَلِيْمٌ ۢ ۙ بِمَا كَانُوْا يَكْذِبُوْنَ ﴿١١﴾ وَ اِذَا قِيْلَ لَهُمْ لَا تُفْسِدُوْا فِي الْاَرْضِ ۙ
قَالُوْۤا اِنَّمَا نَحْنُ مُصْلِحُوْنَ ﴿١١﴾ اَلَاۤ اِنَّهُمْ هُمُ الْمُفْسِدُوْنَ وَلٰكِنْ لَّا
يَشْعُرُوْنَ ﴿١٣﴾ وَ اِذَا قِيْلَ لَهُمْ اٰمِنُوْا كَمَاۤ اٰمَنَ النَّاسُ قَالُوْۤا اَنُؤْمِنُ كَمَاۤ
اٰمَنَ السُّفَهَآءُ ؕ اَلَاۤ اِنَّهُمْ هُمُ السُّفَهَآءُ وَلٰكِنْ لَّا يَعْلَمُوْنَ ﴿١٣﴾ وَ اِذَا
لَقُوا الَّذِيْنَ اٰمَنُوْا قَالُوْۤا اٰمَنَّا ۖۚ وَ اِذَا خَلَوْا اِلٰى شَيٰطِيْنِهِمْ ۙ قَالُوْۤا اِنَّا
مَعَكُمْ ۙ اِنَّمَا نَحْنُ مُسْتَهْزِءُوْنَ ﴿١٥﴾ اَللّٰهُ يَسْتَهْزِئُ بِهِمْ وَيَمُدُّهُمْ فِيْ
طُغْيَانِهِمْ يَعْمَهُوْنَ ﴿١٦﴾ اُولٰٓئِكَ الَّذِيْنَ اشْتَرَوُا الضَّلٰلَةَ بِالْهُدٰى ۠ فَمَا
رَبِحَتْ تِّجَارَتُهُمْ وَمَا كَانُوْا مُهْتَدِيْنَ ﴿١٧﴾

Saturday	Maghrib	Rak'ah	First	Sūrah al- Falaq Ch:113

بِسۡمِ اللّٰهِ الرَّحۡمٰنِ الرَّحِيۡمِ ﴿۱﴾

قُلۡ اَعُوۡذُ بِرَبِّ الۡفَلَقِ ﴿۲﴾ مِنۡ شَرِّ مَا خَلَقَ ﴿۳﴾ وَ مِنۡ شَرِّ غَاسِقٍ اِذَا
وَقَبَ ﴿۴﴾ وَ مِنۡ شَرِّ النَّفّٰثٰتِ فِى الۡعُقَدِ ﴿۵﴾ وَ مِنۡ شَرِّ حَاسِدٍ اِذَا حَسَدَ ﴿۶﴾

Saturday	Maghrib	Rak'ah	Second	Sūrah an-Nās Ch:114

بِسۡمِ اللّٰهِ الرَّحۡمٰنِ الرَّحِيۡمِ ﴿۱﴾

قُلۡ اَعُوۡذُ بِرَبِّ النَّاسِ ﴿۲﴾ مَلِكِ النَّاسِ ﴿۳﴾ اِلٰهِ النَّاسِ ﴿۴﴾ مِنۡ شَرِّ
الۡوَسۡوَاسِ ۙ۵ الۡخَنَّاسِ ﴿۵﴾ الَّذِىۡ يُوَسۡوِسُ فِىۡ صُدُوۡرِ النَّاسِ ﴿۶﴾ مِنَ
الۡجِنَّةِ وَ النَّاسِ ﴿۷﴾

Saturday	‘Ishā’	Rak‘ah	First	Sūrah al-Baqarah 2:256 (Āyatul-Kursī)

اَللّٰهُ لَآ اِلٰهَ اِلَّا هُوَ ۚ اَلْحَيُّ الْقَيُّوْمُ ۚ۬ لَا تَاْخُذُهٗ سِنَةٌ وَّلَا نَوْمٌ ؕ لَهٗ مَا فِي
السَّمٰوٰتِ وَمَا فِي الْاَرْضِ ؕ مَنْ ذَا الَّذِيْ يَشْفَعُ عِنْدَهٗٓ اِلَّا بِاِذْنِهٖ ؕ يَعْلَمُ مَا
بَيْنَ اَيْدِيْهِمْ وَمَا خَلْفَهُمْ ۚ وَلَا يُحِيْطُوْنَ بِشَيْءٍ مِّنْ عِلْمِهٖٓ اِلَّا بِمَا شَآءَ ۚ
وَسِعَ كُرْسِيُّهُ السَّمٰوٰتِ وَالْاَرْضَ ۚ وَلَا يَئُوْدُهٗ حِفْظُهُمَا ۚ وَهُوَ الْعَلِيُّ
الْعَظِيْمُ ﴿٢٥٦﴾

Saturday	‘Ishā’	Rak‘ah	Second	Sūrah al -Baqarah 2:287

لَا يُكَلِّفُ اللّٰهُ نَفْسًا اِلَّا وُسْعَهَا ؕ لَهَا مَا كَسَبَتْ وَعَلَيْهَا مَا
اكْتَسَبَتْ ؕ رَبَّنَا لَا تُؤَاخِذْنَآ اِنْ نَّسِيْنَآ اَوْ اَخْطَاْنَا ۚ رَبَّنَا وَلَا تَحْمِلْ
عَلَيْنَآ اِصْرًا كَمَا حَمَلْتَهٗ عَلَى الَّذِيْنَ مِنْ قَبْلِنَا ۚ رَبَّنَا وَلَا تُحَمِّلْنَا مَا
لَا طَاقَةَ لَنَا بِهٖ ۚ وَاعْفُ عَنَّا ۥ وَاغْفِرْ لَنَا ۥ وَارْحَمْنَا ۥ اَنْتَ مَوْلٰنَا
فَانْصُرْنَا عَلَى الْقَوْمِ الْكٰفِرِيْنَ ﴿٢٨٧﴾

Sunday	Fajr	Rak‘ah	First	Sūrah al-Kahf 18:103-107

اَفَحَسِبَ الَّذِيۡنَ كَفَرُوۡۤا اَنۡ يَّتَّخِذُوۡا عِبَادِىۡ مِنۡ دُوۡنِىۡۤ اَوۡلِيَآءَ ؕ اِنَّاۤ
اَعۡتَدۡنَا جَهَنَّمَ لِلۡكٰفِرِيۡنَ نُزُلًا ﴿١٠٣﴾ قُلۡ هَلۡ نُنَبِّئُكُمۡ بِالۡاَخۡسَرِيۡنَ
اَعۡمَالًا ؕ ﴿١٠٤﴾ اَلَّذِيۡنَ ضَلَّ سَعۡيُهُمۡ فِى الۡحَيٰوةِ الدُّنۡيَا وَ هُمۡ يَحۡسَبُوۡنَ اَنَّهُمۡ
يُحۡسِنُوۡنَ صُنۡعًا ﴿١٠٥﴾ اُولٰٓـئِكَ الَّذِيۡنَ كَفَرُوۡا بِاٰيٰتِ رَبِّهِمۡ وَلِقَآئِهٖ
فَحَبِطَتۡ اَعۡمَالُهُمۡ فَلَا نُقِيۡمُ لَهُمۡ يَوۡمَ الۡقِيٰمَةِ وَزۡنًا ﴿١٠٦﴾ ذٰلِكَ جَزَآؤُهُمۡ
جَهَنَّمُ بِمَا كَفَرُوۡا وَ اتَّخَذُوۡۤا اٰيٰتِىۡ وَ رُسُلِىۡ هُزُوًا ﴿١٠٧﴾

Sunday	Fajr	Rak‘ah	Second	Sūrah al-Kahf 18:108-111

اِنَّ الَّذِيۡنَ اٰمَنُوۡا وَعَمِلُوا الصّٰلِحٰتِ كَانَتۡ لَهُمۡ جَنّٰتُ الۡفِرۡدَوۡسِ
نُزُلًا ۙ ﴿١٠٨﴾ خٰلِدِيۡنَ فِيۡهَا لَا يَبۡغُوۡنَ عَنۡهَا حِوَلًا ﴿١٠٩﴾ قُلۡ لَّوۡ كَانَ الۡبَحۡرُ

مِدَادًا لِّكَلِمٰتِ رَبِّيْ لَنَفِدَ الْبَحْرُ قَبْلَ اَنْ تَنْفَدَ كَلِمٰتُ رَبِّيْ وَلَوْ جِئْنَا

بِمِثْلِهٖ مَدَدًا ﴿١١٠﴾ قُلْ اِنَّمَآ اَنَا بَشَرٌ مِّثْلُكُمْ يُوْحٰٓى اِلَيَّ اَنَّمَآ اِلٰـهُكُمْ

اِلٰهٌ وَّاحِدٌ ۚ فَمَنْ كَانَ يَرْجُوْا لِقَآءَ رَبِّهٖ فَلْيَعْمَلْ عَمَلًا صَالِحًا وَّ لَا

يُشْرِكْ بِعِبَادَةِ رَبِّهٖٓ اَحَدًا ﴿١١١﴾ ع

Sunday	Maghrib	Rak'ah	First	Sūrah al- Falaq Ch:113

بِسْمِ اللّٰهِ الرَّحْمٰنِ الرَّحِيْمِ ﴿١﴾

قُلْ اَعُوْذُ بِرَبِّ الْفَلَقِ ﴿٢﴾ لا مِنْ شَرِّ مَا خَلَقَ ﴿٣﴾ لا وَ مِنْ شَرِّ غَاسِقٍ اِذَا

وَقَبَ ﴿٤﴾ لا وَ مِنْ شَرِّ النَّفّٰثٰتِ فِي الْعُقَدِ ﴿٥﴾ لا وَ مِنْ شَرِّ حَاسِدٍ اِذَا

حَسَدَ ﴿٦﴾ ع

Sunday	Maghrib	Rak‘ah	Second	Sūrah an-Nās Ch:114

بِسۡمِ اللّٰہِ الرَّحۡمٰنِ الرَّحِیۡمِ ﴿۱﴾

قُلۡ اَعُوۡذُ بِرَبِّ النَّاسِ ۙ﴿۲﴾ مَلِکِ النَّاسِ ۙ﴿۳﴾ اِلٰہِ النَّاسِ ۙ﴿۴﴾ مِنۡ شَرِّ
الۡوَسۡوَاسِ ۬ۙ الۡخَنَّاسِ ۪ۙ﴿۵﴾ الَّذِیۡ یُوَسۡوِسُ فِیۡ صُدُوۡرِ النَّاسِ ۙ﴿۶﴾ مِنَ
الۡجِنَّۃِ وَ النَّاسِ ٪﴿۷﴾

Sunday	‘Ishā’	Rak‘ah	First	Sūrah Ḥā Mīm as-Sajdah 41:31-33

اِنَّ الَّذِیۡنَ قَالُوۡا رَبُّنَا اللّٰہُ ثُمَّ اسۡتَقَامُوۡا تَتَنَزَّلُ عَلَیۡہِمُ الۡمَلٰٓئِکَۃُ اَلَّا
تَخَافُوۡا وَ لَا تَحۡزَنُوۡا وَ اَبۡشِرُوۡا بِالۡجَنَّۃِ الَّتِیۡ کُنۡتُمۡ تُوۡعَدُوۡنَ ﴿۳۱﴾ نَحۡنُ
اَوۡلِیٰٓؤُکُمۡ فِی الۡحَیٰوۃِ الدُّنۡیَا وَ فِی الۡاٰخِرَۃِ ۚ وَ لَکُمۡ فِیۡہَا مَا تَشۡتَہِیۡۤ
اَنۡفُسُکُمۡ وَ لَکُمۡ فِیۡہَا مَا تَدَّعُوۡنَ ﴿ؕ۳۲﴾ نُزُلًا مِّنۡ غَفُوۡرٍ رَّحِیۡمٍ ﴿۳۳﴾

Sunday	'Ishā'	Rak'ah	Second	Sūrah Ḥā Mīm as-Sajdah 41:34-37

وَ مَنۡ اَحۡسَنُ قَوۡلًا مِّمَّنۡ دَعَاۤ اِلَى اللّٰهِ وَ عَمِلَ صَالِحًا وَّ قَالَ اِنَّنِیۡ مِنَ

الۡمُسۡلِمِیۡنَ ﴿۳۳﴾ وَلَا تَسۡتَوِی الۡحَسَنَةُ وَلَا السَّیِّئَةُ ؕ اِدۡفَعۡ بِالَّتِیۡ

هِیَ اَحۡسَنُ فَاِذَا الَّذِیۡ بَیۡنَكَ وَ بَیۡنَهٗ عَدَاوَةٌ كَاَنَّهٗ وَلِیٌّ حَمِیۡمٌ ﴿۳۵﴾

وَمَا یُلَقّٰهَاۤ اِلَّا الَّذِیۡنَ صَبَرُوۡا ۚ وَمَا یُلَقّٰهَاۤ اِلَّا ذُوۡ حَظٍّ عَظِیۡمٍ ﴿۳۶﴾

وَ اِمَّا یَنۡزَغَنَّكَ مِنَ الشَّیۡطٰنِ نَزۡغٌ فَاسۡتَعِذۡ بِاللّٰهِ ؕ اِنَّهٗ هُوَ السَّمِیۡعُ

الۡعَلِیۡمُ ﴿۳۷﴾

Monday	Fajr	Rak'ah	First	Sūrah al-Baqarah 2:285-287

لِلّٰهِ مَا فِی السَّمٰوٰتِ وَمَا فِی الۡاَرۡضِ ؕ وَ اِنۡ تُبۡدُوۡا مَا فِیۡۤ اَنۡفُسِكُمۡ اَوۡ

تُخۡفُوۡهُ یُحَاسِبۡكُمۡ بِهِ اللّٰهُ ؕ فَیَغۡفِرُ لِمَنۡ یَّشَآءُ وَیُعَذِّبُ مَنۡ یَّشَآءُ ؕ

وَاللّٰهُ عَلٰی كُلِّ شَیۡءٍ قَدِیۡرٌ ﴿۲۸۵﴾ اٰمَنَ الرَّسُوۡلُ بِمَاۤ اُنۡزِلَ اِلَیۡهِ مِنۡ رَّبِّهٖ

وَالْمُؤْمِنُوْنَ ؕ كُلٌّ اٰمَنَ بِاللّٰهِ وَمَلٰٓئِكَتِهٖ وَ كُتُبِهٖ وَرُسُلِهٖ ۟ لَا نُفَرِّقُ بَيْنَ

اَحَدٍ مِّنْ رُّسُلِهٖ ۟ وَقَالُوْا سَمِعْنَا وَ اَطَعْنَا ۫ غُفْرَانَكَ رَبَّنَا وَ اِلَيْكَ

الْمَصِيْرُ ﴿٢٨٦﴾ لَا يُكَلِّفُ اللّٰهُ نَفْسًا اِلَّا وُسْعَهَا ؕ لَهَا مَا كَسَبَتْ وَعَلَيْهَا

مَا اكْتَسَبَتْ ؕ رَبَّنَا لَا تُؤَاخِذْنَآ اِنْ نَّسِيْنَآ اَوْ اَخْطَاْنَا ۚ رَبَّنَا وَلَا

تَحْمِلْ عَلَيْنَآ اِصْرًا كَمَا حَمَلْتَهٗ عَلَى الَّذِيْنَ مِنْ قَبْلِنَا ۚ رَبَّنَا وَلَا

تُحَمِّلْنَا مَا لَا طَاقَةَ لَنَا بِهٖ ۚ وَاعْفُ عَنَّا ۠ وَاغْفِرْ لَنَا ۠ وَارْحَمْنَا ۠

اَنْتَ مَوْلٰىنَا فَانْصُرْنَا عَلَى الْقَوْمِ الْكٰفِرِيْنَ ﴿٢٨٧﴾ ع

Monday	Fajr	Rak'ah	Second	Sūrah Āl-e-'Imrān 3:191-195

اِنَّ فِیْ خَلْقِ السَّمٰوٰتِ وَالْاَرْضِ وَاخْتِلَافِ الَّيْلِ وَالنَّهَارِ لَاٰيٰتٍ لِّاُولِی

الْاَلْبَابِ ﴿١٩١﴾ لا ج الَّذِيْنَ يَذْكُرُوْنَ اللّٰهَ قِيٰمًا وَّقُعُوْدًا وَّعَلٰی جُنُوْبِهِمْ

وَيَتَفَكَّرُوْنَ فِیْ خَلْقِ السَّمٰوٰتِ وَالْاَرْضِ ۚ رَبَّنَا مَا خَلَقْتَ هٰذَا

بَاطِلًا ۚ سُبْحٰنَكَ فَقِنَا عَذَابَ النَّارِ ﴿١٩٢﴾ رَبَّنَآ اِنَّكَ مَنْ تُدْخِلِ النَّارَ فَقَدْ

اَخْزَيْتَهٗ ؕ وَمَا لِلظّٰلِمِيْنَ مِنْ اَنْصَارٍ ﴿١٩٣﴾ رَبَّنَآ اِنَّنَا سَمِعْنَا مُنَادِيًا
يُّنَادِيْ لِلْاِيْمَانِ اَنْ اٰمِنُوْا بِرَبِّكُمْ فَاٰمَنَّا ۖۗ رَبَّنَا فَاغْفِرْ لَنَا ذُنُوْبَنَا
وَ كَفِّرْ عَنَّا سَيِّاٰتِنَا وَتَوَفَّنَا مَعَ الْاَبْرَارِ ﴿١٩٤﴾ ۚ رَبَّنَا وَاٰتِنَا مَا وَعَدْتَّنَا
عَلٰى رُسُلِكَ وَلَا تُخْزِنَا يَوْمَ الْقِيٰمَةِ ؕ اِنَّكَ لَا تُخْلِفُ الْمِيْعَادَ ﴿١٩٥﴾

Monday	Maghrib	Rak'ah	First	Sūrah al- Falaq Ch:113

بِسْمِ اللّٰهِ الرَّحْمٰنِ الرَّحِيْمِ ﴿١﴾

قُلْ اَعُوْذُ بِرَبِّ الْفَلَقِ ﴿٢﴾ ۙ مِنْ شَرِّ مَا خَلَقَ ﴿٣﴾ ۙ وَ مِنْ شَرِّ غَاسِقٍ اِذَا
وَقَبَ ﴿٤﴾ ۙ وَ مِنْ شَرِّ النَّفّٰثٰتِ فِي الْعُقَدِ ﴿٥﴾ ۙ وَ مِنْ شَرِّ حَاسِدٍ اِذَا
حَسَدَ ﴿٦﴾ ۧ

Monday	Maghrib	Rak'ah	Second	Sūrah an-Nās Ch:114

بِسْمِ اللهِ الرَّحْمٰنِ الرَّحِيْمِ ﴿١﴾

قُلْ اَعُوْذُ بِرَبِّ النَّاسِ ﴿٢﴾ مَلِكِ النَّاسِ ﴿٣﴾ اِلٰهِ النَّاسِ ﴿٤﴾ مِنْ شَرِّ
الْوَسْوَاسِ الْخَنَّاسِ ﴿٥﴾ الَّذِىْ يُوَسْوِسُ فِىْ صُدُوْرِ النَّاسِ ﴿٦﴾ مِنَ
الْجِنَّةِ وَ النَّاسِ ﴿٧﴾

Monday	'Ishā'	Rak'ah	First	Sūrah al-Ḥashr 59:19-22

يٰاَيُّهَا الَّذِيْنَ اٰمَنُوا اتَّقُوا اللهَ وَ لْتَنْظُرْ نَفْسٌ مَّا قَدَّمَتْ لِغَدٍ ۚ وَ اتَّقُوا
اللهَ ۗ اِنَّ اللهَ خَبِيْرٌۢ بِمَا تَعْمَلُوْنَ ﴿١٩﴾ وَ لَا تَكُوْنُوْا كَالَّذِيْنَ نَسُوا اللهَ
فَاَنْسٰهُمْ اَنْفُسَهُمْ ۗ اُولٰٓئِكَ هُمُ الْفٰسِقُوْنَ ﴿٢٠﴾ لَا يَسْتَوِىْٓ اَصْحٰبُ النَّارِ
وَ اَصْحٰبُ الْجَنَّةِ ۗ اَصْحٰبُ الْجَنَّةِ هُمُ الْفَآئِزُوْنَ ﴿٢١﴾ لَوْ اَنْزَلْنَا هٰذَا
الْقُرْاٰنَ عَلٰى جَبَلٍ لَّرَاَيْتَهٗ خَاشِعًا مُّتَصَدِّعًا مِّنْ خَشْيَةِ اللهِ ۗ وَ تِلْكَ
الْاَمْثَالُ نَضْرِبُهَا لِلنَّاسِ لَعَلَّهُمْ يَتَفَكَّرُوْنَ ﴿٢٢﴾

Monday	**'Ishā'**	**Rak'ah**	**Second**	**Sūrah al-Ḥashr 59:23-25**

هُوَ اللّٰهُ الَّذِىْ لَآ اِلٰهَ اِلَّا هُوَ ۚ عٰلِمُ الْغَيْبِ وَ الشَّهَادَةِ ۚ هُوَ الرَّحْمٰنُ

الرَّحِيْمُ ﴿٢٢﴾ هُوَ اللّٰهُ الَّذِىْ لَآ اِلٰهَ اِلَّا هُوَ ۚ اَلْمَلِكُ الْقُدُّوْسُ السَّلٰمُ

الْمُؤْمِنُ الْمُهَيْمِنُ الْعَزِيْزُ الْجَبَّارُ الْمُتَكَبِّرُ ۭ سُبْحٰنَ اللّٰهِ عَمَّا

يُشْرِكُوْنَ ﴿٢٣﴾ هُوَ اللّٰهُ الْخَالِقُ الْبَارِئُ الْمُصَوِّرُ لَهُ الْاَسْمَآءُ الْحُسْنٰى ۭ

يُسَبِّحُ لَهٗ مَا فِى السَّمٰوٰتِ وَ الْاَرْضِ ۚ وَ هُوَ الْعَزِيْزُ الْحَكِيْمُ ﴿٢٤﴾

Tuesday	**Fajr**	**Rak'ah**	**First**	**Sūrah al-Baqarah 2:255-258**

يٰٓاَيُّهَا الَّذِيْنَ اٰمَنُوْٓا اَنْفِقُوْا مِمَّا رَزَقْنٰكُمْ مِّنْ قَبْلِ اَنْ يَّاْتِىَ يَوْمٌ لَّا بَيْعٌ

فِيْهِ وَلَا خُلَّةٌ وَّلَا شَفَاعَةٌ ۭ وَالْكٰفِرُوْنَ هُمُ الظّٰلِمُوْنَ ﴿٢٥٤﴾ اَللّٰهُ لَآ اِلٰهَ اِلَّا

هُوَ ۚ اَلْحَىُّ الْقَيُّوْمُ ۥ لَا تَاْخُذُهٗ سِنَةٌ وَّلَا نَوْمٌ ۭ لَهٗ مَا فِى السَّمٰوٰتِ وَمَا

فِي الْاَرْضِ ؕ مَنْ ذَا الَّذِيْ يَشْفَعُ عِنْدَهٗۤ اِلَّا بِاِذْنِهٖ ؕ يَعْلَمُ مَا بَيْنَ اَيْدِيْهِمْ

وَمَا خَلْفَهُمْ ۚ وَلَا يُحِيْطُوْنَ بِشَيْءٍ مِّنْ عِلْمِهٖۤ اِلَّا بِمَا شَآءَ ۚ وَسِعَ

كُرْسِيُّهُ السَّمٰوٰتِ وَالْاَرْضَ ۚ وَلَا يَـُٔوْدُهٗ حِفْظُهُمَا ۚ وَهُوَ الْعَلِيُّ

الْعَظِيْمُ ﴿٢٥٦﴾ لَآ اِكْرَاهَ فِي الدِّيْنِ ۙۛ قَدْ تَّبَيَّنَ الرُّشْدُ مِنَ الْغَيِّ ۚ فَمَنْ

يَّكْفُرْ بِالطَّاغُوْتِ وَيُؤْمِنْۢ بِاللّٰهِ فَقَدِ اسْتَمْسَكَ بِالْعُرْوَةِ الْوُثْقٰى ۗ

لَا انْفِصَامَ لَهَا ؕ وَاللّٰهُ سَمِيْعٌ عَلِيْمٌ ﴿٢٥٧﴾ اَللّٰهُ وَلِيُّ الَّذِيْنَ اٰمَنُوْا ۙ

يُخْرِجُهُمْ مِّنَ الظُّلُمٰتِ اِلَى النُّوْرِ ؕ۬ وَالَّذِيْنَ كَفَرُوْۤا اَوْلِيٰٓـُٔهُمُ

الطَّاغُوْتُ ۙ يُخْرِجُوْنَهُمْ مِّنَ النُّوْرِ اِلَى الظُّلُمٰتِ ؕ اُولٰٓئِكَ اَصْحٰبُ

النَّارِ ۚ هُمْ فِيْهَا خٰلِدُوْنَ ﴿٢٥٨﴾ ع

Tuesday	Fajr	Rak‘ah	Second	Sūrah Āl-e-‘Imrān 3:26-31

فَكَيْفَ اِذَا جَمَعْنٰهُمْ لِيَوْمٍ لَّا رَيْبَ فِيْهِ قف وَوُفِّيَتْ كُلُّ نَفْسٍ مَّا
كَسَبَتْ وَهُمْ لَا يُظْلَمُوْنَ ﴿٢٦﴾ قُلِ اللّٰهُمَّ مٰلِكَ الْمُلْكِ تُؤْتِی الْمُلْكَ مَنْ
تَشَآءُ وَتَنْزِعُ الْمُلْكَ مِمَّنْ تَشَآءُ ز وَتُعِزُّ مَنْ تَشَآءُ وَتُذِلُّ مَنْ تَشَآءُ ط
بِيَدِكَ الْخَيْرُ ط اِنَّكَ عَلٰی كُلِّ شَیْءٍ قَدِيْرٌ ﴿٢٧﴾ تُوْلِجُ الَّيْلَ فِی النَّهَارِ
وَتُوْلِجُ النَّهَارَ فِی الَّيْلِ ز وَتُخْرِجُ الْحَیَّ مِنَ الْمَيِّتِ وَتُخْرِجُ الْمَيِّتَ مِنَ
الْحَیِّ ز وَتَرْزُقُ مَنْ تَشَآءُ بِغَيْرِ حِسَابٍ ﴿٢٨﴾ لَا يَتَّخِذِ الْمُؤْمِنُوْنَ
الْكٰفِرِيْنَ اَوْلِيَآءَ مِنْ دُوْنِ الْمُؤْمِنِيْنَ ج وَمَنْ يَّفْعَلْ ذٰلِكَ فَلَيْسَ مِنَ اللّٰهِ
فِیْ شَیْءٍ اِلَّآ اَنْ تَتَّقُوْا مِنْهُمْ تُقٰىةً ط وَ يُحَذِّرُكُمُ اللّٰهُ نَفْسَهٗ ط وَ اِلَی اللّٰهِ
الْمَصِيْرُ ﴿٢٩﴾ قُلْ اِنْ تُخْفُوْا مَا فِیْ صُدُوْرِكُمْ اَوْ تُبْدُوْهُ يَعْلَمْهُ اللّٰهُ ط
وَيَعْلَمُ مَا فِی السَّمٰوٰتِ وَمَا فِی الْاَرْضِ ط وَاللّٰهُ عَلٰی كُلِّ شَیْءٍ قَدِيْرٌ ﴿٣٠﴾
يَوْمَ تَجِدُ كُلُّ نَفْسٍ مَّا عَمِلَتْ مِنْ خَيْرٍ مُّحْضَرًا ج وَّمَا عَمِلَتْ مِنْ
سُوْٓءٍ ج تَوَدُّ لَوْ اَنَّ بَيْنَهَا وَبَيْنَهٗٓ اَمَدًا بَعِيْدًا ط وَيُحَذِّرُكُمُ اللّٰهُ نَفْسَهٗ ط
وَاللّٰهُ رَءُوْفٌ بِالْعِبَادِ ﴿٣١﴾

Tuesday	Maghrib	Rak‘ah	First	Sūrah al-Kāfirūn Ch:109

بِسۡمِ اللّٰهِ الرَّحۡمٰنِ الرَّحِیۡمِ ۝۱

قُلۡ یٰۤاَیُّهَا الۡکٰفِرُوۡنَ ۝۲ لَاۤ اَعۡبُدُ مَا تَعۡبُدُوۡنَ ۝۳ وَ لَاۤ اَنۡتُمۡ عٰبِدُوۡنَ مَاۤ
اَعۡبُدُ ۝۴ وَ لَاۤ اَنَا عَابِدٌ مَّا عَبَدۡتُّمۡ ۝۵ وَ لَاۤ اَنۡتُمۡ عٰبِدُوۡنَ مَاۤ اَعۡبُدُ ۝۶
لَکُمۡ دِیۡنُکُمۡ وَلِیَ دِیۡنِ ۝۷

Tuesday	Maghrib	Rak‘ah	Second	Sūrah an-Naṣr Ch:110

بِسۡمِ اللّٰهِ الرَّحۡمٰنِ الرَّحِیۡمِ ۝۱

اِذَا جَآءَ نَصۡرُ اللّٰهِ وَ الۡفَتۡحُ ۝۲ وَ رَاَیۡتَ النَّاسَ یَدۡخُلُوۡنَ فِیۡ دِیۡنِ اللّٰهِ
اَفۡوَاجًا ۝۳ فَسَبِّحۡ بِحَمۡدِ رَبِّکَ وَ اسۡتَغۡفِرۡهُ ؕ اِنَّهٗ کَانَ تَوَّابًا ۝۴

Tuesday	'Ishā'	Rak'ah	First	Sūrah az-Zilzāl Ch:99

بِسۡمِ اللّٰہِ الرَّحۡمٰنِ الرَّحِیۡمِ ﴿۱﴾

اِذَا زُلۡزِلَتِ الۡاَرۡضُ زِلۡزَالَهَا ﴿۲﴾ وَ اَخۡرَجَتِ الۡاَرۡضُ اَثۡقَالَهَا ﴿۳﴾ وَ قَالَ
الۡاِنۡسَانُ مَا لَهَا ﴿۴﴾ یَوۡمَئِذٍ تُحَدِّثُ اَخۡبَارَهَا ﴿۵﴾ بِاَنَّ رَبَّکَ اَوۡحٰی لَهَا ﴿۶﴾
یَوۡمَئِذٍ یَّصۡدُرُ النَّاسُ اَشۡتَاتًا ۬ۙ لِّیُرَوۡا اَعۡمَالَهُمۡ ﴿۷﴾ فَمَنۡ یَّعۡمَلۡ مِثۡقَالَ
ذَرَّۃٍ خَیۡرًا یَّرَهٗ ﴿۸﴾ وَ مَنۡ یَّعۡمَلۡ مِثۡقَالَ ذَرَّۃٍ شَرًّا یَّرَهٗ ﴿۹﴾

Tuesday	'Ishā'	Rak'ah	Second	Sūrah at- Takāthur Ch:102

بِسۡمِ اللّٰہِ الرَّحۡمٰنِ الرَّحِیۡمِ ﴿۱﴾

اَلۡهٰکُمُ التَّکَاثُرُ ﴿۲﴾ حَتّٰی زُرۡتُمُ الۡمَقَابِرَ ﴿۳﴾ کَلَّا سَوۡفَ
تَعۡلَمُوۡنَ ﴿۴﴾ ثُمَّ کَلَّا سَوۡفَ تَعۡلَمُوۡنَ ﴿۵﴾ کَلَّا لَوۡ تَعۡلَمُوۡنَ عِلۡمَ
الۡیَقِیۡنِ ﴿۶﴾ لَتَرَوُنَّ الۡجَحِیۡمَ ﴿۷﴾ ثُمَّ لَتَرَوُنَّهَا عَیۡنَ الۡیَقِیۡنِ ﴿۸﴾ ثُمَّ
لَتُسۡـَٔلُنَّ یَوۡمَئِذٍ عَنِ النَّعِیۡمِ ﴿۹﴾

Wednesday	Fajr	Rak‘ah	First	Sūrah al-Kahf 18:103-107

اَفَحَسِبَ الَّذِيْنَ كَفَرُوْٓا اَنْ يَّتَّخِذُوْا عِبَادِىْ مِنْ دُوْنِىْٓ اَوْلِيَآءَ ؕ اِنَّآ
اَعْتَدْنَا جَهَنَّمَ لِلْكٰفِرِيْنَ نُزُلًا ﴿١٠٣﴾ قُلْ هَلْ نُنَبِّئُكُمْ بِالْاَخْسَرِيْنَ
اَعْمَالًا ؕ ﴿١٠٤﴾ اَلَّذِيْنَ ضَلَّ سَعْيُهُمْ فِى الْحَيٰوةِ الدُّنْيَا وَ هُمْ يَحْسَبُوْنَ اَنَّهُمْ
يُحْسِنُوْنَ صُنْعًا ﴿١٠٥﴾ اُولٰٓئِكَ الَّذِيْنَ كَفَرُوْا بِاٰيٰتِ رَبِّهِمْ وَلِقَآئِهٖ
فَحَبِطَتْ اَعْمَالُهُمْ فَلَا نُقِيْمُ لَهُمْ يَوْمَ الْقِيٰمَةِ وَزْنًا ﴿١٠٦﴾ ذٰلِكَ جَزَآؤُهُمْ
جَهَنَّمُ بِمَا كَفَرُوْا وَ اتَّخَذُوْٓا اٰيٰتِىْ وَ رُسُلِىْ هُزُوًا ﴿١٠٧﴾

Wednesday	Fajr	Rak‘ah	Second	Sūrah al-Kahf 18:108-111

اِنَّ الَّذِيْنَ اٰمَنُوْا وَ عَمِلُوا الصّٰلِحٰتِ كَانَتْ لَهُمْ جَنّٰتُ الْفِرْدَوْسِ نُزُلًا
﴿١٠٨﴾ لا خٰلِدِيْنَ فِيْهَا لَا يَبْغُوْنَ عَنْهَا حِوَلًا ﴿١٠٩﴾ قُلْ لَّوْ كَانَ الْبَحْرُ مِدَادًا
لِّكَلِمٰتِ رَبِّىْ لَنَفِدَ الْبَحْرُ قَبْلَ اَنْ تَنْفَدَ كَلِمٰتُ رَبِّىْ وَلَوْ جِئْنَا بِمِثْلِهٖ
مَدَدًا ﴿١١٠﴾ قُلْ اِنَّمَآ اَنَا بَشَرٌ مِّثْلُكُمْ يُوْحٰٓى اِلَىَّ اَنَّمَآ اِلٰـهُكُمْ اِلٰهٌ

وَّاحِدٌ ۚ فَمَنْ كَانَ يَرْجُوْا لِقَآءَ رَبِّهٖ فَلْيَعْمَلْ عَمَلًا صَالِحًا وَّ لَا يُشْرِكْ

بِعِبَادَةِ رَبِّهٖٓ اَحَدًا ﴿۱۱۰﴾

Wednesday	Maghrib	Rak'ah	First	Sūrah al- Falaq Ch:113

بِسْمِ اللّٰهِ الرَّحْمٰنِ الرَّحِيْمِ ﴿۱﴾

قُلْ اَعُوْذُ بِرَبِّ الْفَلَقِ ﴿۲﴾ مِنْ شَرِّ مَا خَلَقَ ﴿۳﴾ وَ مِنْ شَرِّ غَاسِقٍ اِذَا

وَقَبَ ﴿۴﴾ وَ مِنْ شَرِّ النَّفّٰثٰتِ فِى الْعُقَدِ ﴿۵﴾ وَ مِنْ شَرِّ حَاسِدٍ اِذَا حَسَدَ ﴿۶﴾

Wednesday	Maghrib	Rak'ah	Second	Sūrah an-Nās Ch:114

بِسْمِ اللّٰهِ الرَّحْمٰنِ الرَّحِيْمِ ﴿۱﴾

قُلْ اَعُوْذُ بِرَبِّ النَّاسِ ﴿۲﴾ مَلِكِ النَّاسِ ﴿۳﴾ اِلٰهِ النَّاسِ ﴿۴﴾ مِنْ شَرِّ

الْوَسْوَاسِ ۥ الْخَنَّاسِ ﴿۵﴾ الَّذِىْ يُوَسْوِسُ فِىْ صُدُوْرِ النَّاسِ ﴿۶﴾ مِنَ

الْجِنَّةِ وَ النَّاسِ ﴿۷﴾

Wednesday	‘Ishā’	Rak‘ah	First	Sūrah ash-Shams Ch:91

بِسۡمِ اللّٰهِ الرَّحۡمٰنِ الرَّحِيۡمِ ﴿۱﴾

وَ الشَّمۡسِ وَ ضُحٰهَا ﴿۲﴾ وَ الۡقَمَرِ اِذَا تَلٰهَا ﴿۳﴾ وَ النَّهَارِ اِذَا
جَلّٰهَا ﴿۴﴾ وَ الَّيۡلِ اِذَا يَغۡشٰهَا ﴿۵﴾ وَ السَّمَآءِ وَ مَا بَنٰهَا ﴿۶﴾ وَ
الۡاَرۡضِ وَ مَا طَحٰهَا ﴿۷﴾ وَ نَفۡسٍ وَّ مَا سَوّٰهَا ﴿۸﴾ فَاَلۡهَمَهَا فُجُوۡرَهَا
وَ تَقۡوٰهَا ﴿۹﴾ قَدۡ اَفۡلَحَ مَنۡ زَكّٰهَا ﴿۱۰﴾ وَ قَدۡ خَابَ مَنۡ دَسّٰهَا ﴿۱۱﴾
كَذَّبَتۡ ثَمُوۡدُ بِطَغۡوٰهَآ ﴿۱۲﴾ اِذِ انۡۢبَعَثَ اَشۡقٰهَا ﴿۱۳﴾ فَقَالَ لَهُمۡ رَسُوۡلُ
اللّٰهِ نَاقَةَ اللّٰهِ وَ سُقۡيٰهَا ﴿۱۳﴾ فَكَذَّبُوۡهُ فَعَقَرُوۡهَا ۙ۬ فَدَمۡدَمَ عَلَيۡهِمۡ
رَبُّهُمۡ بِذَنۡۢبِهِمۡ فَسَوّٰهَا ﴿۱۵﴾ وَ لَا يَخَافُ عُقۡبٰهَا ﴿۱۶﴾

Wednesday	‘Ishā’	Rak‘ah	Second	Sūrah aḍ-Ḍuḥā Ch:93

بِسْمِ اللّٰهِ الرَّحْمٰنِ الرَّحِيْمِ ﴿١﴾

وَ الضُّحٰى ﴿٢﴾ وَ الَّيْلِ اِذَا سَجٰى ﴿٣﴾ مَا وَدَّعَكَ رَبُّكَ وَ مَا قَلٰى ﴿٣﴾ وَ
لَلْاٰخِرَةُ خَيْرٌ لَّكَ مِنَ الْاُوْلٰى ﴿٥﴾ وَ لَسَوْفَ يُعْطِيْكَ رَبُّكَ فَتَرْضٰى ﴿٦﴾ اَلَمْ
يَجِدْكَ يَتِيْمًا فَاٰوٰى ﴿٧﴾ وَ وَجَدَكَ ضَآلًّا فَهَدٰى ﴿٨﴾ وَ وَجَدَكَ عَآئِلًا
فَاَغْنٰى ﴿٩﴾ فَاَمَّا الْيَتِيْمَ فَلَا تَقْهَرْ ﴿١٠﴾ وَ اَمَّا السَّآئِلَ فَلَا تَنْهَرْ ﴿١١﴾ وَ
اَمَّا بِنِعْمَةِ رَبِّكَ فَحَدِّثْ ﴿١٢﴾

Thursday	Fajr	Rak‘ah	First	Sūrah al-Baqarah 2:285-287

لِلّٰهِ مَا فِي السَّمٰوٰتِ وَمَا فِي الْاَرْضِ ۗ وَ اِنْ تُبْدُوْا مَا فِيْٓ اَنْفُسِكُمْ اَوْ
تُخْفُوْهُ يُحَاسِبْكُمْ بِهِ اللّٰهُ ۗ فَيَغْفِرُ لِمَنْ يَّشَآءُ وَيُعَذِّبُ مَنْ يَّشَآءُ ۗ
وَاللّٰهُ عَلٰى كُلِّ شَيْءٍ قَدِيْرٌ ﴿٢٨٥﴾ اٰمَنَ الرَّسُوْلُ بِمَآ اُنْزِلَ اِلَيْهِ مِنْ رَّبِّهٖ
وَالْمُؤْمِنُوْنَ ۗ كُلٌّ اٰمَنَ بِاللّٰهِ وَمَلٰٓئِكَتِهٖ وَ كُتُبِهٖ وَرُسُلِهٖ ۛ لَا نُفَرِّقُ بَيْنَ

اَحَدٍ مِّنْ رُّسُلِهٖ قف وَقَالُوْا سَمِعْنَا وَ اَطَعْنَا ق غُفْرَانَكَ رَبَّنَا وَ اِلَيْكَ
الْمَصِيْرُ ﴿٢٨٦﴾ لَا يُكَلِّفُ اللّٰهُ نَفْسًا اِلَّا وُسْعَهَا ط لَهَا مَا كَسَبَتْ وَعَلَيْهَا
مَا اكْتَسَبَتْ ط رَبَّنَا لَا تُؤَاخِذْنَآ اِنْ نَّسِيْنَآ اَوْ اَخْطَاْنَا ج رَبَّنَا وَلَا
تَحْمِلْ عَلَيْنَآ اِصْرًا كَمَا حَمَلْتَهٗ عَلَى الَّذِيْنَ مِنْ قَبْلِنَا ج رَبَّنَا وَلَا
تُحَمِّلْنَا مَا لَا طَاقَةَ لَنَا بِهٖ ج وَاعْفُ عَنَّا وقفة وَاغْفِرْ لَنَا وقفة وَارْحَمْنَا وقفة
اَنْتَ مَوْلٰىنَا فَانْصُرْنَا عَلَى الْقَوْمِ الْكٰفِرِيْنَ ﴿٢٨٧﴾ ع

Thursday	Fajr	Rak‘ah	Second	Sūrah Āl-e-‘Imrān 3:191-195

اِنَّ فِيْ خَلْقِ السَّمٰوٰتِ وَالْاَرْضِ وَاخْتِلَافِ الَّيْلِ وَالنَّهَارِ لَاٰيٰتٍ لِّاُولِي
الْاَلْبَابِ ﴿١٩١﴾ لا ج الَّذِيْنَ يَذْكُرُوْنَ اللّٰهَ قِيٰمًا وَّقُعُوْدًا وَّعَلٰى جُنُوْبِهِمْ
وَيَتَفَكَّرُوْنَ فِيْ خَلْقِ السَّمٰوٰتِ وَالْاَرْضِ ج رَبَّنَا مَا خَلَقْتَ هٰذَا
بَاطِلًا ج سُبْحٰنَكَ فَقِنَا عَذَابَ النَّارِ ﴿١٩٢﴾ رَبَّنَآ اِنَّكَ مَنْ تُدْخِلِ النَّارَ فَقَدْ
اَخْزَيْتَهٗ ط وَمَا لِلظّٰلِمِيْنَ مِنْ اَنْصَارٍ ﴿١٩٣﴾ رَبَّنَآ اِنَّنَا سَمِعْنَا مُنَادِيًا
يُّنَادِيْ لِلْاِيْمَانِ اَنْ اٰمِنُوْا بِرَبِّكُمْ فَاٰمَنَّا صلے ق رَبَّنَا فَاغْفِرْلَنَا ذُنُوْبَنَا

وَ كَفِّرۡ عَنَّا سَيِّاٰتِنَا وَ تَوَفَّنَا مَعَ الۡاَبۡرَارِ ﴿۱۹۳﴾ رَبَّنَا وَ اٰتِنَا مَا وَعَدۡتَّنَا

عَلٰی رُسُلِكَ وَ لَا تُخۡزِنَا يَوۡمَ الۡقِيٰمَةِ ؕ اِنَّكَ لَا تُخۡلِفُ الۡمِيۡعَادَ ﴿۱۹۵﴾

Thursday	Maghrib	Rak'ah	First	Sūrah al- Falaq Ch:113

بِسۡمِ اللّٰهِ الرَّحۡمٰنِ الرَّحِيۡمِ ﴿۱﴾

قُلۡ اَعُوۡذُ بِرَبِّ الۡفَلَقِ ﴿۲﴾ مِنۡ شَرِّ مَا خَلَقَ ﴿۳﴾ وَ مِنۡ شَرِّ غَاسِقٍ اِذَا

وَقَبَ ﴿۴﴾ وَ مِنۡ شَرِّ النَّفّٰثٰتِ فِی الۡعُقَدِ ﴿۵﴾ وَ مِنۡ شَرِّ حَاسِدٍ اِذَا حَسَدَ ﴿۶﴾

Thursday	Maghrib	Rak'ah	Second	Sūrah an-Nās Ch:114

بِسۡمِ اللّٰهِ الرَّحۡمٰنِ الرَّحِيۡمِ ﴿۱﴾

قُلۡ اَعُوۡذُ بِرَبِّ النَّاسِ ﴿۲﴾ مَلِكِ النَّاسِ ﴿۳﴾ اِلٰهِ النَّاسِ ﴿۴﴾ مِنۡ شَرِّ

الۡوَسۡوَاسِ ۬ۙ الۡخَنَّاسِ ﴿۵﴾ الَّذِیۡ يُوَسۡوِسُ فِیۡ صُدُوۡرِ النَّاسِ ﴿۶﴾ مِنَ

الۡجِنَّةِ وَ النَّاسِ ﴿۷﴾

Thursday	‘Ishā’	Rak‘ah	First	Sūrah ad-Ḍuḥā Ch:93

بِسۡمِ اللّٰہِ الرَّحۡمٰنِ الرَّحِیۡمِ ﴿۱﴾

وَ الضُّحٰی ﴿۲﴾ وَ الَّیۡلِ اِذَا سَجٰی ﴿۳﴾ مَا وَدَّعَکَ رَبُّکَ وَ مَا قَلٰی ﴿۴﴾ وَ
لَلۡاٰخِرَۃُ خَیۡرٌ لَّکَ مِنَ الۡاُوۡلٰی ﴿۵﴾ وَ لَسَوۡفَ یُعۡطِیۡکَ رَبُّکَ فَتَرۡضٰی ﴿۶﴾ اَلَمۡ
یَجِدۡکَ یَتِیۡمًا فَاٰوٰی ﴿۷﴾ وَ وَجَدَکَ ضَآلًّا فَہَدٰی ﴿۸﴾ وَ وَجَدَکَ عَآئِلًا
فَاَغۡنٰی ﴿۹﴾ فَاَمَّا الۡیَتِیۡمَ فَلَا تَقۡہَرۡ ﴿۱۰﴾ وَ اَمَّا السَّآئِلَ فَلَا تَنۡہَرۡ ﴿۱۱﴾ وَ
اَمَّا بِنِعۡمَۃِ رَبِّکَ فَحَدِّثۡ ﴿۱۲﴾

Thursday	‘Ishā’	Rak‘ah	Second	Sūrah al-Inshiraḥ Ch:94

بِسۡمِ اللّٰہِ الرَّحۡمٰنِ الرَّحِیۡمِ ﴿۱﴾

اَلَمۡ نَشۡرَحۡ لَکَ صَدۡرَکَ ﴿۲﴾ وَ وَضَعۡنَا عَنۡکَ وِزۡرَکَ ﴿۳﴾ الَّذِیۡۤ اَنۡقَضَ
ظَہۡرَکَ ﴿۴﴾ وَ رَفَعۡنَا لَکَ ذِکۡرَکَ ﴿۵﴾ فَاِنَّ مَعَ الۡعُسۡرِ یُسۡرًا ﴿۶﴾ اِنَّ مَعَ
الۡعُسۡرِ یُسۡرًا ﴿۷﴾ فَاِذَا فَرَغۡتَ فَانۡصَبۡ ﴿۸﴾ وَ اِلٰی رَبِّکَ فَارۡغَبۡ ﴿۹﴾

Jumu‘ah and Eid Prayers	Rak‘ah	First	Sūrah al-A‘lā Ch:87

بِسْمِ اللّٰهِ الرَّحْمٰنِ الرَّحِيْمِ ۝١

سَبِّحِ اسْمَ رَبِّكَ الْاَعْلَى ۙ۝٢ الَّذِىْ خَلَقَ فَسَوّٰى ۙ۝٣ وَ الَّذِىْ قَدَّرَ فَهَدٰى ۙ۝٤
وَ الَّذِىْٓ اَخْرَجَ الْمَرْعٰى ۙ۝٥ فَجَعَلَهٗ غُثَآءً اَحْوٰى ۝٦ۭ سَنُقْرِئُكَ فَلَا
تَنْسٰٓى ۙ۝٧ اِلَّا مَا شَآءَ اللّٰهُ ۭ اِنَّهٗ يَعْلَمُ الْجَهْرَ وَ مَا يَخْفٰى ۝٨ۭ وَ نُيَسِّرُكَ
لِلْيُسْرٰى ۝٩ۚۖ فَذَكِّرْ اِنْ نَّفَعَتِ الذِّكْرٰى ۝١٠ۭ سَيَذَّكَّرُ مَنْ يَّخْشٰى ۙ۝١١ وَ
يَتَجَنَّبُهَا الْاَشْقَى ۙ۝١٢ الَّذِىْ يَصْلَى النَّارَ الْكُبْرٰى ۝١٣ۚ ثُمَّ لَا يَمُوْتُ فِيْهَا
وَ لَا يَحْيٰى ۝١٤ۭ قَدْ اَفْلَحَ مَنْ تَزَكّٰى ۙ۝١٥ وَ ذَكَرَ اسْمَ رَبِّهٖ فَصَلّٰى ۝١٦ۭ بَلْ
تُؤْثِرُوْنَ الْحَيٰوةَ الدُّنْيَا ۝١٧ۖ وَ الْاٰخِرَةُ خَيْرٌ وَّ اَبْقٰى ۝١٨ۭ اِنَّ هٰذَا لَفِى
الصُّحُفِ الْاُوْلٰى ۙ۝١٩ صُحُفِ اِبْرٰهِيْمَ وَ مُوْسٰى ۝٢٠ع

Jumu‘ah and Eid Prayers	Rak‘ah	Second	Sūrah al-Ghāshiyah Ch:88

بِسۡمِ اللّٰهِ الرَّحۡمٰنِ الرَّحِيۡمِ ﴿١﴾

هَلۡ اَتٰىكَ حَدِيۡثُ الۡغَاشِيَةِ ﴿٢﴾ وُجُوۡهٌ يَّوۡمَئِذٍ خَاشِعَةٌ ﴿٣﴾ عَامِلَةٌ
نَّاصِبَةٌ ﴿٤﴾ تَصۡلٰى نَارًا حَامِيَةً ﴿٥﴾ تُسۡقٰى مِنۡ عَيۡنٍ اٰنِيَةٍ ﴿٦﴾ لَيۡسَ لَهُمۡ
طَعَامٌ اِلَّا مِنۡ ضَرِيۡعٍ ﴿٧﴾ لَّا يُسۡمِنُ وَ لَا يُغۡنِىۡ مِنۡ جُوۡعٍ ﴿٨﴾ وُجُوۡهٌ
يَّوۡمَئِذٍ نَّاعِمَةٌ ﴿٩﴾ لِّسَعۡيِهَا رَاضِيَةٌ ﴿١٠﴾ فِىۡ جَنَّةٍ عَالِيَةٍ ﴿١١﴾ لَّا تَسۡمَعُ
فِيۡهَا لَاغِيَةً ﴿١٢﴾ فِيۡهَا عَيۡنٌ جَارِيَةٌ ﴿١٣﴾ فِيۡهَا سُرُرٌ مَّرۡفُوۡعَةٌ ﴿١٤﴾ وَّ
اَكۡوَابٌ مَّوۡضُوۡعَةٌ ﴿١٥﴾ وَّ نَمَارِقُ مَصۡفُوۡفَةٌ ﴿١٦﴾ وَّ زَرَابِىُّ مَبۡثُوۡثَةٌ ﴿١٧﴾
اَفَلَا يَنۡظُرُوۡنَ اِلَى الۡاِبِلِ كَيۡفَ خُلِقَتۡ ﴿١٨﴾ وَ اِلَى السَّمَآءِ كَيۡفَ رُفِعَتۡ
﴿١٩﴾ وَ اِلَى الۡجِبَالِ كَيۡفَ نُصِبَتۡ ﴿٢٠﴾ وَ اِلَى الۡاَرۡضِ كَيۡفَ سُطِحَتۡ ﴿٢١﴾
فَذَكِّرۡ ۟ اِنَّمَاۤ اَنۡتَ مُذَكِّرٌ ﴿٢٢﴾ لَسۡتَ عَلَيۡهِمۡ بِمُصَيۡطِرٍ ﴿٢٣﴾ اِلَّا مَنۡ
تَوَلّٰى وَ كَفَرَ ﴿٢٤﴾ فَيُعَذِّبُهُ اللّٰهُ الۡعَذَابَ الۡاَكۡبَرَ ﴿٢٥﴾ اِنَّ اِلَيۡنَاۤ اِيَابَهُمۡ ﴿٢٦﴾
ثُمَّ اِنَّ عَلَيۡنَا حِسَابَهُمۡ ﴿٢٧﴾

تمت بالخير